MT. McKINLEY
THE PIONEER CLIMBS

MT. McKINLEY
THE PIONEER CLIMBS
By TERRIS MOORE

THE MOUNTAINEERS, SEATTLE
for
THE UNIVERSITY OF ALASKA

The Mountaineers: Organized in 1906 ". . . to explore, study, preserve, and enjoy the natural beauty of the Northwest."

Second edition, 1981, published by The Mountaineers, 719 Pike Street, Seattle, Washington 98101

Originally published in 1967 by University of Alaska

Published simultaneously in Canada by Douglas & McIntyre Ltd., 1615 Venables Street, Vancouver, British Columbia V5L 2H1

Manufactured in the United States of America

Cover: Author on McKinley climb, 1942. *Photo by Bradford Washburn.*

Title Page: Aerial photo of Mt. McKinley from 13,000 feet. *Photo by Terris Moore.*

Library of Congress Cataloging in Publication Data

Moore, Terris.
Mt. McKinley, the pioneer climbs.

Bibliography: p.
Includes index.
1. Mountaineering—Alaska—McKinley, Mount—History. 2. McKinley, Mount (Alaska)—Description.
I. Title.
GV199.42.A42M325 1981 917.98'3 81-1002
ISBN 0-89886-021-0 AACR2

Publisher's Note for the New Edition:

Since first published by the University of Alaska Press in 1967, Terris Moore's comprehensive history of the exploration and climbing of North America's highest peak has been a virtually indispensable reference for the ever-increasing numbers of those who climb on or near the mountain. We are grateful for the cooperation of Dr. Moore and the University that enables us to publish this edition, keeping this significant and important information readily available to climbers throughout the world, so they may fully appreciate the significance of those who preceded them to the summit of "Denali."

The Mountaineers
1981

Mt. McKinley . . .
The Pioneer Climbs

Contents

Publisher's Note

AS the University of Alaska celebrates its fiftieth anniversary in 1967, it is appropriate that the fledgling University of Alaska Press should publish *Mt. McKinley: The Pioneer Climbs.* Its distinguished author, Terris Moore, served as the University's second president from 1949 to 1953.

In addition to presenting the fascinating story of the exploration and earliest ascents of Mt. McKinley for the first time in a single book, we feel that Dr. Moore makes a contribution to a related subject: a modern interpretation of the great controversy regarding the discovery of the North Pole which was such a storm center of popular discussion half a century ago. A key point in that dispute was its relation to Alaska's Mount McKinley.

We find it remarkable that among the dozens of writers who have defended or attacked Dr. Frederick A. Cook in that dispute, Terris Moore seems to be the only one who personally has visited the scenes of both of Dr. Cook's curiously related claims: the summit of Mount McKinley and also the Canadian High Arctic region about Ellesmere and Axel Heiberg Islands from which Dr. Cook departed on his still mysterious journey toward the Pole. That a detailed familiarity with both claims is necessary to an understanding of what really went on during the polar controversy is shown by Dr. Cook's own book, *My Attainment of the Pole,* whose most passionately written chapter is the one he entitled "The Mount McKinley Bribery—Forged News Items—Money Powers Encourage Perjury—Mt. McKinley Honestly Climbed . . ." etc.

We think that from his unique perspective, Dr. Moore reaches an interpretation of both Mt. McKinley and polar claims which, in the long run, will come to be the generally accepted view.

University of Alaska
College, Alaska

Acknowledgments and Dedication

THREE principal acknowledgments must be made for assistance in researching and preparing this book. First we must salute and thank Francis P. Farquhar, the grand old man and historian of western mountaineering, for having assembled and preserved an extraordinary collection of magazine articles, newspaper accounts, diaries and private letters bearing on Mount McKinley, at the time the events described in this book occurred. Books are readily available in libraries, but this is not true of magazine and newspaper stories and private papers, which often give the more lively atmosphere of what was going on. To undertake their assembly years later would have been a hopeless task. We applaud him for having done this at the time; and at the completion of our own book, we intend to entrust this collection (which he so kindly sent to me in Cambridge, Massachusetts in 1965), to the University of Alaska's Library, where, appropriately, it is assured of an appreciative and permanent home.

To the American Alpine Club, especially the successive editors of its *American Alpine Journal,* we must also express our gratitude. Thanks for permission to quote from the copyright articles in the *American Alpine Journal* is only the perfunctory part of a very real appreciation for its role of historian in keeping the record of Mount McKinley's climbs as correct and complete as possible. This acknowledgment includes the Appalachian Mountain Club and its publication *Appalachia,* for the two clubs and publications were a single club and a single publication in the nineteenth and early twentieth century years when many of the early Mount McKinley expeditions took place. To the Sierra Club and its *Bulletin*, and to the Mazamas, and to the American Geographical Society we also extend our full thanks.

To Dr. Bradford Washburn, for his very excellent *Mount McKinley and the Alaska Range in Literature,* the loan of some of his conveniently situated library books and films, and the generous gift of his time, our other major acknowledgement must be made. But of this, more below.

To Dr. Robert H. Bates, with whom I shared a climbing rope on that unforgettable day when we stood on McKinley's summit together, go hearty thanks for reading the entire manuscript and making several excellent suggestions.

I almost feel as if I had shared a climbing rope up and down McKinley's slopes with B.G. Olson of the University of Alaska, when I recall the vicissitudes he and I endured together in guiding this book through the press from opposite ends of the continent! For the many hours of expert attention he gave this work go our sincere thanks.

I also thank my cousin Henry D. M. Sherrerd, Jr., for reading chapter six in manuscript and making useful comments from the general reader's viewpoint.

Not only for inspiration in undertaking this book do I thank my long gone friend Belmore Browne, great artist as well as great climber. But more specifically grateful thanks are due his family (especially his daughter-in-law Mrs. Hugh Robinson) for permission to reproduce as the frontispiece of this book his hauntingly beautiful and never-before-published painting of mountain sheep, with Pioneer Ridge and the North and South Peaks of the great mountain above.*

Copyright permission acknowledgments in this book are few for the reason that virtually all the important early material has by now moved into the public domain and permissions are no longer necessary. Where specifically appropriate, copyright permissions are acknowledged on the particular page.

Many libraries and librarians have been helpful. Miss Marie Tremaine, editor of the Arctic Institute of North America's *Arctic Bibliography,* extended vital assistance in securing translations of some Russian material; as did Mrs. Sophia Bonnell of the Russian Research Center at Harvard. The librarians of the

*This painting is not included in the second edition.

University of Alaska, of the Appalachian Mountain Club, of the Bancroft Library at the University of California, Berkeley, and of the Houghton Library, Harvard, all provided valuable help.

Finally, in a most personal way I must acknowledge the two individuals closest to me in the preparation of this book. By chance the three of us also were trail companions together nearly thirty years ago in the first ascent of Alaska's Mount Sanford: but that of course is quite another story. For the readers of *Mount McKinley—The Pioneer Climbs,* if they find its pages interesting, then for them let me convey the thanks due my wife Katrina, for her role as "the research staff", for critically reading, and for endlessly typing and retyping the tentative copy for this book. At times I suggested that the book should be regarded as a full collaboration and her name appear with mine as joint author; but then when inevitable differences of view would arise as to what representative parts of the vast literature about Mount McKinley's early explorations and climbs and their relations to the North Pole controversy the book should offer, what voluminous material we would spare the reader, and finally just how to phrase the presentation of those early climbs, we concluded that since I had been there I would make the decisions and take the responsibility.

And now lastly and most importantly, to our friend Brad Washburn, tireless and ever cheerful companion on many a long mountain trail—on the ground and in the air—Katrina and I affectionately dedicate this book.

Terris Moore
Cambridge, Massachusetts
January, 1967

MAGAZINE SECTION

The New York Times.

SUNDAY, JUNE 5, 1910.

FIRST ACCOUNT OF CONQUERING MT. McKINLEY

Thomas Lloyd, Leader of the Successful Expedition, Tells How He and His Comrades Planted the Stars and Stripes on the Heretofore Baffling Peak, the Highest Point on the American Continent.

By W. F. Thompson.

The Twin Peaks of Mt. McKinley Photographed Before the Final Climb. The Dotted Line Shows the Route Traveled. The Two Peaks Are of Equal Height, and the Party Scaled Both of Them. The Flag Was Planted on the One Marked with a Circle Which Was of Rocky Formation and Admitted of Firmly Fixing the Flagpole.

Tom Lloyd and the Dog Team Arriving at Chena, Alaska. Lloyd Is the First Figure at the Left.

"Buster," the Dog That Climbed Up 15,000 Feet.

The "Pothole" Camp on 10,000 Foot Level of Wall Street Glacier.

DRAMATIC STORY OF THOMAS LLOYD

He Reinforces His Simple Narrative of the Remarkable Climb with His Diary of Each Day's Journey.

Newspaper account of the Sourdough Expedition, *The New York Times*, June 5, 1910.

Introduction by Francis Farquhar

IN writing the history of a great mountain such as Mount McKinley there are two important requisites. The writer must have an intimate knowledge of its character through personal experience; and he should be widely and intensively acquainted with the documentary record, with the narratives and descriptions as well as maps. Both of these requisites are possessed by Dr. Terris Moore to an extraordinary degree. As President of the University of Alaska he lived for a number of years within sight of the mountain. To be sure, it was a long way off and not visible every day, but it was always a conscious presence. Not content with merely looking at it, Terris Moore made frequent visits to it. In 1942, he had taken part in an expedition of several weeks to its upper regions, in the course of which he himself climbed to its highest summit. On later occasions he piloted his own airplane around the flanks of the mountain and made repeated landings high on one of its more inaccessible glaciers.

Dr. Moore knew and often talked with many of Mount McKinley's early explorers and climbers and has sought out and read with a critical understanding all the published accounts. More than any other writer he has studied the narratives and charts of the Russian explorers who first brought to geographical knowledge the remote mysterious mountains dimly seen from the coast.

The accounts of the Russians and of the first Americans to penetrate into the interior of Alaska are a necessary prelude to the climbing history of the great mountain. The whole period, from the first sighting of the range to the attainment of its summit, as well as detailed mapping, is comprised in an incredibly short time, comparable only to the exploration of the Himalaya and the mountains of Africa. In the latter instances the mountains were known to exist long before they were visited, but in the case of the Alaskan mountains the entire history is compacted into a single century, and most of it into the latter portion.

Much has been written about Mount McKinley, including the accounts of those who have attempted to climb it—with varying success. Sometimes the claim of success has been challenged, and in these challenges we find the two "suspense stories" that form the central theme of this book. No one doubts the accounts of Brooks and Wickersham, for they did not claim more than they accomplished. The near miss of Parker, Browne, and La Voy is acknowledged by them; the ultimate success of Karstens, Stuck, Tatum, and the native Alaskan Walter Harper is established beyond question. The two great "suspense stories" are another matter.

There is the "Sourdough" climb of 1910. When first published in the newspapers the account was regarded by many as entirely acceptable. But as time went on more and more doubts were expressed. Old-time Alaskans in Fairbanks knew perfectly well that Tom Lloyd, who gave out the story, was incapable of climbing any such mountain. The discredit cast upon Lloyd began to reflect upon other members of the party, although no one questioned the capabilities or the integrity of such tough old-timers as Billy Taylor, Charley McGonagall, or Pete Anderson. Nevertheless, the question persisted: "Did any of these pioneer Sourdoughs reach the top of Mount McKinley?" The rise and fall of opinion is followed in fascinating detail by Dr. Moore. We leave the conclusion to him.

The other suspense story is of greater proportions and reaches international fame. It is tied to the North Pole controversy and is, as the reader may guess, the story of Dr. Cook. It is handled by Moore with masterly skill, worthy of the most accomplished mystery-story writers. Dr. Cook's accounts, both of the Pole and of the McKinley climb, receive full and fair treatment, devoid of hasty judgment. Nevertheless, in the McKinley case a definite conclusion is reached, and the reader can hardly fail to agree with Terry Moore (as he is known to his intimates), who stood in a position of authority on the summit of Mount McKinley on July 23, 1942.

Berkeley, California
October, 1966

Author's Foreword

ALL my life I've longed for the luxury of enough time to research out and write this book. I happen to have been born in 1908, in the midst of the period when so many of the dramatic events here described were taking place, and the older generation of my family were reading and talking about them. During those years American families who read widely followed the events of geographical exploration to unknown parts of the earth with as much attention as space exploration receives today.

In 1930, when visiting Alaska for the first time, I came to know and talk with many of the diverse and colorful figures who appear in the pages of this book. Most intimately I knew Allen Carpé and Andy Taylor, for we shared in the first ascents of Mount Bona and Mount Fairweather. In 1931 at the old Explorers Club in New York (when we were located at 110th Street and Cathedral Parkway and could live with other members in the clubhouse) I came to know and greatly admire Captain Bob Bartlett who had gone with Peary to 87° 47′, and Matt Henson who had been with him all the way to the Pole. Belmore Browne, Merl LaVoy, and Ed Beckwith I also came to know there. But my acquaintance with Harry Karstens and Charley McGonagall developed much later when I was able to discuss their McKinley climbs with them during the four winters and five summers I lived at the University of Alaska, in Fairbanks, where I was taken into honorary membership in The Pioneers of Alaska. Alfred Lindley, Joe Crosson, Grant Pearson and Erling Strom were more distant acquaintances I would like to have known better; but from each I had a direct bit of conversation or a letter about his Mount McKinley experiences. Nine of these eleven early Mount McKinley explorers, and all of the North Pole figures of history except for Admiral MacMillan, are now gone. The time has come to do this book while there is still a direct touch with living memory of the people and events which occurred in Mount McKinley's early days, and their relation to the great Polar Controversy which so occupied men's minds in the early decades of this century.

The remarkable connection of Alaska's great mountain with this strange event always fascinated me; especially when in recent years I was brought to realize by our Canadian friends that this controversy is still very much alive. They enabled me to participate in the Canadian International Geophysical Year program in northern Ellesmere Island at the very top of Canada, in the course of which I flew my own small Cub aircraft in that remote, seldom visited region, where, from the north end of Axel Heiberg Island Dr. Cook is known to have set forth over the Polar Sea toward his much disputed destination.

However the reader comes to regard Frederick Albert Cook he will find the Doctor inevitably the most obtrusive figure in this book. It was he who brought the worldwide Polar Controversy into the great mountain's history, and we cannot remove or ignore it. For on the very day, October 15, 1909, when Dr. Cook at a great public reception was officially honored with the keys and the freedom of the city of New York, reportedly the first American to be thus distinguished, the morning newspapers were carrying the headline: "Barrill Says Cook Never on M'Kinley's Top!" All this we shall review in the pages which follow.

* * *

Now at the end of Alaska's first American century, more than two hundred individuals, seven of them women, have reached the top of Mt. McKinley.* The post-war rush to the mountain became so great indeed that the national park authorities have had to impose detailed restrictive regulations for those wishing to climb the mountain. And even the count of those who have reached its summit can no longer be made with certainty, for at least one "outlaw expedition" is now known to have climbed the mountain surreptitiously without the permission of the Park Superintendent.

McKinley's summit has moreover, now been reached by about a dozen new routes, some of them *tres difficile*. The first of these new routes was pioneered by Washburn in 1951; and the author of this book participated to the extent of flying half the members

*By the time this paperback edition was published in 1981, approximately 1000 people had climbed the peak.

of that expedition to the upper Kahiltna Glacier, and after the climb removing all by Cub ski-plane from the ten-thousand-foot level.

But our book is not about these modern climbers and the many new routes on Mount McKinley they have introduced since those years. For this reason we have not drawn upon Bradford Washburn's magnificent modern aerial photographs which revealed these new routes and inspired the climbs—a subject alone worthy of a whole mountaineering book. Rather, our book which follows is *for* modern climbers, and for the many Alaskan enthusiasts who also might like to explore our great mountain with the handful of early pioneers, in those long forgotten days before aerial photography, when all was so different.

Toward that distant elusive goal, the summit of America's highest peak, our narrative now moves forward.

I

Prologue: Tenada and the Tschigmit Mountains, 1839

FOR a century and a half after the first Europeans reached Alaska, the highest peak in North America, rising more than 20,000 feet into the sky and clearly visible from salt water, continued to elude geographers and mapmakers. In 1741 Vitus Bering's Russian expedition had discovered mainland Alaska, when he and his ship's company sighted 18,000-foot Mount St. Elias looming out of the sea to the North. They made no attempt to visit the mainland, however, and could not possibly have seen the great peaks of the interior.

In 1778 the renowned English navigator, Captain James Cook, sailed up into the treacherous tides of the Inlet now named for him. But he does not mention seeing distant inland mountains. Captain George Vancouver, however, engaged in charting the northwest coast of America for the British Admiralty in 1794, seems to have had better weather. From Knik Arm he writes that on May 6th he could see on the far northwest horizon "distant stupendous mountains covered with snow, and apparently detached from one another." This is generally accepted as the first mention in literature of Mount McKinley and its companion peak Mount Foraker.

The earliest Russian fur traders who cruised the Aleutian Islands and later the mainland coast for sea-otters, were not geographers. Mountains to them were merely obstructions to travel, and their crude maps were based in large part on casual observation and hearsay. By 1830, though, the Russian American Company, which held a monopoly on Alaska's fur trade by imperial charter, was seeking to expand its traffic into the interior; the newly appointed Governor, Baron Ferdinand P. von Wrangell, an admiral in the Russian Navy, already was distinguished for his Arctic explorations in Siberia. Wrangell promptly set about collecting such information as already was available on Alaska's interior, from the Company traders who had penetrated a few of its great rivers, including the Copper, the Susitna, the Kwikpak (the Russian name for the Yukon), and the Kuskokwim. The Governor himself sent out Company employees trained in navigation, with instructions to get accurate information on the topography, natural resources, and native tribes of the interior. They organized and sent all this material back to headquarters in St. Petersburg for publication by the Imperial Academy of Sciences. Governor Wrangell's *Statistical and Ethnographic Information on the Russian Possessions on the Northwest Coast of America,* produced in 1839, is the first book (in German) of a 44-volume encyclopedia on the Russian Empire. The remaining volumes were completed in ensuing decades. The Imperial Academy's editor at St. Petersburg offers the book, and its accompanying map, as "for the first time giving detailed knowledge of the interior of Northwest America, a work welcome to geographers."

The accompanying map which Wrangell personally compiled is reproduced here. Its coastal outlines largely follow the well-known and reliable earlier British charts, made by Captains Cook and Vancouver, but the interior features, developed by the Russian explorers, produced real news. The Kwikpak (Yukon) is shown entering the sea through its vast delta (which Captain Cook had missed entirely because of foggy weather). The Kuskokwim is traced for hundreds of miles into the interior. The Susitna falls into Cook Inlet. Dividing the watersheds of these two rivers appears a cluster of mountains marked Tenada and Tschigmit which can only be our Mount McKinley, Mount Foraker, and their satellite peaks.

Three enterprising Russian American Company explorers were chiefly responsible for these additions. All were creoles (the Russian term at that time for the son of a Russian father and a native Aleut or Indian mother), who had received training in navigation in the Company's school at Sitka. Alexander Kolmakov had led an expedition up the Kuskokwim in 1832, setting up a new trading-post. His talented assistant, Semyon Lukeen, made trading journeys still further into the interior, reaching the Takotna River, near the site of present-day McGrath. The third, Andrei Glazunov, who had been the first to enter the lower Kwikpak (Yukon) River, made a remarkable journey from that river overland to the Kuskokwim and into the unknown country to the east, in an attempt to open up a new trade route through the mountains to Kenai Bay (Cook Inlet). He traveled up the frozen Kuskokwim by dogteam. His journal reports that on March 7, 1834, nearing the mouth of the tributary Tschalchuk River which entered from the east, he and his companions "saw a great mountain called Tenada, to the northeast, at a distance of 70 to 80 versts (about 50 miles)."

They pressed on up the Tschalchuk, where no natives were willing to guide them, hoping to cross the mountains to the east, until starvation forced them to turn back. Finally, to save their lives, they ate the last of their dogs and then the dog harness, barely getting back to the Kuskokwim settlement alive.

Just how far up the Kuskokwim Glazunov had reached when he saw the great mountain depends upon one's identification of the Tschalchuk River on today's map. But it is accepted that at least Kolmakov and Lukeen both reached the Takotna, and that "the zealous Lukeen explored for several tens of miles the chief tributaries of the Kuskokwim". It was the field work of these three men which provided the detail for the western side of today's Alaska Range on Wrangell's 1839 map. Apparently Malakoff's journey up the Susitna River did the same for the eastern side of the Range.

Later Tenada and the Tschigmit mountains disappeared rather curiously from subsequent Russian and American maps. When Wrangell returned to Russia at the end of his term as Governor, he continued his interest in the mapping of the huge unknown territory. It seems to have been through his influence that in 1842 a young naval officer, Lieutenant Lavrenti Zagoskin, was sent out by the Russian-American Company to carry out scientific mapping of the Kwikpak (Yukon), and if possible to make the crossing, which Glazunov had attempted, from the Kuskowim across the mountains to Cook Inlet.

This crossing Zagoskin also failed to accomplish. It was not to be done by literate men until the eighteen nineties. But Zagoskin did spend three very successful years in interior Alaska travel-

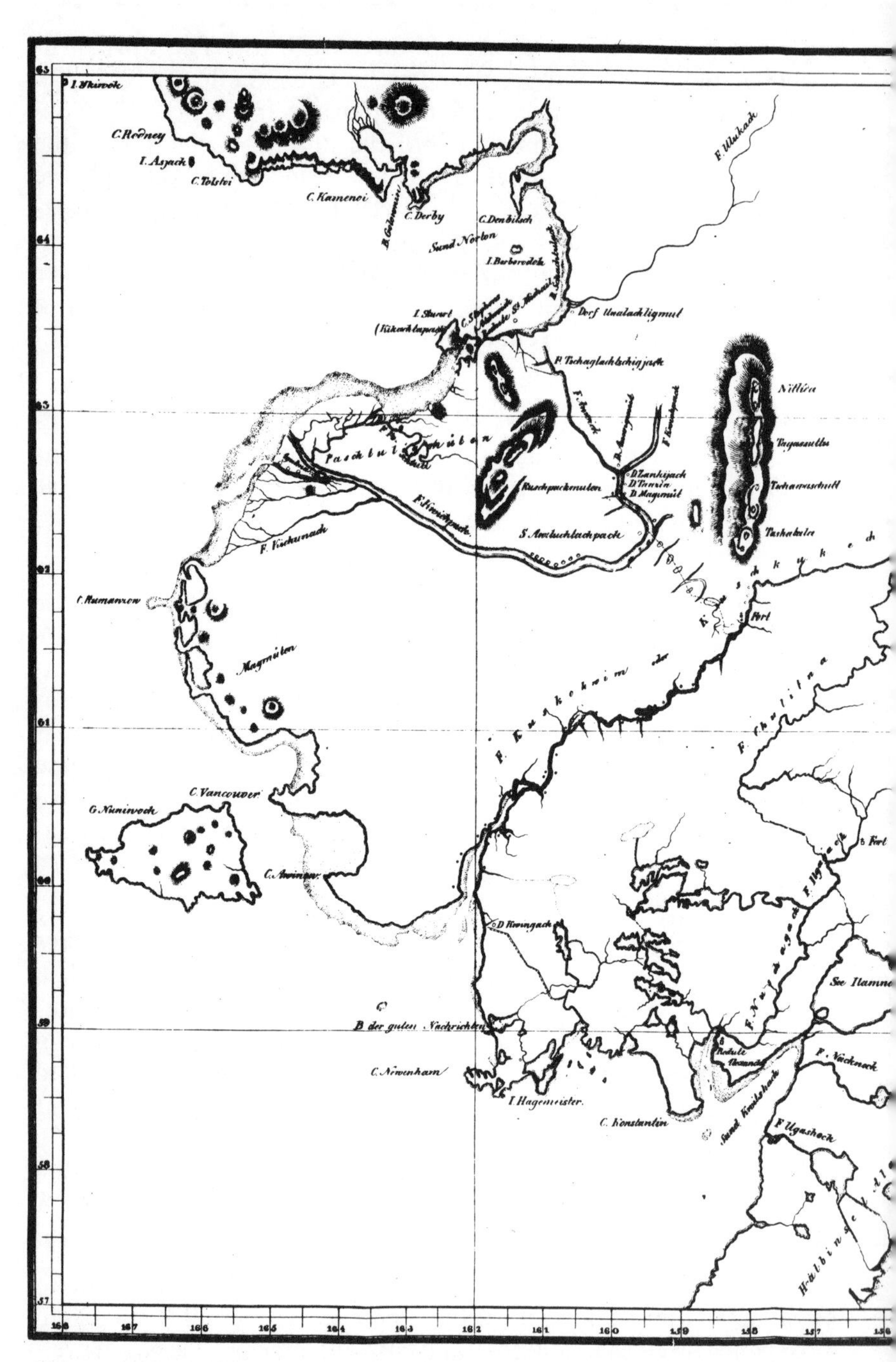

Governor Wrangell's map of 1839 (greatly reduced). "Tenada" in the upper right of the map is today's Mt. McKinley, "Sund Kanai" just below it is Cook

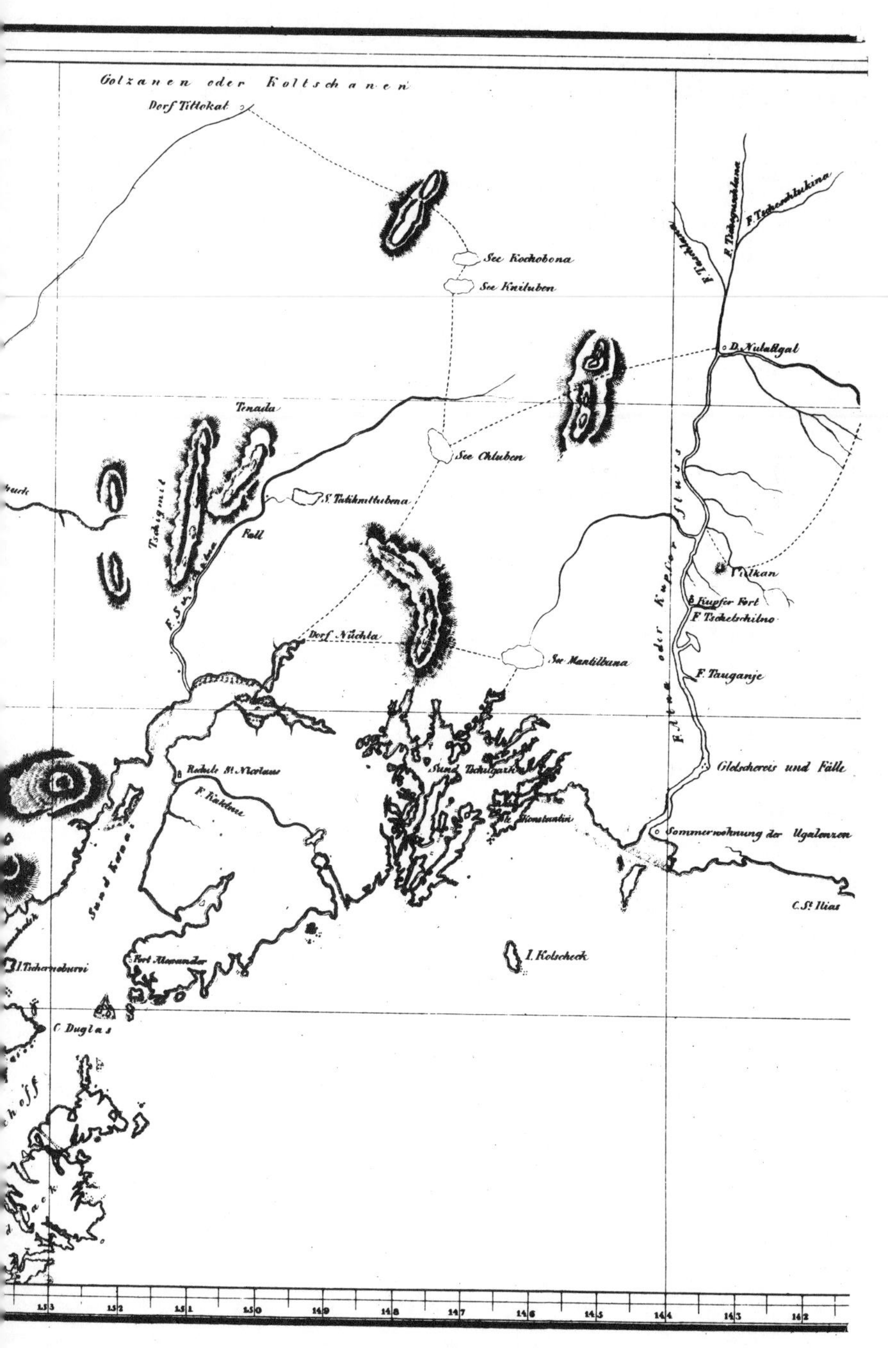

Inlet, and "Redute St. Nicolaus" is the village of Kenai. (From *Dictionary of Alaska Place Names* by Donald Orth.)

ling by skin boat in summer and by dog-team in winter, covering thousands of miles, making painstaking surveys, and collecting much information of great interest and value about native customs and traditions. He mapped the Yukon up nearly to the mouth of the Tanana, crossed overland to the lower Kuskowim, and ascended the latter to the mouth of the Takotna. From there Zagoskin also had the great view of the inland front of the Alaska Range, which, like his predecessors, he learned was called by the natives the Tschigmit Mountains.

He entered the nearer, or the lower end, of these on his map with this name. But as a naval officer his great interest for his map was accuracy, especially for the watercourses on which he personally travelled and whose key points he determined astronomically for latitude and longitude. He makes clear in his book that for this reason he only entered upon his map those features of whose position he was certain. Thus he did not enter mountains seen at a great distance, leaving those areas blank instead. Zagoskin's 1847 map is therefore more accurate and even more detailed where he gives coverage, than Wrangell's of 1839; and for this very reason Zagoskin left the region around the great peak "Tenada" a blank.

Then, when in 1861, Tikhmenief published his *History of the Russian American Company*, he understandably chose for his accompanying map Zagoskin's and not Wrangell's detail, for the interior of Alaska. Apparently, to be yet more sure of accuracy he even omitted Zagoskin's speculative detail about the lower end of the Tschigmit Mountains, leaving the entire region of today's Alaska Range a complete blank. When the United States purchased Alaska in 1867 it was the map offered by Tikhmenief, the great historian of the Russian American Company, which was regarded as the latest and most reliable Russian map of interior Alaska. Thus the early mapping by Russian explorers of the Tschigmit Mountains with the high peak "Tenada", dropped from the notice of geographers and historians. Even the earliest recorded name of our great mountain came to be forgotten.

II

Prospectors Name the Great Ice Mountain

"WHAT the country north of Cook's Inlet is like, no civilized man can tell, as in the years of occupation of the coast by the Caucasian race it has remained a sealed book. The Indians tell us that the rivers lead into lakes, and that the lakes are connected by rivers with other lakes again, until finally the waters flow into the basins of the Tennanah and the Yukon. But conflicting with this intermingling of the waters are stories of mountains visible for hundreds of miles. The natives living north of this *terra incognita* give a similar description, a description that may be accepted until reliable explorers are enabled to penetrate the region."

This outline written for the Tenth United States Census of 1880, well portrays the lack of geographical knowledge about the mysterious high mountains in central Alaska at that time. After the Russian explorers and mapmakers, twenty-one-year-old William H. Dall of Boston became the first American scientist to study and write about interior Alaska. He traveled up the Yukon River, in fact in 1866, while the territory was still Russian America. In company with the English artist Frederick Whymper (brother of Edward Whymper of Matterhorn fame), Dall paddled up the Yukon in a skin boat bidarka, exploring and collecting natural history specimens. Dall was entirely familiar with Wrangell's 1839 book, but by preference carried with him Zagoskin's 1847 map as being more recent, more accurate, and much more informative about the lower Yukon River.

From near the mouth of the Tanana River on the Yukon, Dall and Whymper viewed the full sweep of Alaska's great interior mountain range. The entire arc of that long mountainous chain appears on the map which Dall published in 1870, where it is labelled by him the "Alaskan Range". But viewing this range of mountains from the vast distance of one hundred and fifty or more miles away, Dall could not appreciate the remarkable dimensions of the highest peak, and, indeed, he did not attempt to note any single peak specifically. He and Whymper completed their expedition up the river to the Hudson's Bay Company post at Fort Yukon, and returned to St. Michael and the States, still mistakenly believing St. Elias to be the highest mountain in Alaska, and so reporting it.

Dall, who went on to become one of the most distinguished of Alaskan scientists of his day is generally credited with being the man who first named the great Alaska Range on American maps.[1] He is also remembered as the first naturalist to recognize that the Alaska Range seems to form the natural barrier between the western flora and fauna confined south of the Range, and the easterly Canadian forms prevailing north of the Range.

In 1875 Arthur Harper, Irish-born prospector and trader, made the first known journey by a white man along the Tanana River, and saw the view of the Alaska Range and Mount McKinley so familiar to present day Fairbanksans and the University of Alaska community. We are especially interested in Harper because it was his son, a generation later, who first set foot on the summit of Mount McKinley itself. From his 1875 rafting trip down the Tanana with Bates, and his 1878 upstream expedition with Mayo, Arthur Harper reported seeing "the great ice mountain to the south". He also discovered alluvial gold in the gravel bars of the Tanana, and is often referred to as the discoverer of gold along the Yukon, though in such limited amounts that it never enriched him

It was American prospectors who gave the Great Ice Mountain its English name, and their first name for it was not McKinley; nor was it Denali. The early pioneers along the Tanana and Yukon rivers had become increasingly aware of the mountain's impressive mass, so plainly visible on clear days to the southwest. In 1889, a party led by Frank Densmore crossed from the Tanana River to the Kuskowim by way of Lake Minchumina, where they enjoyed the magnificent view of the great ice mountain and its satellite peaks which this closer approach provided. We are told that it was Densmore's enthusiastic descriptions of the mountain which led the Yukon pioneers to name it "Densmore's Mountain". As such it was known on the Yukon long before anyone realized its altitude.

"Denali" is, of course, the well-known name today thought by most people to have been the one used by the interior Indians. The first literate man to visit the local native tribes in the immediate vicinity of the great peak, and in 1902 the first to set foot upon its slopes, was Dr. Alfred H. Brooks of the U. S. Geological Survey. He observes that "The Alaskan Indian has no fixed nomenclature for the larger geographic features. A river will have half a dozen names depending upon the direction from which it is approached. The cartographers who cover Alaskan maps with unpronounceable names, imagining that these are based on local usage, are often misled. Thus the Yukon natives called the White River the Yukokon, the Tanana natives called it the Nazenka, and the coastal tribe of Chilkats had still another name for it. None of these can be said to have merited precedence over any other. In this way the natives of the interior knew the mountain under the name of Denali, while the Susitna tribes called it Doleyka, and the Cook Inlet natives, Traleyka. Thus it was that long before Mount McKinley appeared on any map, it already had five names Denali, Doleyka, Traleyka, Bulshaia Gora (Russian for Great Mountain), and Densmore's Peak. Though at least a hundred white men had seen it, no one seemed to realize its stupendous height, nor had any cartographer taken note of it."[2]

It was a minor gold rush in 1895 which attracted the Princeton-educated prospector William A. Dickey, who first appreciated our great mountain's true height, gave it the name by which we know it today, and in 1897 first brought it to national attention. His account of this, and his own life story, well merit a place in Alaska's history.

Dickey had graduated from Princeton University at twenty-three, in the class of 1885. The class secretary later wrote: "His career at Princeton was featured by his winning personality, his ability as a baseball pitcher, and by his mathematical genius. He had many admiring friends. Though originally from New Hampshire, Dickey after graduation went west in 1886, his choice Seattle. He did business for a period in the real estate line, and as a pleasing diversion, played baseball—he was one of the first curve ball pitchers in Seattle—and camped out in the favorite camping spots. In 1888 he was engaged in a wholesale and retail grocery business, and was sending goods as far as Alaska. Then in June, 1889, he lost his business through the destructive Seattle fire. Next we find him engaged in banking in Montesano, not far from Seattle. But his banking and real estate interests failed to produce as he had anticipated; he therefore repaired to Alaska."

Dickey's experiences there soon made news all over the country. We read about these in his dispatch to the New York Sun of January 24, 1897:

> The largest unexplored region in the United States is the district north of Cook's Inlet, Alaska . . . Large muddy rivers, draining great glaciers, are at flood height through the short summer season. The difficulty of making headway against such swift streams, the clouds of gnats and mosquitoes, the reputed fierceness of the interior Indians (the Apaches of the North) have all served to keep out both the explorer and that most venturesome of all investigators, the prospector.
>
> The discovery of paying placer mines on Cooks Inlet in the fall of 1895 brought about 2,000 prospectors to its shores last summer. They swarmed over Kenai Peninsula, staking out claims in the deep snow, and the surplus ventured into the Knik and Sushitna valleys, both unexplored districts. Over one hundred parties entered the Sushitna River, but only five attained any great distance up the river. One party, provisioned for two years, proclaimed that they were prepared to ascend the Sushitna to its source, and if they found nothing there they would go on to the Tanana; if still unsuccessful, they would keep on northward to the Arctic Ocean. In five days they were back, saying they thought there must be some easier way to the North Pole. Another party gave up the attempt after nearly losing their lives, their boat, driven by the swift current, jerking them off the bank from which they were towing. One young man from Boston turned back after he and his mate had been about a week on the river without reaching the Station,[3] giving as a reason his unwillingness to prospect a country where he was obliged to tie up his head in a gunny sack every night in order to escape the mosquitoes.
>
> We landed at Tyonick, near the head of Cooks Inlet, the first week in May, 1896, in about two feet of snow, thick blocks of ice lining the shores, and awaited the opening of the Sushitna. Our object in prospecting the Sushitna was the hope of finding placer mines on its upper waters. There were several reasons leading to this conclusion. One of the most important was that anywhere on the shores of Cooks Inlet a few colors of fine

gold could be found. Probably this gold came from the largest stream entering the inlet; then the Copper River, rising in the same district, was reported to be rich in gold and copper.

Cooks Inlet is like the Bay of Fundy. It is shallow, with high, swift tides, the extreme being about sixty-five feet. It is often visited by violent storms, so violent that the natives pack many miles along its beach rather than venture out in boats.

Starting in an open dory, with the incoming tide, we reached the broad mud flats extending some fifteen miles from the mouths of the Sushitna. All night and a greater portion of the next day we spent on the flats hunting for the entrance of the river, for the Sushitna, like many Arctic rivers, has quite an extensive delta, which, with its network of channels, is eight or ten miles wide. Inside the entrance, the swift current, low, muddy, and caving banks, covered with thick brush and cottonwood trees, render progress very difficult. Many unable with oars to stem the mighty flood have given up the struggle before reaching the trading post thirty miles above tidewater on the river.

The river at the Station has two channels: the eastern as measured on the ice is 855 yards wide, and flows swift and deep from shore to shore; the other channel is nearly as large, but not so swift and deep. Just above are the first high banks, perpendicular promontories of rock on each side, against which the stream rushes with great force. Whirlpools in the current seemed to threaten to engulf our boat, but as suddenly as they form they disappear, and we crossed in safety. Finding our sea dory too heavy to handle, we stopped at the Station long enough to whipsaw lumber and make two river boats, such as are used on the Yukon, 25 feet in length over all, 18 inches wide on the bottom, and 40 inches at the top. Not having any tar, we pitched the seams with spruce gum and grease. Our equipment consisted of paddles, poles, and tow lines.

While building the boat we witnessed the annual run of candle-fish, a species of smelt so fat that when dried they will burn like a candle. The natives stand on the bank with rude dips made of willow roots and catch quantities of them, which are dried on long racks in the sun. Indeed, the river was so full of the fish that it was impossible to dip a bucket of water without catching some of the little beauties. The lean Eskimo dogs put on a layer of fat during candle-fish season. They stand on the bank and expertly paw the fish out of the water.

A short distance above the Station a great branch comes in from the west. The Indians say that this branch runs around the head of Cooks Inlet and rises in a high range of mountains which we had seen from Tyonick. Above this fork the river again spreads out into many channels, so that it is difficult to tell where to go, the low banks affording no clue as to the probable main course of the river. Twenty miles further another large branch comes in from the west, the main river bearing almost due north. For two weeks we travelled amid islands and sloughs, the river at times several miles wide across its many channels.

On the east were the mountains that form the watershed between the Knik and Sushitna valleys, a low but rugged range from 3000 to 6000 feet in altitude. From these mountains several small rivers flow into the Sushitna, but they did not prospect as well as the main stream, which gave us from six to 200 colors per pan, it being almost impossible to get a pan which did not have some colors.

On the clearing up of the weather we obtained our first good view of the great mountain, occasional glimpses of which we had had before, the first from near Tyonick, where we saw its cloudlike summit over (much lower) Sushitna Mountain. The great mountain is far in the interior from Cook's Inlet, and almost due north of Tyonick. All the Indians of Cooks Inlet call it the "Bulshoe" Mountain, which is their word for anything very large. As it now appeared to us, its huge peak towering far above the high, rugged range encircling its base, it compelled our unbounded admiration. On Cooks Inlet we had seen Iliamna's still smoking summit, 12,066 feet above us, rising precipitously from the salt water. Inland is a continuation of the same range, and even higher, probably 14,000 to 15,000 feet in altitude. On Puget Sound for years we had been admirers of Mount Rainier, over 14,000 feet high, but never before had we seen anything to compare with this mountain. My companion in the boat, Mr. Monks, was one of the few who made the ascent of Rainier the previous summer. In his opinion Rainier was about the same altitude as the range this side of the huge peak, which towered at least 6000 feet above its neighbors. For days we had glorious views of this mountain range, many of whose glaciers emptied apparently into our river.

According to our journal, 100 miles above the trading station, the river again forked, this time into three branches. The branch from the northwest apparently drains the southern slope of the great range, and like a flowing sea of mud spreads out in many channels about two miles wide. The branch from the northeast is as white as milk, while the middle stream, which we concluded was the main river, was nearly clear. This last river had good towing banks, and but few channels, and we soon entered a narrow valley, almost a cañon, between the mountains, which now enclosed us on both sides. Ascending one of the highest of these that stood out into the valley, we had a splendid view of the river valley below, and solved a question which had previously given us much study, namely, why such large branches came in from the west, where the Government chart of Alaska shows a great range of mountains.

The fact is, there is no range there, but a broad, flat valley extending westward as far as the eye could reach, heavily timbered with spruce and birch. It is apparently a continuation of the flat country that surrounds the upper portion of Cooks Inlet. I should estimate the dimensions of this valley as being nearly 100 miles each way. In the south, Mount Sushitna, some 5,000 or 6,000 feet high, marked the mouth of the river. In the east was the rugged but low range that separated us from the Knik Valley. In the northeast was an apparent gap in the range, through which our river ran, and whose course we could trace for thirty or forty miles. In the northwest was the greatest range of mountains we had ever seen, of which the great mountain previously mentioned was the culminating point.

We were amazed at the fine growth of grass, which in the short time since the snow had been gone, had attained a height of nearly four feet. In any open glade one could make most excellent hay. It is hard to understand why, with such fine feed in a country so sparsely inhabited, there are no more moose and reindeer. Perhaps it is due to the rigorous climate and the abundance of fierce timber wolves and a large brown bear as large and dangerous as the Rocky Mountain grizzly.

The river now had many boulders and rapids. On one side we passed a high bank in which were seams of coal of fair quality, eight or ten feet thick, to which a steamer could extend its gangplank and get a load with pick and wheelbarrow. After passing this coal formation the river entered a long series of cañons with slate walls. Back of these, some seven or eight miles, were low granite mountains. Some of this granite is a rich green, the most beautiful I have ever seen. About seventy miles from the great forks we came to a small village of the Kuilchau, or Copper River Indians, tall and fine looking, and great hunters. Throughout the long and arduous winter they camp on the trail of the caribou. They build huge fires of logs, then erect a reflector of skins back from the fire, between which reflector and the fire they sleep, practically out of doors, although the temperature reaches 50° below zero. We were surprised to find them outfitted with cooking stoves, planes, saws, axes, knives, sleds sixteen feet in length, 1894 model rifles, etc. They were encamped near a fish trap which they had constructed across a small side stream, and were catching and drying red salmon. They had no permanent houses, living in Russian tents, with the entrance arranged like our own to keep out the gnats and mosquitoes. They informed us that we could go no further with our boats, as the Sushitna now entered an impassable cañon, whose upper end was blocked by a high waterfall. "Bulshoe!" they exclaimed, raising both hands high above their heads.

The river at the highest point we reached was about 200 yards across, deep from shore to shore, with a millrace current. From the maps which the Indians made for us of the continuation of the river above the falls, we inferred that it ran a long distance to the northeast, probably from 150 to 200 miles, though none of the natives had been to its source. The Kuilchaus, who trade at the Knik station of the Alaska Commercial Company, say that some of the tribes live on a lake that empties into the headwaters of Copper River, and the balance on a lake not far distant, in which the Sushitna rises, and that it is only a short portage from either lake into the Tanana.

At all events, from the size of the Sushitna at the falls and from its direction it must flow nearly from the Copper River. Other prospectors who ascended the muddy western branch informed us that about forty miles from the great forks it branched, one stream flowing northward around the base of the great range from whose many glaciers it receives several tributaries: the other, flowing west, drains the southern side of the great range, finally turning back into the flat valley that runs a long way to the west. From a mountain top they could trace its course in the flat country for many miles. To the north they could see a stream apparently flowing west, which they thought was the Kuskokwim. One glacier at the forks came down almost to the river's bank, and was the source of a large stream. They could trace the glacier far back toward the great mountain.

Unable to pass the falls on the main river we turned down the stream to the great forks. It was very exciting and dangerous running the rapids among the big boulders, the race-horse speed at which we travelled giving us no time to examine the river ahead. The boiling waves several times entered our boats, and we were constantly on the jump to keep them from swamping. We could make a greater distance down the stream in an hour than we could up in a day.

. . . We ascended Mount Sushitna near the mouth of the river and confirmed our previous observations on the upper river, namely, the extent of the broad, flat country, and the total absence of the great Alaska range as marked on the Government charts of Alaska.

We named our great peak Mount McKinley, after William McKinley of Ohio, who had been nominated for the Presidency, and that fact was the first news we received on our way out of that wonderful wilderness. We have no doubt that this peak is the highest in North America, and estimate that it is over 20,000 feet high. We have talked with seven different parties who saw the mountain this summer, and they estimate its height at over 20,000 feet. Most of them think it is nearly 25,000 feet in altitude. Our last view of its towering summit was from one of the tideland islands at the mouth of the Sushitna. Here on a glorious evening we had a fine view of Iliamna, 100 miles south, and Mount McKinley, to the north. Field glasses brought out the details on Iliamna, but made no change in the appearance of Mount McKinley, which was nearly twice the distance away. Notwithstanding its great distance, Mount McKinley looked much the higher of the two peaks.

The natives on Cooks Inlet are devout Greek Catholics. Every village has its church and even the Copper River Indians fear the priests. Last winter some of the Copper River Indians who came down to trade at the Knik station had several wives. This the Greek priest said was wrong, and ordered them to put away all but the woman they had married first. Too superstitious to refuse, the Indians sent their extra wives away, but on the departure of the priest for other parishes the banished wives, who had only retired a short distance, promptly returned to their former lords.

Many Indians were killed or seriously wounded by the great brown bear, which they hold in great respect. They never bring in the head or claws, although they would bring higher prices at the store with them left on the skin. At Kuskutan last spring a hunter did not return to the village after his daily trips of inspection to his traps. The next morning another brave, axe in hand, went to search for him. He also failed to return, and the next day the whole village went in search of the missing. They found nothing except the axe and huge bear tracks. A few days later an enormous bear chased some of the natives to their very doors, notwithstanding the many wounds inflicted by rifles of the pursued. After that he hung about the village, and although shot many times he would soon return. Just after dark one evening he suddenly appeared at a window of one of the cabins, smashed in the glass, and gave the lamp inside a knock that sent it across the room. Without further ceremony the monster proceeded to climb into the room. Luckily all escaped through the door, and the men finally drove the bear away with no further damage than the wrecking of the furniture. All were now afraid, for surely this must be an evil spirit or shaman, and not an ordinary bear, as bullets seemed to have no effect on him. As a last resort they took some bullets to the church, had special prayers recited and holy water sprinkled over them; then they marched three times around

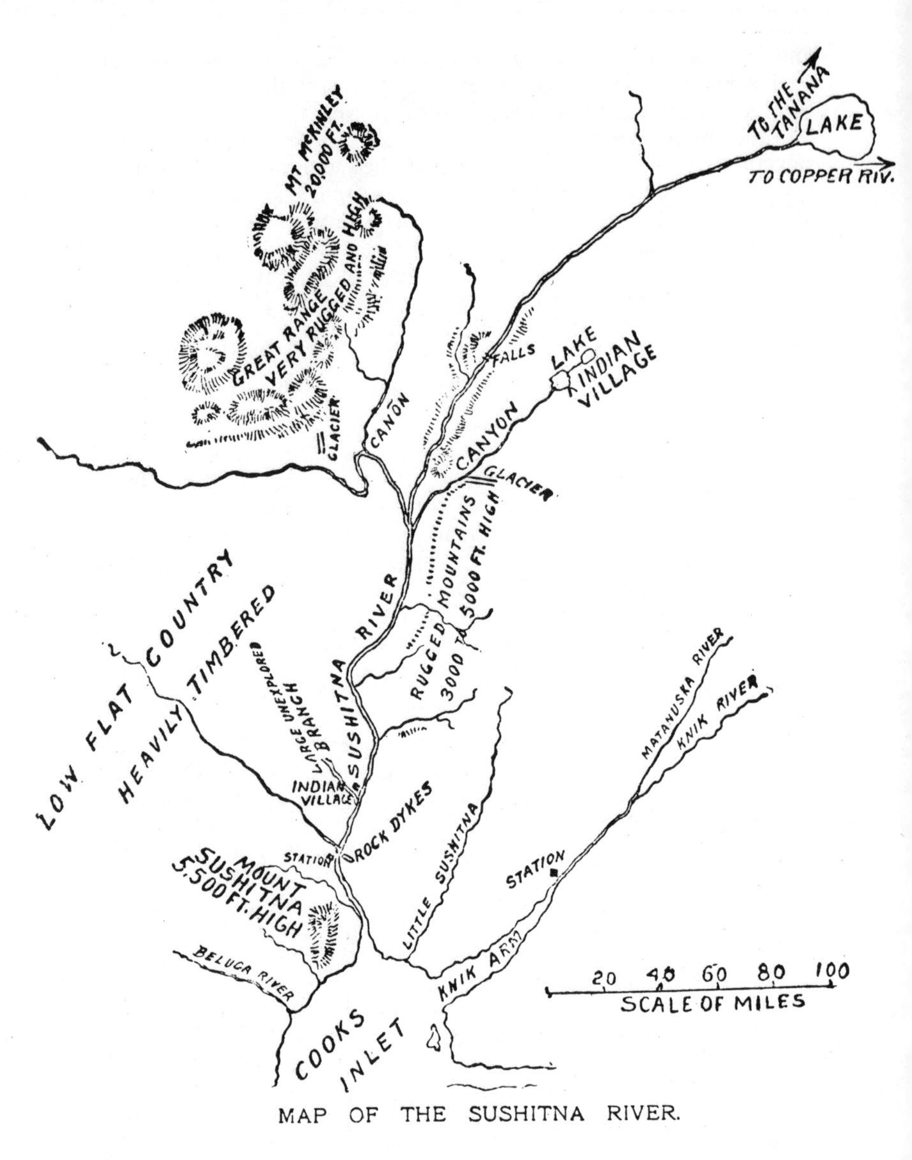

The first appearance of the name Mt. McKinley, Dickey's sketch map, 1897. The scale of miles is greatly in error; the actual distance from Mt. McKinley to Cook Inlet is only 125 miles.

> the church carrying the sacred candles and praying for deliverance from the shaman. The next time the bear appeared one of the holy bullets found a mortal spot, and the huge bear came crashing to the earth. "God killed the bear and not our bullets," cried the old chief who told us the story, as he reverently stood with hands uplifted. I counted thirty-two bullet holes in the hide which he showed us; one hole in the head undoubtedly did the work.
>
> Some idea of the remoteness of Cooks Inlet can be gained by the fact that it was more than seven weeks from the time we commenced our homeward voyage before we finally reached Seattle, much benefited by our summer's outing in unexplored Alaska.

Mr. Dickey was later asked why he named the mountain McKinley. Dickey answered that while they were in the wilderness he and his partner fell in with two prospectors who were rabid champions of free silver, and after listening to their arguments for many weary days, he retaliated by naming the mountain after the champion of the gold standard.

In 1898 Dickey returned to Alaska where he packed over the Dyea Pass, went to Dawson and there located the richest claim on King Solomon Hill, but finally lost it in litigation with Canadian Government officials. This claim was sold for $100,000 the next winter; and more than $250,000 profit, which, it is claimed should have been his, was then taken out of the grounds. In 1899 he was a member of the famous Harriman-Alaska Expedition. Later he located the copper property at Landlock Bay, Latouche Island and Knights Island in Prince William Sound which he operated successfully thereafter.

Two years after Dickey's explorations about Mount McKinley a party of the U. S. Geological Survey disputed his claim to the naming of this peak, but the *N. Y. Sun* promptly called their attention to the two-year priority of the map and Dickey's naming of the peak which that newspaper had already published and widely circulated in 1897.

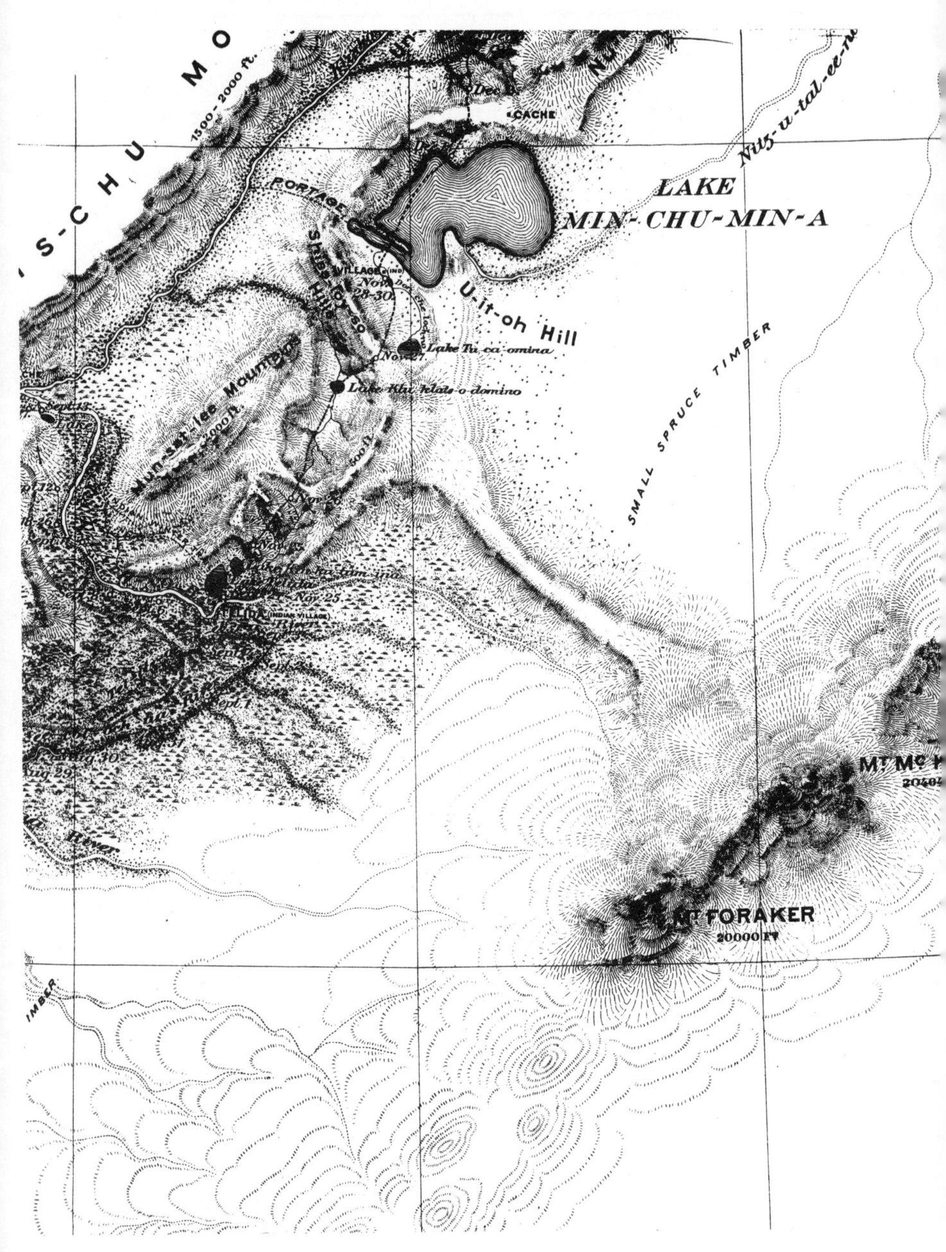

A portion of Herron's map (greatly reduced) shows the first appearance of McKinley's companion, Mt. Foraker. Seen from the west, it appeared to be 20,000 feet high, but we now know it to be only 17,300 feet.

III

McKinley's Height Measured; Mt. Foraker (Denali's Wife) Discovered

AT the same time that the gold-rushers of 1898 were stampeding north, the early expeditions of the U.S. Geological Survey were arriving in Alaska. One of these, in the summer of that historic year, was sent out from Washington to measure the exact height of the newly discovered Mount McKinley, estimated to be anywhere from 20,000 to 25,000 feet high. With George Eldridge of the Survey in charge, and Robert Muldrow to make the altitude determinations (both men subsequently commemorated by the glaciers which today bear their names), their party of eight ran a surveyors' stadia line up the Susitna River, and from six different locations along this line, at distances ranging between 43½ and 89 miles, triangulated the vertical angles to the top of the mountain's South Peak. Others in the party explored Broad Pass east of Mount McKinley. Eldridge carried a rough survey line all the way through to the Nenana River.

Muldrow's computations confirmed that Mount McKinley did indeed rise well over 20,000 feet. His figure of 20,464 came remarkably close to today's accepted altitude of 20,320 feet above sea-level (determined by Bradford Washburn with much more precise equipment many decades later). At the turn of the century in a world whose geography still had been only partially explored, McKinley's unique uplift above its base, its vast mass, situated at the edge of the Arctic—nothing like it anywhere else in the world at so high a latitude—for a while marked this region in interior Alaska as an object of exploratory interest second only to the North Pole region itself. A series of expeditions were sent out by the government through the U. S. Geological Survey, and through the U. S. Army. Private parties also were attracted to explore the unknown still to be found in and around the McKinley region.

Denali's magnificent companion peak, referred to by many of the native people in their language as "Denali's Wife", came to the attention of explorers in 1899. The first to gain a nearby view was young Lieutenant Joseph S. Herron of the 8th U. S. Cavalry. The Klondike gold rush had brought pressure upon the government in Washington to locate an "All-American" route, bypassing Canadian territory entirely, from the Pacific Ocean ports of the south Alaskan coast to the interior gold fields of the upper Yukon. Herron was placed in command of a six-man exploring party, furnished with fifteen horses and with orders for travel from Cook Inlet up the Yentna River, then across the unknown mountainous region close around the west end of the McKinley massif. From there he was to continue northward across unexplored territory to Fort Gibbon on the Yukon (the site of present-day Tanana.)

Excerpts from the Lieutenant's official account describe this journey, the first ever made overland from Cook Inlet to the Yukon River:

> Shortly after noon, June 30, 1899, the boat left us on the upper Yentna, six white and two red men, camped in a fringe of alder and spruce timber on the north bank of the river. The fifteen pack horses, tied on a picket line, were fed their last ration of oats, and over 3,000 pounds of our rations and other impedimenta were piled up on the ground. The country, as will be seen, being wild and overgrown, exacted from us extraordinary labor at every step, and from this time on until winter the daily routine was as follows: a reconnoissance for the best route for the day's march; a search for fords, crossings, detours around or passages through ravines, swamps, and other obstacles; . . . fording or swimming the pack train over the rivers encountered, and the building of spar bridges for the horses where mud-bottom creeks interposed which were too shallow to swim yet too deep to corduroy, too soft-bottomed to ford and too wide to jump; investigation for wood, water, grass, and, if possible, a breezy location for camp, wind as an additional requisite, minimizing the mosquitoes, gnats, horse-

flies, and mooseflies; packing the horses in the morning; driving, racing, dragging, or other wise hustling them into and along the trail, and adjusting or repacking shifted packs during the day; and at night, unpacking, washing backs, and oiling ears, eyes, and other favorite mosquito resorts.

Before packing each morning the herd had to be rounded up, driven to camp and caught up, and previous to the roundup it had to be found—a difficult task after its night's wanderings in search of feed and relief from mosquitoes—notwithstanding the conservative disposition of the bell horse "Shorty". Besides energetically nodding his intelligent head and making the most of the cow bell strapped around his neck, "Shorty's" strong point, as the bell horse and leader of the herd, was that he was no leader at all, but the best kind of a follower. Though "Cooley", "Bitter Root", "Minnie", and other restless spirits led the herd on long excursions away from camp, "Shorty" was always present in the rear of the bunch, where his filibustering tactics saved many miles of pursuit for us. Nevertheless, the daily round-up involved much tedious trailing . . . and scouring the country for miles around.

In addition to the above daily duties, a reconnoissance survey of the country passed over was made, specimens of plants were collected, photographs were taken and carried through under many adverse circumstances. Making and breaking camp and cooking meals were details. Sharpening axes for the day's trailcutting was necessary each morning, and drying wet blankets and clothes each night.

The first objective was to get through the Alaskan Range, a mass of enormous peaks and glaciers about 70 miles wide extending across Alaska and constituting the chief barrier to the interior. We consumed the month of July exploring through these mountains.

The first day's march was through dense timber and over soft ground. The packs were heavy, the lash ropes stiff, and the horses frolicsome. They stampeded back on the trail at every opportunity, raced through the woods, knocked off packs, plunged into mudholes, bogged down, and it required eleven hours of patient toil to make that short march. Upon making camp the back trail was blocked by felling trees across it, the herd turned out, and for this night only, the more restless ones were hobbled . . .

July 10, 1899. The Indians informed me that it would be impossible to get the horses over the divide, and that it consisted of vertical rock cliffs, and that the Indians who crossed had to use their hands in climbing over. I told them we should make efforts to get over. This day one of the horses fell, knocked over Webster, and both rolled down a steep bluff together, but luckily escaped serious injury.

During the next six days the Indians informed me that they "saveyed" (knew) the country no further. I proposed climbing to the top of the mountains for a reconnoissance, and devoted the afternoon of the 16th to doing so. The Indians still wanted to go back, repeatedly warned me "one month snow" and made efforts each day to persuade me to abandon the trip . . .

We were nearing the headwaters . . . when on the 19th, the monotony was relieved by the discovery of the pass over the divide. (Simpson Pass on Herron's map.) The formation, the locality, and game trails of antiquity all indicated I had found the pass I sought. I asked my Indians their opinion, but I received a reply of "No savey." I camped in the last clump of trees, our elevation now being at the timber line, and prepared to reconnoiter the pass.

Stepan shot, about a mile from this camp, a large bull moose. The animal was not far from 20 hands high and very fat, the antlers in velvet state. The fresh meat was welcome after a diet of bacon. The Indians consider the soft outer edge of the horns a great delicacy, likewise the nose, the sole of the hoof, the intestines, and the marrow of the bones.

While in this pass we came upon two enormous brown bears, asleep. Led by the Indian, Slinkta, I crawled around to the leeward, and then approached them too near, I thought to myself, as I had a poor gun, only a few cartridges, and the nearest tree was 5 miles away. Slinkta whistled and awoke the bears while I fired and shot the larger one in the head, but only staggered him. He arose and passed a swinging righthander at the other bear, but missed him. They got away. The same day Jones and Webster were chased by a brown bear, near the glacier at the head of the river.

The 22nd of July we crossed the crest of the divide and started down the other side of the watershed. East of the divide the drainage is into the Pacific Ocean; west of it into Bering Sea.

In the vicinity of camp, July 23, hundreds of mountain sheep were visible, high up near the summit. Jones, Carter and Slinkta climbed the mountains and shot two.

July 28, 1899. Having exhausted all their arguments to persuade me to turn back, Slinkta and Stepan, theretofore faithful and energetic, slipped out of camp, deserted, and went back to the coast. There being no other Indians in that section of the country at that time, the loss of my natives was a severe blow to the expedition. It was not unexpected, however. I had previously considered the question of putting a guard over them day and night, but had decided it to be impracticable. I proceeded, all of us redoubling our efforts, did my own guiding, and travelled by compass and the sun.

August 8, 1899. Left our valley and turned to the northeast. We found two Indian villages, both deserted. The village at the mouth of the Tonsona was also deserted.

For two weeks in August I was disabled by a sprained ankle caused by a pack horse jumping and falling on me, afoot, in a mudhole; but continued the march, riding a pack horse during the interval.

August 18, 1899. Deserted village on the Chedotlothno. It consisted of two cabins of hewn logs, a cache, and a graveyard. In one cabin was a sled, a pair of snowshoes, a stove, a knife, spearhead, and some pictures of Russian divinities and prophets.

August 25, 1899. Lost two pack horses by their having been snagged, one in the abdomen, and one in a lung. I was obliged to abandon the canvas canoe here on that account. This day to September 1st brought us to higher and firmer ground.

About September 1st, frosts at night killed off the mosquitoes; also the leaves and grass. September 3d a violent earthquake occurred at 2 p.m.; a sack of evaporated potatoes was punctured and leaked out on the trail about this time, which ended our potato diet.

September 4, 1899. I cached some bacon, rice, matches and other supplies in order to reconnoiter from high ground. While we were away a bear knocked down our cache and ate our remaining 50 lbs. of bacon. Later, an Indian wholly unknown to us crossed his trail, tracked him to his hole, killed him, discovered to his astonishment that the bear had been indulging in bacon, and started out to find the white man. It was the first time the Indian had any idea white men were in his country. We subsequently owed much to that bear, and later (September 19) as we helped to eat him, we were not much out by the loss of the bacon.

September 8, 1899. Rations getting so low that I finally ordered the pack saddles and horse equipment permanently cached, turned out the horses to fend for themselves, and started to explore down the river on rafts.

The river in this locality is crooked, swift, full of snags and sweepers, and dangerous for rafting. Eight miles down began a series of log jams extending entirely across the river. Rafting proved to be a series of collisions and clashes, one raft actually being turned bottom up twice, and some of us knocked over by snags and sweepers. That trip cost us some more rations, spoiled by wetting and the coffeepot, bread pan, a bucket, camp hatchet and a frying pan, which went to the bottom, though they had been lashed on.

We had nearly cut through the first log jam when the discovery of others below made rafting there out of the question. I made another cache at this point.

The expedition was now reduced to the last resort, that of becoming its own pack train. We filed along like coolies with fifteen days' food and other impedimenta harnessed on our backs, making packs so large and heavy that progress was a continuous performance of wrestling, the pack having the advantage of a double-Nelson hold and the assistance of the brush and timber.

The first damp snowfall loaded the trees until they bent under its weight. Then, as we pushed through the brush, each tree dropped a small avalance on our heads and kept our clothes wet, while snow on the ground added to the labor and discomfort of walking and kept our feet wet.

September 16th, 1899. Fresh blazes on the trees and other signs led us to believe we were now near Indians on this river.

September 19th, 1899. We found an Indian, who I learned actually found us, being the Indian who killed the bear which had robbed our cache. It is needless to say that we gave him a welcome, sincere if not verbose, our mutual vocabulary consisting of three words, "yes", "no," and "good"; and the Indian seemed to think them synonymous at times, but the deficiency was made good by pantomime. I learned his name to be "Shesoie". Eight days were spent in negotiations to hire him for a guide and setting a time to start. On the 27th we packed 25 miles to Shesoie's village, "Telida." And I proceeded to go into camp there for two months, until we could get winter clothes and socks made of our horse blankets, procure mitts, fur caps, moccasins, and snowshoes for the party from the Indians, and to wait until conditions were favorable for snowshoe travel.

Our food during this period was chiefly moose, bear, beaver, fish and tea. The Indians were hospitable but childish, requiring careful management. In our condition we were in their power and knew it, but they were our prisoners and they did not know it. There was to be no deserting us this time. Before the two months had elapsed, however, we had gained their entire confidence and friendship.

November 25th, 1899, with four Indians as guides, I resumed

> the exploration of the last 171 miles on snowshoes, cutting and blazing the trail and mapping the country as before. The transportation consisted of dogs and sleds—9 dogs and 3 sleds.
>
> We bivouacked on the ground, digging through the snow, using our snowshoes as shovels, piling shelters of spruce trees around us, and keeping the fire going all night, as we had few blankets and few clothes.
>
> We ran out of food on the trip, and hunting netted only a few ptarmigan, but, luckily, we intercepted the fresh trail of a party of Tanana Indians, overtook them after a hard all day chase, and obtained enough moose meat and dried fish from them to last us through.
>
> I reached the junction of the Tanana and Yukon with my detachment on December 11, making five months and eleven days on the trail and total of over 1,000 miles traveled.
>
> I enjoyed unequalled opportunities for observing the McKinley Range for months; the view from the west has the advantage of having no intervening mountains to obstruct it. I discovered a second great mountain in the range, 20,000 feet high, which I named Mount Foraker.

As in so many original explorations, Herron's altitudes and distances subsequently turned out to be somewhat in error. We now know that the altitude of Mount Foraker is very close to 17,395 feet, not "20,000 feet"; and that the distances between some of the key points on Herron's map north of the McKinley Foraker range do not match today's more closely measured detail—for example, his Telida-Mount Foraker distance measures 46 miles against 67 miles on today's maps. But his was the first crossing from Cook Inlet to the Yukon; and the first mapping exploration of the upper Kuskokwim region; and ensuing scientific expeditions were to learn from the detailed reports of Herron's trials and tribulations what to plan for and how to travel in that region.

* * *

Next came the 1902 scientific party of the U. S. Geological Survey headed by Alfred H. Brooks, soon to be the first man to set foot on McKinley's slopes, and the first to propose a plan for climbing to its summit.

Brooks was a member of the Harvard class of 1894, graduating with a science degree in geology. While in Paris, studying at the

Sorbonne, he had been invited by cable to join the U. S. Geological Survey's program in 1898 for its first season of systematic geological surveys in Alaska. He had actively participated with the Survey for four successive seasons in the eastern part of the Territory. For his fifth year, in 1902, his assignment called for a traverse from Cook Inlet to the Yukon River which would connect with the immediately preceding U.S.G.S. surveys made along the Susitna, Kuskokwim and Tanana Rivers. Taking D. L. Reaburn his professional colleague, five other men, and 20 pack horses, Brooks led a memorable expedition northwest from Cook Inlet that summer. Following Herron's route in part—up the Susitna, the Yentna and the Kichatna Rivers—but going through the Alaska Range via Rainy Pass, which he named, Brooks then turned easterly along the northern rim of McKinley's unexplored foothills.

The party had left tidewater on June 2, and by August 3 had travelled the long distance around and through the range to these northern foothills. Brooks' official instructions directed him to "bend close to the base of Mount McKinley." At the headwaters of what on the map today is named Slippery Creek, he and his party made their camp "in a broad shallow valley . . . drained by a stream which found its source in the ice-clad slopes of the high mountain." Brooks continues:

> "We had reached the base of the peak, and a part of our mission was accomplished, with a margin of six weeks left for its completion. This bade us make haste, for we must still traverse some four hundred miles of unexplored region before we could hope to reach even the outposts of civilization. Notwithstanding all of this, we decided to allow ourselves one day's delay so that we might actually set foot on the slopes of the mountain. The ascent of Mount McKinley had not been part of our plan, for our mission was exploratory and surveying, not mountaineering; but it now seemed very hard to us that we had neither time nor equipment to attempt the mastery of this highest peak of the continent.
>
> "The next morning (August 6, 1902) dawned clear and bright. Climbing the bluff above our camp, I overlooked the upper part of the valley, spread before me like a broad amphitheatre, its sides formed by the slopes of the mountain and its spurs. Here and there glistened in the sun the white surfaces of glaciers which found their way down from peaks above. The great mountain rose 17,000 feet above our camp, apparently almost sheer from the flat valley floor. Its domeshaped

Alfred H. Brooks of the U.S. Geological Survey was the first man to set foot on the slopes of Mt. McKinley, August 6, 1902.

summit and upper slopes were white with snow, relieved here and there by black areas which marked cliffs too steep for snow to lie upon.

"A two hours' walk across the valley, through several deep glacial streams, brought me to the very base of the mountain. As I approached, the top was soon lost to view; the slopes were steep and I had to scramble as best I could. Soon all vegetation was left behind me, and my way zigzagged across smooth, bare rocks and talus slopes of broken fragments. My objective point was a shoulder of the mountain about 10,000 feet high; but, at three in the afternoon, I found my route blocked by a smooth expanse of ice. With the aid of my geologic pick I managed to cut steps in the slippery surface, and thus climbed a hundred feet higher; then the angle of slope became steeper, and as the ridge on which the glacier lay fell off at the sides in sheer cliffs, a slip would have been fatal. Convinced at length that it would be utterly foolhardy, alone as I was, to attempt to reach the shoulder for which I was headed, at 7,500 feet I turned and cautiously retraced my steps, finding the descent to bare ground more perilous than the ascent.

"I had now consumed all the time that could be spared to explore this mountain which had been reached at the expense of so much preparation and hard toil; but at least I must leave a record to mark our highest point. On a prominent cliff near the base of the glacier which had turned me back, I built a cairn in which I buried a cartridge-shell from my pistol, containing a brief account of the journey together with a roster of the party.[1]

"By this time I was forcibly reminded of the fact that I had forgotten to eat my lunch. As I sat resting from my labors, I surveyed a striking scene. Around me were bare rock, ice and snow; not a sign of life—the silence broken now and then by the roar of an avalanche loosened by the midday sun, tumbling like a waterfall over some cliff to find a resting place thousands of feet below. I gazed along the precipitous slopes of the mountain and tried again to realize its great altitude, with a thrill of satisfaction at being the first man to approach the summit, which was only nine miles from where I smoked my pipe. No white man had ever before reached the base, and I was far beyond, where the moccasined foot of the roving Indian had never trod. The Alaskan native seldom goes beyond the limit of smooth walking and has a superstitious horror of even approaching glacial ice."

Brooks and his party successfully completed the remaining 400 of their 800-mile scientific expedition. The maps and geologic data which subsequently resulted were, half a century later, still being called "the most complete and reliable single work on the McKinley region." But his very first publication from this expedition was an article entitled "Plan for Climbing Mount McKinley" which appeared in the January, 1903 issue of the *National Geographic Magazine.* In this Brooks suggested that the best way to ensure a mountaineering success would be to approach the mountain from the north. It would require wintering over on the north side of the range. But, after his 1902 experience, Brooks believed that the excessively long approach from the Cook Inlet side would be a mistake for a climbing expedition.

His recommendation proved to be remarkably prescient. Of the eleven Mount McKinley expeditions during the next decade, those which made their approach from the Cook Inlet side of the mountain exhausted themselves, their time and provisions. But three of the four expeditions which wintered north of the range, as Brooks proposed, were able progressively to locate the ultimately successful route, in 1910 to make the ascent of the North Peak, and in 1913 to reach the top of the South Peak, the mountain's true summit.

IV

Judge Wickersham Makes the First Climbing Attempt; and Dr. Cook Makes the Second—1903

MANY accounts of mountaineering expeditions to Mount McKinley have appeared during the six decades since the first climbing party left Fairbanks, heading for those distant glittering slopes. But none equal the charm of this first narrative, for it took place in the spring of 1903, when the Alaskan world was young, and is described for us by the man destined to become Alaska's best loved and most versatile citizen of his generation—Judge James Wickersham, leader of the party.

In 1900 the Hon. James Wickersham of Seattle became United States District Judge for Alaska. In September, 1901, he was the special judge sent to Nome to clear up the legal tangles resulting from the notorious claim-jumping decisions of Judge Noyes; and he finally succeeded in bringing civil law and order to that turbulent mining camp. In Wickersham's future lay fourteen years of service as Alaska's lone Delegate to Congress, one of the terms being thirty years after his attempt to climb Mount McKinley. In later life, he received an honorary degree from the University of Alaska, and today one of the fine buildings on the University campus is named in his honor.

The Fairbanks boom mining camp of "more than a thousand persons and three hundred and eighty-seven buildings by actual count" had sprung up during the nine months following Felix Pedro's rich gold strike of 1902. Federal Judge Wickersham moved his court, originally held at Eagle on the Yukon, to the new town of Fairbanks realizing that because of the extent and location of the strike, the resulting community was likely to become the future commercial center of interior Alaska. By early May of 1903 he had completed his new Court organization, and assisted in establishing the civil government of the new town.

The next Court session being announced for late July, Judge Wickersham writes, "there was time to look around and consider what to do next. To me the most interesting object on the horizon was the massive dome which dominates the valley of the Tanana, the Yukon and the Kuskokwim—that monarch of North American mountains, Mount McKinley. From the bluff point at Chena, one gets a superb view. The oftener one gazes upon its stupendous mass, the stronger becomes the inclination to visit its base and spy out its surroundings. From the moment we reached the Tanana Valley, the longing to approach it had been in my mind; now the opportunity was at hand."

Wickersham organized his expedition from among his friends at Fairbanks.

> "Many adventurous persons offered to go, but only the young and vigorous were accepted—men who were physically sound and would go from love of adventure and pay their share of the expense. George Jeffrey, Court stenographer and a good amateur photographer, his friend Mort Stevens, and Charlie Webb, packer and woodsman, were accepted. They chose the fourth and last man: John McLeod, interpreter, son of a Hudson Bay Company trader, born on the Liard River, spoke all the northern Tena dialects, knew the wilderness as well as his foster brothers the Indians. The two other members of the party were Mark and Hannah, thoroughbred Kentucky mules, male and female, young and strong [named, tongue in cheek, for then prominent Senator Marcus A. Hanna!]; their owners, in their enthusiasm, had offered them as transporters, and carriers of packs, the only mules to be had in the Tanana Valley. The personnel of our party was thus completed!"

Wickersham's party engaged passage on the mail steamer, the *Tanana Chief,* as soon as the river ice should be safely out. It would take them down the Tanana "to the mouth of a small river, which the Indians called Kantishna, and told us its source was near the great mountain. Captain Hendricks had said that if the lower Tanana should still be filled with ice, he would be willing to make a side journey and take us one day's travel up the Kantishna in his steamer, because he was curious to learn whether the Kantishna was navigable for small boats."

Their departure from Fairbanks took place May 16th. "The people of Fairbanks are greatly interested in our expedition. They escorted us with flags flying and the dance hall band."

The steamer, the *Tanana Chief,* was loaded and waiting at Chena. "Our supplies consisted of flour, bacon, beans, dried applies, prunes, three hundred feet of good ropes, alpenstocks, footwear, and one hundred pounds of rolled oats and a bale of hay for the mules. The *Chief* is pushing a small barge into whose open hold we loaded our packs and the mules.

"Ducks and geese are resting on every sandbar, and clouds of these summer visitors are winging their way to their northern nesting places. Heavy ice is piled up on the bars and river banks, for the break-up passed this part of the Tanana only three days ago."

Next day they reached the mouth of the Kantishna, and Captain Hendricks undertook to run them one day's journey up the river.

"Owing to the swift current at the mouth of the Kantishna, we had much trouble and delay in getting into its stream, but finally after much puffing and smoking our craft worked up to the point where the current was more confined and regular, the river deeper and the navigation easier."

"Our craft chugged along all night, and when we turned out this morning at six o'clock (May 18, 1903) we were delighted to find we were in a lake-like expanse of quiet water, five or six hundred feet wide, and apparently quite deep. We are making good speed, and the river stretches out in the general direction of Mount McKinley.

"The Kantishna shores are well timbered and fertile. It is a beautiful virgin country, and our steamer is the first to enter its waters. It is a glorious spring day; birds sing in the birch and spruce forests along the river banks; innumerable waterfowl—ducks, geese, and swan—are in the sky. Far across the evergreen valley ahead of us the distant summits of the snowy range sparkle in the sunshine. The landscape bears no resemblance to an Arctic land; it more nearly resembles a scene in the lower valley of the Mississippi.

"Sail ho! The *Tanana Chief* cast anchor in midstream as a canoe came alongside. The solitary occupant greeted us with surprise but evident pleasure. His name is Butte Aitken and he tells he has hunted and trapped along the river near the Toclat all winter. His boat is filled with bales of furs gathered on his lonely expedition, which has now lasted for nearly a year. He quit his hunting and trapping camp and started downstream for civilization after the ice went out three days ago. He intends to follow it down to Tanana and thence to St. Michael, where he will take the steamer for the States to dispose of his catch. He says there are no other white men in the valley, though there is an Indian camp about fifteen miles upstream, and he informed us it is about forty miles to the Toclat. He asked a few questions, gave us some general information about the river, and floated downstream for the great Outside.

"About ten o'clock we reached the vicinity of the Indian camp on the right bank of the river. Our boat is now out of fuel and tied to the bank somewhat below the camp, near a good bunch of dry timber burned over last summer by forest fires. All hands turned out with axes and for an hour we felled dry trees, cut cordwood and carried enough on board to enable the captain to run the ship back. The Indians came down and gathered around in evident astonishment at the sight of a steamer on the Kantishna in the midst of their hunting grounds.

"When we had 'coaled ship' the boat pushed on to the Indian camp and we unloaded our mules and supplies. We thanked Captain Hendricks for his assistance and courtesy, and gave him some letters to mail, and bade him and the crew goodbye. He turned the nose of his craft downstream and went around the nearest bend at full speed, while his boat's shrill whistle filled the luminous midnight stillness with strange wild echoes never before heard in this valley. We are now cast loose in the wilderness with our supplies in our packs. We hastily put up a cache in some trees near our camp, hoisted our supplies thereon above reach of marauding malemutes, and turned in.

"May 19, 1903. We awoke this morning while fifty Athabascans and a hundred malemute dogs gazed at us enquiringly. When our mules were put off last night, the natives had gathered in open-mouthed wonder. Neither the natives nor the dogs had ever before seen a mule. Mark and Hannah were at once dubbed 'White Man's Moose'; and when too closely examined Mark's heels hit the skyline. There was a scurrying to safer distance and loud commands from their wise chief. Every malemute strained at his leash eager for the chase. After a solemn midnight treaty we employed a guard to watch our animals while we slept. A loosened malemute might have run them into the swamp or crippled them beyond further use.

"Next morning the Indians gathered round us to learn whence, whither, and why. Our interpreter informed us they were from the mouth of the Tanana, and brought forward two young men who had some schooling with the missionaries. We tell them of our journey to the big mountain and our wish to reach its summit. Incredulity appeared on every unwashed face at the statement of our purpose. 'What for you go top—gold?' No, we go merely to see the top, to be the first men to reach the summit. This information imparted by the interpreter caused their wise man to remark in brief Indian phrases, which translated for us after the rude laughter had subsided, was 'He says you are a fool.' Having learned our business in the wilderness and given their opinion of it, they turned away to attend to their own. A few interested squaws watched us make bread in the flour sack and cook our breakfast over the coals.

"Soon after we arrived yesterday afternoon we called at old Koonah's wigwam to pay our respect to the sachem. When we entered he rose and received us with a native modesty and simplicity that adorns and ennobles primitive man. He is blind, slender and rather tall, well proportioned, and about fifty years of age. He enjoys the blessings and labor of two wives; the youngest is an active and bright eyed Indian Hebe, who keeps the chieftain's home cheerful and neat and his moccasins dry; the elder tans mephitic moose hides, and prepares odorous salmon for the drying rack, beneath which she keeps the fire asmudge that the fish may be dry and brittle for the well worn teeth of her master, and keeps away fish-loving malemute dogs with a club and a raucous voice. In civilized lands, or in a Circle City court, the old lady would have had the law on the co-respondent long ago, and possibly alimony of at least two of Koonah's best dogs and one moose hide per annum, but here in Tenaland she snares rabbits for the household and sleeps by the blaze under the fish rack.

"Today we put Mark and Hannah across the Kantishna river, which is threateningly at high water, much against their will. A mule dislikes the water as a cat does, but like that animal can swim if thrown into the stream. We first led Hannah gently to the high bank above the wide and rolling torrent and kindly invited her to enter and swim, as if it were an ordinary everyday matter, but she backed away, shaking her big ears in violent negation. Again and again we courteously led her to the jumping-off place, begging and pleading with her to 'be nice, old girl, it's all right', only to be denied in the most positive manner. Finally Webb made an unsportsmanlike hitch over her head with a long, heavy rope, the other end of which lay coiled in the stern of the *Mudlark,* which was hanging to the bank. Another rope was arranged behind her, with pressure to come where it would be most efficacious, and with all hands on the hoisting rope we gave her a sudden rush over the bank, and landed her broadside in the river current. The crew of the *Mudlark* hastily pushed off as they saw her strike the water, and drawing her headrope taut, towed her across and ashore. We made short work of Mark, and thus brought our quadrupedal companions into the village, whose inhabitants, biped and canine, lined the home bank and howled in happy unison at the first circus performance ever exhibited in Tenaland.

"We note that present day general maps of this region are incorrect in extending the headwaters of the Kuskokwim to the Chitsia range. We climbed the bluffs this afternoon (May 26, 1903) to study the country in company with the Indian chief and old Ivan, who have for many years hunted around the heads of the streams toward Denali. These hunters pointed out the gaps in the hills through which we must go to reach the great glacier which they tell us comes down from its summit. After consultation with the Indian chief and his aged hunters we have determined to cache our boat at this place, and go across the Chitsia hills toward the base of Denali. We now (May 27) are rearranging and repacking our outfit for the overland journey. Our base of supplies from this time forward will be in our packs, in those on the broader backs of Mark and Hannah, and in our rifles. We will not see any more Indians or Indian camps before we return to the Kantishna.

"Today we had our first sight of a symmetrical high peak to the west of Mount McKinley, to which it is joined by a tremendous ridge. We supposed for a time we had discovered a new giant, but it proved to be Mount Foraker, as we subsequently ascertained, which Lieut. Herron, U. S. A., saw and named in 1899.

"Our camp tonight is on the bank of a dashing stream, the outlet of a lake on the birch bench—a beautiful place in the grove on high ground, from which we can see far and wide across the Kantishna valley. Through the soft haze of fog, spreading low over the lakes and swamps in the valley at our feet, we could see muskrats quietly parting the waters as they moved in search of an evening meal; the warm south wind gently moved the waving branches of the surrounding birch; the incessant movement of migrants from the southland; the glow of resurrection in the balmy airs of returning spring and the vast wilderness landscape, disclose the joy of life that primitive man has in his surroundings. Whether man is happier as a wanderer in the wilds, or as a cog in the complicated machinery of civilization, is a question."

On June first they reached more open country; and coming among caribou herds "took two, cut poles, built a drying rack and began jerking and drying caribou cutlets for use on the journey. While two of us remained in camp to do this work, three of our party went over to prospect Chitsia creek for gold.

They returned in the evening reporting prospects of placer gold and ruby sand. The next day we staked placer claims for each member of our party and for Captain Hendricks of the *Tanana Chief*. These are the first mining claims in this region."

The mountain now really loomed up ahead of them. They pushed on and by June 14th emerged onto the broad gravel plain of the upper McKinley fork of the Kantishna, and found an unexpected bounty of fuel.

"We had assumed that one of the main difficulties in approaching the mountain would be the scarcity of fuel—that the mountain would stand on a base so high as to be treeless, but we were relieved to find that a large spruce forest skirts the east side of the McKinley fork. It extends to within four miles of the perpendicular inner walls of McKinley which rise up from the valley glacier at their foot. We made our camp in a small grove of these spruces on the east bank of the stream.

"A glorious summer day (June 18,1903) without a cloud. We loaded one mule with wood and the other with our packs, and set out for the upper end of the glacier virtually underneath McKinley's walls, which covered with ice and snow rise almost fifteen thousand feet above our heads. We made our high camp on a little meadow, near a stream of clear water, with two fat caribou carcasses by our kitchen fire. We unloaded our wood and packs, and sent the mules back down the moraine to our lower camp under charge of McLeod. We are at least 4,000 feet high in this camp and we can see the glacier continues to rise as it turns an acute angle to the southwest. We will make a permanent camp here and carry our packs forward from this point. Tomorrow evening we will start the upward climb, when the sun gets so far down in the north as to permit the snow to set and stop the snowslides.

"In making camp we were careful to get far enough away from the mountain to avoid possible slides, which frequently plunge down its slopes. During the night, although the sun was shining, we were alarmed by the thundering noises of an avalanche that came down some distance ahead of us. Great masses of snow and ice broke loose far up the mountain, and with accelerating speed shot down its ice-encrusted slope, now striking a jutting angle of mountain wall and turning its course, and finally leaping clear of the high wall and falling thousands of feet, like a great white cloud, upon the surface of the glacier. Its millions of tons of rock and snow spread wide on the glacier below.

"June 20, 1903. A cloudless summer day. We left camp last night at 10 o'clock, Webb, Jeffrey, Stevens and I, each with a knapsack filled with provisions—bread and meat, dried and jerked caribou, chocolate, an assortment of good substantial grub,—enough to last us three or four days. Each man carried a hundred feet of small but strong rope and an alpenstock, armed at one end with a sharp point of iron, and with pick and cutting edge on the other. I carried the glasses and Jeffrey the small camera, but otherwise we were limited to necessities. We crossed to the center of the main glacier opposite our camp, and thence followed the medial moraine which bore a general southerly course, between the walls of McKinley on the left and the lower frontal mountain range on the right.

"About five miles up the main glacier above its acute angle, we came to the confluence of a branch glacier on the left hand side, coming down from a high bench on McKinley. It ran parallel to the main glacier, which emerged from a great canyon, and was here opened up into many bottomless crevasses. The left ascending bench glacier seemed good travelling and more directly headed for the altitudes which we desired to reach.

"Along the main glacier, on both sides, up the mouth of the canyon, there are extraordinary forms of ice movement. Great seracs hovering far overhead, pushed forward by the slow moving but constant pressure of rearward accumulations of ice, threaten to leap into space, and when they do, carry with them thousands of tons of rock and ice which they cast on the glacier below with the crash of thunder. From steep but short couloirs, along the sides of the lower range, waterfalls pour over the walls in dissolving spray, making rainbows in the summer sunshine, to be lost down bottomless moulins or glacier mills. Beneath, in the depths of the main glacier, their waters join the drainage stream in its ice caverns along bedrock and finally swell the flood of McKinley Fork where it emerges at our lower camp.

"The left-hand glacier which we have chosen to follow, rapidly ascends the bench on the mountainside and climbs higher and higher towards the much desired ridge which may lead to the summit; and we toiled up its soft snow carpet during the long sunlit summer night. We were forced to cross several bad crevasses, but were careful at these bottomless pits to be roped with our long, safe lifelines. We walked fifty feet apart in Indian file. The leader kept sounding for crevasses with the long hickory handle of his alpenstock, and when he found one, sought for the safest snow bridge, which he crossed carefully on his hands and knees, those behind holding his lifeline loosely, but so nearly taut as to catch his weight and break the drop should he fall through into the depths of the mighty ice crack. The second man, fifty feet from the leader, and the same distance ahead of the third man, would follow in the same careful way, and thus each man was eased safely across several bad places where bottomless crevasses were exposed.

"After travelling for nine hours without rest, at about seven o'clock in the morning we reached an arete or sharp ridge of bare rock at the extreme upper end of the bench glacier, and found, to our intense disappointment, that the glacier did not connect with the high ridge we were seeking to reach, and which yet seemed as far above us as when we began the ascent.

"We are now about 10,000 feet above sea-level[1] on a sharp ridge of rock. Here our bench glacier roadway ends, for over this arete which juts out from the mountain wall, the descent is almost perpendicular to the great bergs of the main glacier far below as they crowd over each other to enter the narrow gorge. Above us is a tremendous precipice beyond which we cannot go. Our only line of further ascent would be to climb the vertical wall of the mountain at our left, and that is impossible.

"We can now see that the main glacier, far below on the right, instead of swinging around to climb McKinley as we had hoped it might, spreads out fan shape into a tremendous amphitheater filled with snow and ice that extends for many miles out between McKinley and Mount Foraker to the west.

"Our present position on the bare rocks is, happily, safe from snow slides. But high above us, resting insecurely on a sloping shelf, are great angular blocks of ancient ice, yellow and discolored by the wash from higher altitudes. Some are as large as city blocks. The noise we had heard at our last camp was evidently caused by one of these which dropped a thousand feet or more over the adjacent vertical wall upon the bench glacier near where we are now marooned. Others overlap and tremble on the dizzy height and seem likely to fall at any moment. Here we remained all day in the hot sun.

"About two o'clock this afternoon a thunderstorm added its downpour to the already perspiring mountain. The long, beautiful cloudless summer days had already made the mountain sweat. Torrents of water and melting snow are now pouring down its ice-enshrouded body. The seracs and snowfields on edge are so undermined by the warm winds, the sun's rays, and the warm rain of last night, that we recognize we are inviting destruction by staying here, and have reluctantly concluded there is no possible chance of further ascent on this side of Denali, this season.

"June 21, 1903. Clear. We left our rocky perch last night at 9 o'clock, while far overhead the dome of Denali glowed like a great friendly light. Down, down to the glacier and back along

> its high medial moraine we trudged. The midnight sun which lighted our way home, although far down in the north, was yet high enough above the horizon to tint the upper half of Denali a soft rose color.[2] We reached our previous camping place at 'The Elbow' at five o'clock this morning, all but exhausted from the strain of the three days and nights journey, and from long hours of wakefulness under the glare of incessant sunshine. We threw ourselves upon the grass on a dry spot and slept.
>
> "We have organized an Alaska Board on Geographic Names," Wickersham writes in his journal, "to christen a few of the most interesting natural phenomena in sight. Of course the Washington officials may reverse our baptismal judgements, but that shall not deter us. My companions insist that since we are the first to view this new glacial world, we may name the features we are the first white men to see, especially since the Indians were unable to give us any particular names, other than for the mountain itself."

Some of these names they gave were in fact reversed—and for good reason, Alfred H. Brooks having preceded Wickersham with some naming the year before—but many have become permanent. The great glacier up which Wickersham's party was the first to travel, they named the Hanna Glacier. This name did subsequently appear on some government maps, and indeed in the literature of the mountain so late as the 1947 issue of the *American Alpine Journal.* But Brooks previously had named this same glacier (which in 1902 he had been the first man to see), the Peters Glacier for one of his companions on an earlier Alaskan expedition. This is its name today. The small Jeffrey Glacier, up which Wickersham's party climbed to reach their highest point on the mountain, still retains this name. Appropriately the great north wall of the mountain—not named by Wickersham at all—has been known and referred to in all the mountain literature ever since, as Wickersham Wall.

Dr. Cook's 1903 Expedition

Within two months of the Wickersham party's departure from the northern slopes of Mount McKinley, another expedition unexpectedly came upon the site of their abandoned base camp. This 1903 McKinley attempt by Dr. Frederick A. Cook became number two of no less than eleven different expeditions which

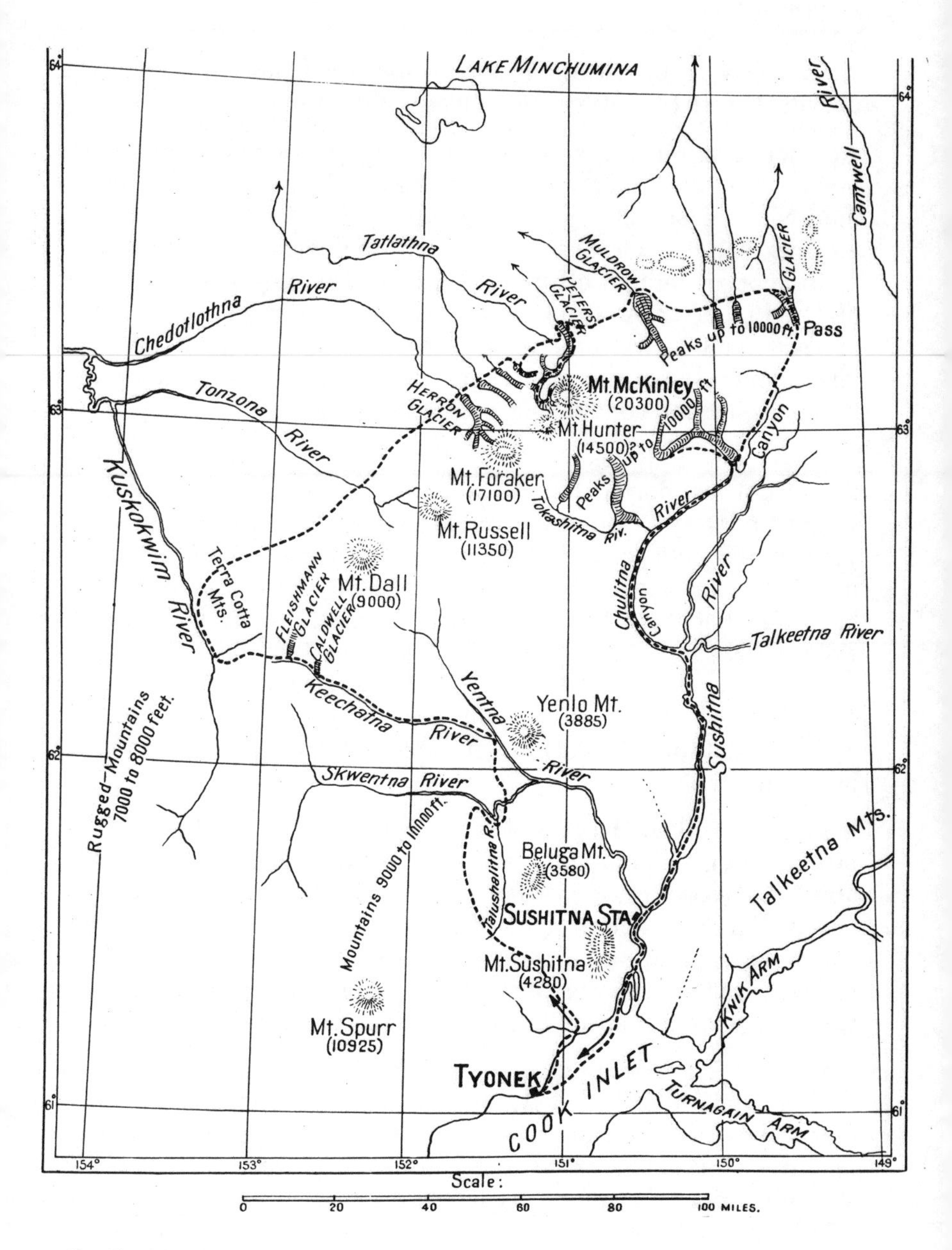

Dr. Cook's 1903 expedition, whose route is traced here on Robert Dunn's map, accomplished the first circumnavigation of Mt. McKinley by land.

were to try to climb to the top of the great mountain during a decade, before that mystic point was finally reached.

All eleven published accounts of their adventures, some wrote books, and each party, trying a different route or a different method, had something new to report, for the region was still an unexplored wilderness. Set out chronologically, a curious kaleidoscope of human effort is revealed. The enigmatic character of Dr. Frederick A. Cook, leader of this second expedition, now appears for the first time in the mountain's story. To understand him, one must see the man as he then appeared, for to that date his entire life and conduct had seemed exemplary.

The son of a physician who had died leaving him fatherless at five, Cook supported himself in his teens at miscellaneous jobs, worked his way through Columbia University and then through a year of its College of Physicians and Surgeons, completing his medical education at New York University in 1890. In 1891 he had joined Robert E. Peary's first attempt to reach the North Pole. Cook and Peary got along well that year; after 130 miles of hard travel, with other members failing, Peary referred to Dr. Cook as "the first to volunteer to go on. Always helpful and an indefatigable worker with unruffled patience and coolness in an emergency."

Cook returned to Greenland in 1893 to continue studies of Eskimo ethnology, upon which Peary later commented: "Most valuable. A record of the tribe unapproached in ethnological archives." In 1894 Cook again distinguished himself in the Arctic when the expedition ship on which he was travelling struck an iceberg, and he courageously sailed some ninety miles through ice-laden waters in a small open boat to summon help.

Next he became a member of the Belgian Antarctic expedition of 1897 on which Roald Amundsen was beginning his polar career. Unexpectedly caught in the ice and unprepared for wintering over, the entire ship's company suffered terribly. Of Cook, the ship's doctor, Amundsen later wrote: "He was the one man of unfaltering courage, unfailing hope, endless cheerfulness and unwearied kindness. Cook was beloved and respected by all, upright, capable, and conscientious in the extreme."

Amundsen even went so far as to credit Cook principally for the survival of the party while they waited for winter's end to release the ship. All this was the admirable doctor in Cook's Jekyll-Hyde dual personality, who on return from his first Alaskan expedition in 1903, published only the truth, and forthrightly compared the difficulty of reaching McKinley's unclimbed summit with the difficulties of attaining the still unreached North Pole. The other personality latent in Cook's dual nature was not to emerge visibly until three years later.

Dr. Cook organized his 1903 expedition to Mount McKinley in part with funds from *Harpers Magazine.* Of the other four members, three are of particular interest to us: Fred Printz, horse-packer, who had had charge of Alfred Brooks' packtrain over the same route the previous year; and Robert Dunn, journalist, who was to be the expedition's chronicler; Ralph Shainwald, botanist, from whom we hear again years later; Walter Miller, photographer, and Jack Carroll, completed the party.

Robert Dunn was the Harvard-educated newspaper man who had gained Alaskan experience in the gold stampede and had been introduced to Dr. Cook by Lincoln Steffens, the crusading editor. Cook had taken Dunn on as second-in-command. Alfred Brooks in Washington had told Dunn, "You have a good fighting chance to get to the top of McKinley." Steffens however had a different interest: "You must write exactly what happens," he told Dunn. "Whether you reach the top or not, be the first to tell the whole truth about exploring. The rows, the bickering—" And Dunn, ever the reporter, did not disappoint his old mentor. Dunn's subsequent series of articles in *Outing* Magazine, and his following book *The Shameless Diary of an Explorer,* became a classic of exploration exposés.

From the very outset the contrast is sharp with the light-hearted wilderness picnic atmosphere of Judge Wickersham and his companions. Dr. Cook set off at about the same time, in mid-May, but from New York, with a train journey and a seavoyage totalling 4,000 miles before even coming within sight of Alaska. Dr. Cook's transport had to be acquired on the way; he bought fifteen pack horses, mostly unbroken, from the Yakima Indian Reservation. Embarked on the steamer *Santa Ana* at Seattle, these animals were taken north with the expedition, to Tyonek, then the only settlement on Cook Inlet. Here they were steam-winched off the ship's yardarm, then swum ashore, and were promptly attacked and put to rout by the local dog population.

The summer season was nearly over when at last, after "some 450 miles through trail-less forests and over tundra, under the curse of mosquitoes and bulldog flies" they finally reached the terminus of the Peters Glacier—far around on the north side of the mountain—the beginning of Alfred Brooks' suggested climbing route.

They had been more than nine weeks on the trail in their long swing from the south around the west of the range, and their food supplies were by now very low. Dunn made no secret of his distrust of the leader: "The man hasn't the least idea of a horse's needs, or of Alaskan travel. He can't make up his mind. Can't seem to grasp the situation. He's simply afraid or unable to make up his mind beforehand."

It was past the middle of August when to their astonishment, approaching Peters Glacier, they stumbled upon the place where the Judge's party had camped, and delightedly salvaged a red coffee can full of salt, the one item they completely lacked.

Only a few days were now left to attempt the actual climb, for Dr. Cook's party was not prepared to winter over, and the long return journey to the coast must be made before freeze-up. In the long history of Mount McKinley, their climbing accomplishment was that they explored much farther up the Peters Glacier than Wickersham had done; that they reached 2,000 to 3,000 feet higher than he had, that is, to between 10,000 and 11,000 feet, and on a different route, this being the West Buttress of the North Peak.

Dr. Cook's 1903 expedition also is remembered for the naming of McKinley's nearby companion peak, Mount Hunter (14,850 feet), one of Alaska's great mountains. Dunn tells the story. On August 30, 1903, the four climbers have reached about 10,000 feet on the steep Western Buttress of the North Peak:

> "Doctor is in the lead. It was my turn to cut steps in the ice-slope but he did not seem inclined to give me the ice-axe. I couldn't tell if he withheld the axe because he thought I'd rather stay behind, or didn't want to give it up. I was content enough behind; but I felt he thought he was sort of sacrificing himself to me. 'It's all ice here. Look out,' he would say calmly between most deliberate steps; and stopping to hack a little deeper. 'Are they too far apart?'—just the things I should say ahead there, but I was not saying them; that made

"We roped up the side by a crafty combination of pinnacles." *(Photo by Robert Dunn.)*

me feel guilty; I admired him mightily. Fred and Ralph never spoke, except at the rests, and then horrible little commonplaces. Everything was ice, not an inch of névé. It seemed to take ten minutes to cut each step, which then held one toe, or one inch of mushy in-trod boot sole. There was nothing for mittened hands to grip. . . We kept on as before. 'It's getting a little leveler', said the doctor. It was. And then I would ply him with questions about that, laughingly fishing for more assurances. 'Rocks ahead, the edge of a ridge, something, see them,' he said. So there were. 'Thank you, thank you,' I said, as if that were all the Doctor's doing. 'God! I admire the way you take this slope,' I'd exclaim. And by heaven, with all these mean pages behind, I still do.

"We could dig a seat now, on the corniced brow of the rock ridge, a thousand feet sheer down, then down another fifteen hundred feet of black porcupine-like spires. Lunch? No, no one was hungry. As usual we asked for the barometer. As usual, the Doctor said, 'It can't have responded yet,' drawing it from his belt. It was not quite 10,000 feet. . . .

"We have now camped, and on less than ten square feet of primeval level. We've dug into the névé wall to get enough flatness to spike the tent, and contorted ourselves to places within again, I still on the windy side. And the wind is rising from the darkening white ridges and each unplanetary depth, the silk overhead shivers like a cobweb, and jam down my head and cover up as best I can, it nevertheless steals through and jabs. Even in our warmth we're numb, tired, disappointed. We have come only half as high as the Doctor hoped; we are only halfway to the top of the great snow spur, the camp for the final climb, where the cache is to be made.

"The old cooking, squirming, sock-changing game is on. I am digging névé to melt—'finest imported névé'—with a teaspoon from a hole at my head, preferably where the kerosene has not spilt to flavor it. Fred glum. Ralph at the stove. The doctor is scribbling in his notebook. The barometer has adjusted itself to 10,000 feet. . . .

"How warmly the tea went down! . . . 'Here's your ration, Dunn' . . . Ralph is now telling how to run an auto; we are all laughing. This is all a great joke; there is something devilish about just being here. Everyone is in a bully humor, more tolerant of his fellow than ever before on the trip. Aren't we the only ones in all this dastardly white world? How would it pay for the only four creatures in the universe to be the least at odds? We depend on one another. . . .

"I have just been outside, forgetting to undo the safety-pin that holds the flap, and nearly tearing down the tent—like Fred. The finnsku (mukluks) do not give a sanded footing, and you slip around on the inches of our little ledge, expecting to be floating down through mid-air, your stomach inside out. . . . Far below not an acre of the tundra was to be seen. Through the gap which leads west of Foraker, sleeps a billowy floor of cloud, into which the sun is blazing a vermilion way—lighting the gentle natives of Bristol Bay far west perhaps, or a slow-smoking island off the coast of Asia. That vast glimmering floor of cloud! The silvery lining for us of what may be gloom to all the world below, an enchanted plane soft and feathery, yet strong and bright like opal—for us and us alone, veined and rippled, dyed with threads of purple, rose and blue, where Foraker rises pale with late sunlight. . .

"We hang our snow-glasses on the tent-pole, knotting the string around it so they dangle down. They look very funny up there, motionless above me—four of them, mine the lowest. . . .

"I can feel the deathlike silence. No one is asleep, yet no one dares move lest he tell his neighbors he's awake. A cold blue from the nether world forms with the awful twilight a sort of ring about the tent, which magnifies the texture of the silk, and rises and falls as I lift my head from the pillow of trousers and pack. . . The world below is swinging on through space quite independently of us, at least. I am not cold, but I shiver and shiver; think and think over everything I have thought and feared today, and the little of it put down here. And if I doze, I seem to be at the very instant of slipping off our little ledge. . . .

"Not a word as we crawled from the tent toward nine next day and draped our shelf with tarpaulins wet from underneath the tent, and sleeping bags damp from feet and breath. Fred and I had been awake as usual from a small hour, shooting anxious glances at the Doctor, knowing it was useless to rouse his sigh—till I remarked aloud that the sun wouldn't reach this shelf until 4 p.m.; so he turned over, threw us our pemmican, Ralph lit the stove, and we told our dreams.

"Fred, starting ahead, settled our direction, straight up, a bit to the right (S.E.). Packs were the same, numb shoulders ached under the same weight. . . We crawled along a crack in the sheer névé, where you had to punch holes for frozen hands in the crumbly stuff, and look down sheer three thousand feet. . .

"I led at last with Ralph's axe, straight up toward the rock slope objective. We were now above the balconies over last night's camp. Soon the surface improved to let you step sometimes without step cutting, then all was as steep as ever. On the east, as we climbed, a huge ridge paralleled ours, depressed in the middle with a squarish gap, through which a dark greenish line wavered in the sunlit haze—low peaks of the Susitna Valley to the south flecking the distant horizon.

"Then toward Foraker, quite nearby through the gap, gathering all the southern ridges about the final bend in Peters Glacier, rose and rose a turret-like summit, smooth, white, specked with bergschrunds to a terrifying height. 'There's a hell of a high mountain over there,' I shouted, 'Just appearing, you can't see it yet.' 'Yes sir, yes sir,' said Fred, catching up, and we sat down to gaze and gnaw pemmican."

This new peak, discovered at the high point of their climb, they named Mount Hunter, in honor of Dunn's aunt, who had been one of their financial backers.

"But in half an hour we stood on the narrow knife of the spur top, facing failure. Here, where the black ridge leading to the top of the pink cliffs should have flattened, all was

> absolutely sheer, and a hanging glacier, bearded and dripping with bergschrunds, filled the angle between. . . I heard Fred say, 'It ain't that we can't find a way that's possible, takin' chances. There ain't *no* way.'
>
> "We were checkmated by steepness at 11,300 feet with eight days' mountain food on our hands. But remember this: also with scarce two weeks' provisions below on which to reach the coast, and winter coming. The foolishness of the situation, and the fascination, lies in the fact that except in this fair weather, unknown in Alaska at this season, we might have perished either night in those two exposed camps. Even the light wind nearly collapsed the tent, and any alpinist will tell you what storm and six inches of snow on that sheer slope would have meant. I don't think the slope we did climb would have worried an experienced mountaineer, who might succeed another time."

Even Dr. Cook admitted defeat; "Thwarted by an insurmountable wall at 11,300 feet." They turned back to the glaciers in the valley below to begin a remarkable return journey. They completed the circumnavigation of the mountain, by finding on the east a pass unnamed even today, south into the headwaters of the Chulitna River. Here they abandoned their horses, built rafts, and on these ran the river down to the settlement at Susitna Station, which they reached on September 24.

Curiously, the name "Hunter" did not remain on the mountain they had just discovered and attempted to name. Instead, on today's maps "Mount Hunter" designates a much higher mountain; but it is one farther around on the south side of Mt. McKinley which they could not possibly have seen from their position. But that is another story.

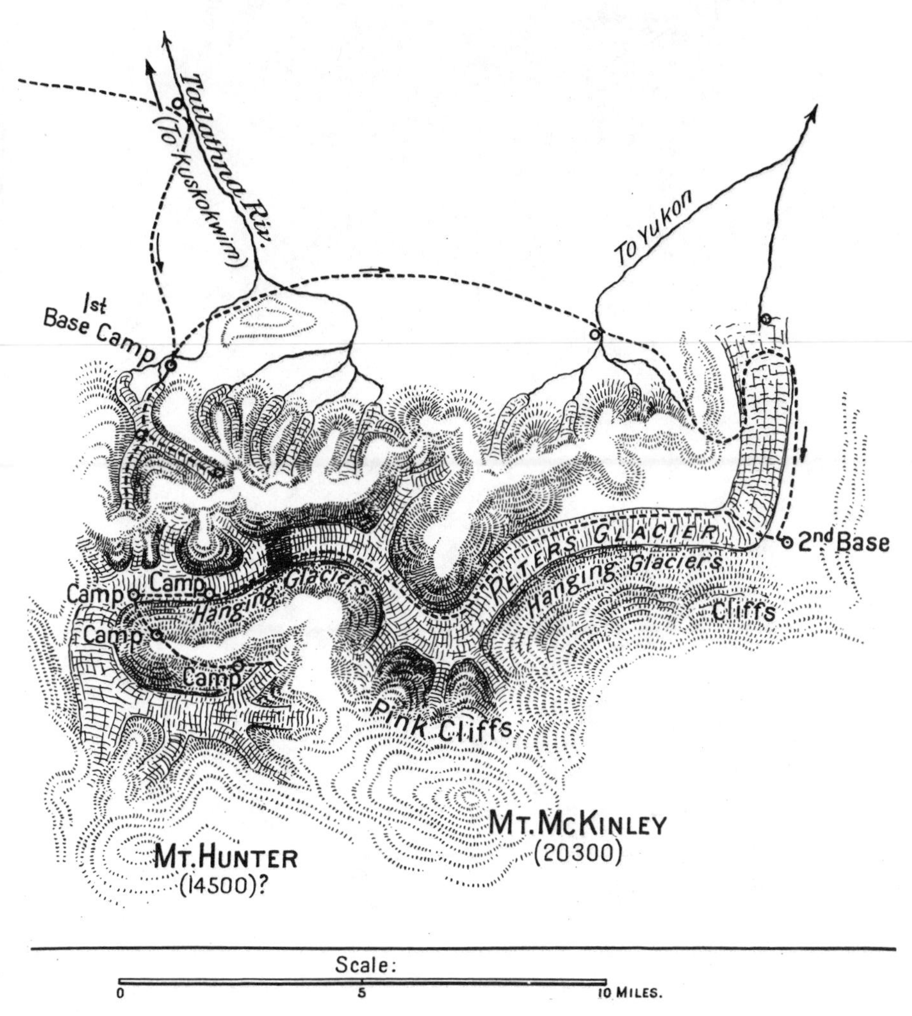

This map, tracing the Cook-Dunn climb in 1903, also encompasses the area of the earlier Wickersham camp which was close to Cook's "2nd base camp."

The 1906 Cook expedition, swimming the packtrain across the Yentna River. *(From a drawing by Belmore Browne.)*

V

Dr. Cook's Claim: Mount McKinley, 1906; and the North Pole 1908

EXPLORATION of the great mountain now shifted to its south slopes. It was felt that the Wickersham and Cook expeditions of 1903 must have made a pretty fair examination of the climbing possibilities along the north approaches of the mountain. Those attempts had ended in disappointment. So the summer of 1906 was devoted to close-in survey of the still unknown details of the mountain's southern glaciers and ridges.

Dr. Frederick Cook's 1903 attempt on Mount McKinley had further enhanced his already excellent reputation. Robert Dunn's "debunk-the-explorers" series of articles in *Outing* magazine about the expedition with Cook, was read in 1904 along with Dr. Cook's parallel series "America's Unconquered Mountain" in *Harpers Monthly Magazine.* Fascinating though Dunn's exposé was to the general reader, Cook's dignified presentation of the geographical achievements of the 1903 trip, his generous and kindly treatment of his companions including Dunn, created a generally favorable impression of Cook as a leader and traveling companion. He was honored with memberships in various learned societies, geographical and alpine clubs, including the presidency of the Explorers' Club in New York in which position he succeeded the greatly respected General A. W. Greely. Consequently, when Dr. Cook announced plans for another expedition to try to climb Mount McKinley in 1906, this time via new explorations to be made from the south, he immediately had a number of capable applicants from whom to choose.

Professor Herschel C. Parker, of the department of physics at Columbia University, and Belmore Browne, a well-known artist and experienced out-of-doorsman, both with impressive climbing records, joined Dr. Cook's party which sailed north from Seattle in May, 1906. So did Russell W. Porter, topographer of the recent Baldwin-Ziegler Polar expedition, later to become a distinguished astronomer. And both Walter Miller, the photographer, and Fred Printz, the horse packer, former companions of Dr. Cook during the impressive 1903 circumnavigation of the mountain, joined him again. But not Robert Dunn who, one may suppose, was not invited.

With twenty-two pack horses, and a 40-foot, 25-horsepower motor launch named the *Bolshaia* for ascending the Susitna River and its tributaries, Cook's amphibious expedition now carefully approached the southern bastions of the McKinley massif. The horsepacking party by land, and the river party, making frequent rendezvous with each other, explored and mapped the upper Yentna, the upper Kahiltna, and the upper Chulitna rivers, each of which drains McKinley's southern glaciers. After two months of this, beset by mosquitoes, struggling through alders and devil's club thorns, and finding that none of the many glaciers above these rivers offered any promise of a route to McKinley's summit, the expedition returned to Cook Inlet by August 15th, convinced that not on the south side, but only on the still partially unexplored northeast, was there any remaining hope of a route to the summit.

Excellent geographical exploration and mapping of McKinley's southern foothills had been accomplished by this 1906 party despite the disappointing conclusion. And had Dr. Cook merely returned to New York at this point reporting what had been accomplished, he would have been a greatly respected man, and could no doubt have returned another year to lead an expedition to success on the northeast, the Muldrow Glacier approach. But—and it is still curiously incredible—Dr. Cook now instead embarked upon a very strange journey indeed. Belmore Browne, who happened to be close to the event, has described it for us:

> "With all thought of climbing Mount McKinley put aside for another year, our party broke up in mid-August, 1906, at Tyonek on Cook Inlet. Porter was left to finish up some topo-

graphical work, Professor Parker returned to New York, and Dr. Cook asked me to make a side trip up the Matanuska River into the Chugach Mountains to secure some museum specimens. I told him that if he contemplated exploring the southern foothills of Mount McKinley I would prefer going with him. He answered that he would do no exploring outside of seeing whether or not the water route was practicable. Barrill (assistant horsepacker on the expedition just ended) and some prospectors picked up at Susitna station now accompanied the doctor.

"Before leaving Tyonek I invited Dr. Cook aboard to take luncheon with me, and while he was on board or while the boat was at Seldovia he sent the following telegram to a well-known business man of New York City: 'AM PREPARING FOR A LAST DESPERATE ATTEMPT ON MOUNT MCKINLEY.'

"Some weeks later at the appointed time in early September, 1906, we met at Seldovia on the Kenai Peninsula. Printz and Miller were the first to join me. At this time we heard the rumor that Dr. Cook and Barrill had reached the top of Mount McKinley, but we paid little attention to it, as rumors in Alaska are as thick as mosquitoes. But at last the Doctor joined us, and to my surprise confirmed the report.

"I now took Barrill aside, and we walked up the Seldovia beach. Barrill and I had been through some hard times together, I liked Barrill and I knew that he was fond of me, for we were tied by the strong bond of having suffered together. As soon as we were alone I turned to him and asked him what he knew about Mount McKinley, and after a moment's hesitation he answered: 'I can tell you all about the big peaks just south of the mountain, but if you want to know about McKinley, go and ask Cook.' I had felt all along that Barrill would tell me the truth.

"I now found myself in an embarrassing position. I knew the character of the country that guarded the southern face of the big mountain, had travelled in that country, and knew that the time that Dr. Cook had been absent was too short to allow of his even reaching the mountain. I knew that Dr. Cook had not climbed Mount McKinley, in the same way that a New Yorker would know that no man could walk from the Brooklyn Bridge to Grant's Tomb in ten minutes.

"This knowledge, however, did not constitute proof, and I knew that I should have to collect some facts. I wrote immediately on my return to Professor Parker telling him my opinions and knowledge concerning the climb, and I received

> a reply from him saying that the climb under the conditions was impossible. I returned to New York."

On September 27th, 1906, Dr. Cook sent a telegram from Alaska to one of his financial backers in New York, Herbert L. Bridgman, which the latter naturally released to the newspapers: WE HAVE REACHED THE SUMMIT OF MOUNT MCKINLEY BY A NEW ROUTE FROM THE NORTH.

Browne says: "Professor Parker and I now stated our convictions to members of the American Geographical Society and the Explorers Club. Many of these men were warm friends of Dr. Cook. We, however, knew the question was above partisanship. Nothing official had as yet been written by Dr. Cook . . . It was necessary to wait until his account of the climb was published."

Upon his return to the states, Cook next began giving lectures about his "first ascent" of Mount McKinley, lectures which were, of course, reported in the press. Soon, however, it became inside knowledge in the mountaineering fraternity that Professor Parker and Belmore Browne, Dr. Cook's companions for most of the past summer, doubted the truth of his statements. And pressure soon mounted upon them either to publish their reasons for doubt, or else cease to slander the Doctor. They ceased. But it was with impatience that they waited for Dr. Cook's account of the climb to be published.

To many, even in mountaineering circles, Belmore Browne's disbelief at this time, appeared to be nothing more than one man doubting another's word. For after all, what was so impossible about climbing a 20,000-foot mountain in eight days and getting back in four? Mont Blanc in the Alps, nearly 16,000 feet high, is constantly climbed up and back in a few days. Parker and Browne earlier in the summer of 1906 at Mount McKinley might have seen no way to do this; but in September after they had separated, perhaps Dr. Cook *had* found such a way?

What Dr. Cook needed was proof—preferably photographic. A panorama of overlapping photographs taken from the summit on a clear day should provide solid evidence of the ascent. Failing that, pictures of the new route Dr. Cook had found would suffice.

Did he have any photographs? Yes, he did, said the Doctor, and in due time they would be published. Meanwhile he used these pictures as slides to illustrate his lectures. And increasingly except for a small but growing group of skeptics in the little-known American Alpine Club—Dr. Cook with his long reputation as an Arctic and Antarctic explorer, projecting his Mount McKinley "summit" pictures, seemed to give satisfaction to his public audiences.

He was widely accepted, initially even by Robert E. Peary, his old Arctic leader, and by the National Geographic Society, where his lecture was introduced by Dr. Alexander Graham Bell. Alfred H. Brooks, director of the U. S. Geological Survey's Alaska Division, let it be known that he was contributing a chapter on geology to Dr. Cook's forthcoming book on the first ascent of Mount McKinley. Charles Sheldon, the naturalist, offered a chapter concerning the mammalogy and ethnology of the region. Also about this time Alfred Brooks wrote his friend the Rev. Hudson Stuck, the Alaskan missionary in Fairbanks with whom he had a bet. Stuck had bet that Dr. Cook would not get to the top of McKinley in 1906 from the south. Brooks called upon Stuck to "pay up," because Dr. Cook had succeeded. The $2.50 amount was trifling, but the principle was large.

In this atmosphere Professor Parker and Belmore Browne continued wary about the danger of possible libel or slander action, refrained from challenging Dr. Cook's lectures and lantern slides, and waited for his printed publication.

When at last Dr. Cook's illustrated article appeared, nearly a year had gone by. The piece, published in the May, 1907, issue of *Harpers Monthly Magazine* included a photograph captioned "The Summit of Mt. McKinley, 20,300 feet above sea-level" showing Ed Barrill standing there waving the American flag; a photograph of glaciated terrain titled "The View from 16,000 Feet"; and a map of the Mount McKinley region showing explicitly the detail of Dr. Cook's and Barrill's purported route to the summit. The dotted line of this "route" approaches McKinley from the south, runs from the upper Susitna and Chulitna Rivers, up the Ruth Glacier, then through the immense tangle of glaciers and peaks around the east side of McKinley, northerly all the way to a point about twenty miles northeast of McKinley's summit to the region of the middle Muldrow Glacier.

From there it turns sharply southwest along today's well-known Muldrow Glacier route southwest to the summit.

At last Belmore Browne and Professor Parker had a tangible, specific, published claim by Dr. Cook which could be studied carefully and objectively. Close examination persuaded them even more than before that neither Dr. Cook and Ed Barrill nor anyone else could physically have forced their way over any such route in twelve days—up in eight and back in four. And they noted other reasons for doubt.

But Dr. Cook could not be reached. During the winter of 1906-7 he had persuaded the millionaire sportsman John R. Bradley to finance an Arctic expedition, and the two of them departed, about the time the article appeared, "quietly and without fanfare"—secretly in Parker's and Browne's view—in the 110-ton fishing schooner Bradley had bought for the purpose. When Bradley returned to New York at the end of the summer season from northwest Greenland, he brought back with him a letter for the Explorers Club from Dr. Cook. It read: "I find I have a good opportunity to try for the Pole. I will stay here for a year, and hope to get back to the Explorers Club in September, 1908, with the record of the Pole".

Professor Parker and Belmore Browne now decided they were unwilling to challenge the integrity of a fellow Club member before the Club while he was absent, unable to defend himself. They held their charges, awaiting Dr. Cook's return to New York.

The next event was the appearance, in 1908, while Dr. Cook was still in the Arctic, of his book *To the Top of the Continent,* published in New York by Doubleday Page, and later in London by Hodder & Stoughton. Alfred H. Brooks' impressive contribution in geology, and the greatly respected Charles Sheldon's chapter on natural history, added substance to the book. The *Alpine Journal* (London) in its review accepted without challenge the claim to a first ascent of McKinley, thus strengthening Dr. Cook's position considerably. The *A. J.'s* editor did, to be sure, complain about the fact that the accompanying map failed to show Cook's and Barrill's specific route to the summit (noteworthy, since the same map in the earlier magazine article had shown it), but that journal's review gained acceptance for Dr.

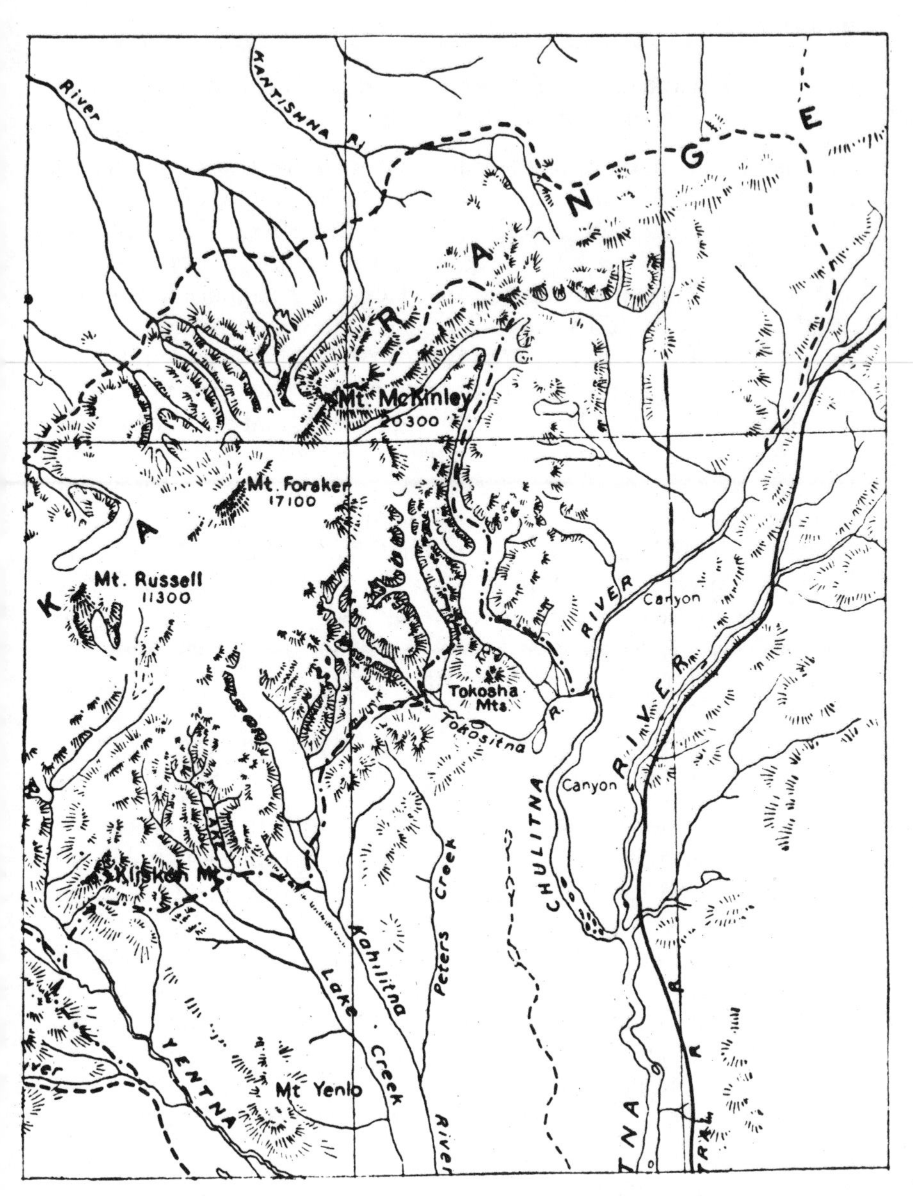

Part of Dr. Cook's map accompanying his May 1907 *Harper's Monthly Magazine* article. It was the only detailed route map to McKinley's summit he ever published. It is at least consistent with his most detailed verbal description: ("We made the first ascent by the most eastern of the three north ridges. . . . Parker in 1912 started from the north [and] reached the upper part of the same ridge upon which our climb was made from the east.") Of the hundreds of climbers who have now reached McKinley's summit by a dozen different routes, no one has yet been able to do it Dr. Cook's way.

Cook in European alpinist circles, which in those years were rather remote from the American scene.

To Parker's and Browne's small group of knowledgeable friends in the American Alpine Club, however, Dr. Cook's *To the Top of the Continent* had exactly the opposite effect. The new detail disclosed by the book related to the "summit" photograph showing Ed Barrill waving the American flag supposedly on top of McKinley's 20,300 foot south peak. The same photograph in the May, 1907, *Harpers Magazine* article had been guided to press by Dr. Cook himself; but in the case of the 1908 book, this had been done by others. It now appeared that the "summit" photograph in the magazine must have been cropped or retouched along its right-hand edge. For in the book's "summit" picture, not cropped or retouched in this way, a bit of another peak now emerged in the right-hand background. No horizon is visible anywhere in this picture which might provide a clue as to the inclination of the camera, and thus whether or not the background peak actually was higher or lower than the purported "summit" on which Barrill is seen standing. But by chance enough detailed rib structure appears on the face of the background peak, so that the expert may be able to make a tentative identification.

Professor Parker and Belmore Browne immediately proceeded to do just this by a careful study of all photographs about Mount McKinley published by Dr. Cook in the 1907 magazine article and the 1908 book. One of these soon provided the clue for which they were looking: the picture in the magazine article entitled "The View from 16,000 Feet", which appeared again in the book, but this time with the caption "Scene of Glaciers, Peaks and Cliffs—Shoulder of Mt. McKinley, a cliff of 8,000 Feet." The middle peak of three in the background of this picture matched the telltale one along the edge of the purported "summit" picture!

From this, other related details, and their own knowledge of the country, Parker and Browne were now persuaded that Dr. Cook's "summit" photograph had not been taken anywhere near the top of Mount McKinley. Indeed, as Browne later wrote, "When *To the Top of the Continent* was published it enabled us to locate Dr. Cook's fake peak before leaving New York, and later events showed we were only about one hundred yards out of the way in our reckoning." They identified the fake peak to be nothing more than a partially snow-covered rock pinnacle in a foothill range southeast of Mount McKinley, distant about twenty miles from its actual summit.

But Dr. Cook's return from the Arctic to a private, grim confrontation with his fellow Explorers Club members in New York, turned out to be quite otherwise from that expected. What happened next is still remembered history. On September 1, 1909, the American Minister in Copenhagen, Denmark, interrupted the entertainment of his guests at tea to read aloud a cablegram just handed him by a messenger from the Danish Foreign Office. Dispatched from Lerwick in the Shetland Islands to the Danish Government by the master of the homeward bound Danish Greenland service vessel *Hans Egede,* the message read: DR. COOK REACHED THE NORTH POLE APRIL 21, 1908. ARRIVED MAY 1909 AT UPERNIVIK FROM CAPE YORK. THE CAPE YORKERS CONFIRM TO RASMUSSEN THE VOYAGE OF COOK.

As the American Minister later wrote: "Nobody questioned the truth of the story, for Knud Rasmussen's name is a talisman, and the officials in Greenland do not take travellers' tales seriously unless the travellers have serious claims."

So Cook's statement that he had reached the North Pole was now immediately accepted and believed in Copenhagen. From that moment on, Dr. Frederick A. Cook became the subject of excited and thrilling headlines throughout the world. *The New York Herald* carried the story in three lines of big type across seven columns. And during the remaining three days it took for the little Danish Government steamer to reach Copenhagen the newspapers searched out and set forth the newly famous explorer's background.

The public learned: that he was already a respected figure in the world of Polar and mountain exploration, that he had just had a book published in both New York and London about his latest Alaskan explorations, on the title page of which there was listed the fact that he was a Member of the Belgian Geographical Society and a Chevalier of the Order of Leopold I.

Later the American Minister commented, "because I in earlier days had also been decorated by King Leopold, I felt a burst

Dr. Cook's photographs, such as this one, prove he travelled the first minor portion of his claimed route.

"Camping on a sixty degree slope, sketched, from description, by R.W. Porter," was the caption for this drawing in Cook's 1907 magazine article and his 1908 book, *To the Top of the Continent*.

This, the first of the two famous summit flag pictures, is the one that appeared in Dr. Cook's May 1907 magazine article, labelled by him "The Flag on the Summit of Mt. McKinley."

This second famous summit flag picture, labelled "The Summit of Mt. McKinley," appeared in Dr. Cook's 1908 book. Note the bit of a background peak on the right hand margin.

of sympathy for Dr. Cook". The Minister wired the U. S. State Department in Washington that Dr. Cook's story was officially accepted in Copenhagen, and himself set to work with the Danes to organize a great official reception.

The result—a carnival of mass hero-worship comparable only to the similar one which ocurred eighteen years later for the real hero who flew the Atlantic and landed his plane in Paris—took Dr. Cook himself completely by surprise. A more conventional personality would perhaps have been bowled off his feet. But modestly, and moreover with dignity, Dr. Cook submitted to ensuing days of world adulation, led off by the Danish Royal family and the faculty of the University of Copenhagen, which awarded him an honorary doctorate.

Back at the Explorers Club in New York however, where questioning awaited Dr. Cook about Mount McKinley 1906, a very different sort of private reception was brewing for him. It has long been clear that had Dr. Cook returned from Greenland direct to New York in September, 1909, instead of to Copenhagen, the whole Cook-Peary polar controversy would have followed a very different pattern. But the way it actually developed, with Denmark and indeed all Europe now accepting Dr. Cook's North Pole claim as fact and wildly cheering him, the American public, especially at New York where he was about to land on return, was not going to be outdone.

If a little rival group of explorers in Alaska in 1906 had doubts about Cook's McKinley climb which they were not willing to publish, this counted for nothing now. What did receive attention at this point however was a cable from Robert E. Peary, originating at Battle Harbor, Labrador, on September 6th, five days after the Cook story had first broken. It announced that he finally had reached the North Pole in April 1909. As to Dr. Cook's claim to have been there a year earlier in April, 1908, there was a special wire for the Associated Press: COOK'S STORY SHOULD NOT BE TAKEN TOO SERIOUSLY. THE TWO ESKIMOS WHO ACCOMPANIED HIM SAY HE WENT NO DISTANCE NORTH AND NOT OUT OF SIGHT OF LAND. OTHER MEMBERS OF THE TRIBE CORROBORATE THEIR STORY.

The initial effect of this was not so much to create doubt about

Dr. Cook, but rather to cause the American authorities to rejoice that they had, not one, but two, North Pole heroes, the second regrettably jealous of the first. The Danish *National Tidende* newspaper in Copenhagen set the tone about Dr. Cook for the moment by editorializing: "Doubtless Knud Rasmussen has means of producing reliable evidence, and when he says Cook must be trusted, that opinion counts for more than Peary's statement of what Eskimos told him. Peary is too much a party to the case for his word to be accepted unconditionally."

So when the *Oscar II* with Dr. Cook aboard dropped anchor off Quarantine in lower New York Bay, September 21, 1909, a score or more of boats, crowded with cheering passengers, soon surrounded her. One of them was a tug, carrying Dr. Cook's wife and two daughters. To this he was transferred and the four of them were then taken aboard the *Grand Republic,* an excursion steamer chartered by a Brooklyn welcoming committee. As they started up the bay for a tour of the harbor a band on the ship played "Hail to the Chief" to wild cheering. Summing up, the *New York Herald* the next day referred to Dr. Cook's tumultuous reception as "a demonstration of popular confidence and enthusiasm without parallel in the history of this city". Some days later, when the "freedom of the city" was officially bestowed upon him, that paper further noted: "Dr. Cook is the first American to whom the keys of the city have been given".

But during the next six weeks, all fell into ghastly disarray for the Doctor, his friends and supporters. The University of Copenhagen and learned geographical societies in the United States began to call for proof of Dr. Cook's North Pole claim. It soon emerged however, that he really had none, and the responses of the still primitive Eskimos to questioning were soon recognized as being inconclusive either way, as to whether Dr. Cook had been to the North Pole or not. Moreover, photographs —even if Dr. Cook had had a wealth of them—could prove little because the Arctic ice-pack everywhere looks so much alike. It became increasingly clear that Dr. Cook's North Pole claim rested upon scarcely more than his own personal statements and observations as to where he had been.

And just how credible were these statements and observations? Good enough, quite possibly, to be accepted in full if Dr. Cook had hitherto had an unblemished record for intellectual honesty.

But this was the very thing now being challenged even by Ed Barrill, Dr. Cook's sole companion on McKinley's "summit".

Dr. Cook soon met, as requested, with a committee chosen by the Explorers Club. Both Professor Parker and Belmore Browne were called as witnesses and Dr. Cook appeared. "The chairman opened the meeting by telling Dr. Cook he was not to consider himself in the light of a guilty man being tried to prove his innocence, but rather as an honest man who was being given a chance by his friends to clear himself from suspicion. But Dr. Cook refused to testify before the committee. He said his hardships in the long Polar night had affected his memory and that he could not answer any questions without consulting his diary. He asked for two weeks' time. Before the expiration of that time he had disappeared."

It was decided at the Explorers Club, late in 1909, not to make public any of these private charges of Professor Parker and Belmore Browne against Dr. Cook, but instead to organize the Club's own expedition jointly with the American Geographical Society for the purpose of further exploring Mount McKinley the next summer, 1910. The committee meanwhile continued to wait, vainly, for Dr. Cook to reappear and answer questions.

Months passed during the winter of 1909-10; the newspapers offered rewards of up to $1,000, for information which would locate Dr. Cook. But he had vanished. Late in December, 1909 the Explorers Club dropped Dr. Cook from membership. So did the American Alpine Club, and the various geographical and learned societies in the United States. Peary, in contrast, was now honored by these same organizations at their annual dinners that winter.

The facts about these private rejections of Cook and honors for Peary were of course picked up by the newspapers, and had the effect of greatly exacerbating the Peary-Cook polar controversy raging in the press. The public still could not be given the real reasons for what was going on in private: there was a moral but not yet any legal certainty and the possibility of libel suits kept the matter private during this period. Those in the know agreed upon releasing nothing publicly until after the forthcoming 1910 expedition should return from McKinley with its own pictures and its own findings.

Gradually a new, and somewhat ugly, situation developed. The public, not knowing the background, began to suspect that their recent hero, Dr. Cook, who had now mysteriously disappeared, was somehow being unfairly treated for sinister reasons. Thus, when at this point a group of millionaires publicly bestowed upon Peary a sum of $10,000 as a token of their esteem, and a bill was introduced into the Congress designed to give Peary a life retirement as Rear Admiral, the pro-Cook portion of the public, which apparently was still very much in the majority, worked itself up to a pitch of acrimony and outrage. For awhile it resembled in public indignation the then recent Dreyfus Affair in France. Newspapers in several parts of the country conducted public opinion polls on the subject of the Cook-Peary polar controversy. The *Pittsburgh Press* reported a straw vote on the following statements as follows:

Cook discovered North Pole in 1908	73,238 votes
Peary discovered North Pole in 1909	2,814
Cook did not reach North Pole	2,814
Peary did not reach North Pole	58,009

The *Toledo Blade* reported "550 votes for Cook, 10 for Peary"; the *Watertown, N.Y., Times*, "three to one for Cook".

It was from this background that three expeditions, one made up of Alaskans from Fairbanks, one organized by the Mazamas of Portland, Oregon, and the Explorers Club-American Geographical Society Expedition from New York, all attacked Mount McKinley in 1910—with Dr. Cook and his claims uppermost in their minds.

VI

Tom Lloyd's Sourdough North Peak Expedition—1910

THE pioneer town of Fairbanks, Alaska, read the newspaper wire dispatches of the great Cook-Peary polar controversy of 1909 and 1910, with the same fascinated attention as the rest of the world. But, unlike most of their fellow Americans "Outside", who had only the published newspaper accounts, Fairbanksans also had the "inside" view. The community then, as today, was small enough for those with the direct contacts to share these with their neighbors and the private news got around quickly.

Hudson Stuck writes that he "well remembers the eagerness in Fairbanks with which Dr. Cook's book *To the Top of the Continent* was perused by man after man from the Kantishna diggings, and the acute way in which they detected the place where vague 'fine writing' began to be substituted for definite description."

Both Alfred H. Brooks and Charles Sheldon, who had written supplementary chapters in Dr. Cook's book, promptly got in touch with their friends at the Explorers Club, American Geographical Society, and American Alpine Club as soon as the Cook-Peary polar controversy broke out. Intimately familiar with Mount McKinley, both Brooks and Sheldon were soon persuaded by the details which Professor Parker and Belmore Browne pointed out, and by Dr. Cook's unsatisfactory response on his return from Copenhagen to New York, that their contributions to the book had placed them in a highly embarrassing position. Now they too became aware of the personality breakdown that must have occurred in Dr. Cook. They ceased to be "Cook supporters".

Fairbanksans had three close personal ties and correspondence to the inside of the situation: Hudson Stuck in Fairbanks with Alfred H. Brooks; Harry Karstens with Charles Sheldon, the eastern naturalist; and other Alaskans with Fred Printz and Ed Barrill, who had returned to their native Montana.

"Some of these men", continues Stuck about Dr. Cook's book, "convinced that the ascent had never been made, now decided upon proving it in the only way in which it could be proved—by making the ascent themselves." The result, perhaps the most interesting of all Alaskan mountain expeditions, is still, more than half a century later, in part a mystery.

Specifically who got to the top of which peak; and was there or was there not a *second* Sourdough North Peak Expedition in 1910? It is the most often told McKinley story, still controversial, a truly human document. It was organized with an enthusiasm built not only upon the general indignation in Fairbanks against Dr. Cook's claims believed to be false, but also the determination to prove that Alaskans could themselves perform the feat, and honestly.

The organizer and leader of the Sourdough party was Tom Lloyd. He, Pete Anderson, Billy Taylor, and Charley McGonagall, all were experienced Fairbanks miners and prospectors. When the party left Fairbanks it included E. C. Davidson, a qualified surveyor who four years later became the official Surveyor-General of Alaska, and two of Davidson's friends, Horne and W. Lloyd.

In the *Fairbanks Daily Times* of December 22, 1909, we read, "Cheers Are Given as Climbers Leave". The farewell ceremony took place in front of the Pioneer Hotel as the expedition set forth on the winter trail, with dog teams, horses, and a mule.

The undertaking was well planned, and all seemed auspicious. This was not just two or three impulsive prospectors starting off on a shoestring. Fifteen hundred dollars, from three Fairbanks businessmen, financed equipment and supplies. Further enlivening the prospect was a large bet—$5,000 according to the N.Y. *Sun*—reported to have been placed between William H. McPhee, a financial backer, and Dave Petree, a doubter, that some member of the expedition would reach the top of Mount McKinley before July 4, 1910. To complete the send-off the *Fairbanks Times* in the same issue ran an editorial indignantly denouncing Dr. Cook for his false claims concerning McKinley in 1906, and the North Pole in 1908. "Our boys will succeed, they've got the route figured out, and they'll show up Dr. Cook and the other 'Outside' doctors and expeditions".

And well they might have. For though the "Outside doctors and expeditions"—Brooks in 1902 and Cook in 1903—had passed nearby without realizing that the upper Muldrow Glacier gives access to the high basin from which either the North or South Peak may readily be climbed, the Lloyd 1910 Sourdough party was well aware of this possibility. They had learned the key secret of the probable successful route during their years of prospecting in the Kantishna and Toklat districts.

For in 1906 Charles Sheldon had dog-sledded out onto the Muldrow Glacier to a point where all this becomes clear, and looking at the mountain Sheldon and his sourdough companion, Harry Karstens, at that time had discussed it with Lloyd and his friends. Even Dr. Cook, who obviously must have got the idea from Charles Sheldon in the winter of 1906-7, shows this northeast climb up the Muldrow as *his* final route to the summit in his May, 1907, *Harpers* magazine article wherein he first published his claim.

Certainly all might have gone well for Lloyd's 1910 Sourdough Party. They had the right idea, the right people, were adequately equipped, and had favorable weather. Their competent surveyor, Davidson, could, and doubtless would, have pointed out that the two-mile-distant but 850-foot higher South Peak was the true summit and would have to be climbed for a complete first ascent. Also, a photographer, probably he would have succeeded in bringing back summit photographs adequate to prove the ascent.

Lloyd's party established a winter base camp at Cache Creek, and occupied the first of their mountain camps on February 27th. Then they returned to the flats to get firewood and to kill caribou and moose for more food. But Tom Lloyd now antagonized Davidson. One report mentions a fist fight. The expedition's surveyor, with his two friends Horne and W. Lloyd, packed up and departed for Fairbanks. This was truly unfortunate. For, as Dr. Stuck, who knew them all in Fairbanks pointed out: "The loss of Davidson was a fatal blow to anything beyond a 'sporting ascent'. He was the only man in the party with any scientific bent, or who knew so much as the manipulation of a photographic camera." (Photography in those years was almost as complicated and specialized as surveying.)

Now comes the tragically ironic part of it all. Fairbanks heard no further news of the expedition until April 11th, on which day Tom Lloyd reappeared in town, alone, but with the story that *all four* of them had reached the top of *both* peaks of Mount McKinley, the true summit, "the South Peak at 3:25 pm on April 3, 1910." The other three men on their return had remained behind at Kantishna to do some necessary work on their mining claims. Lloyd asserted that his party was the first to make the ascent, because the summit did not resemble Dr. Cook's picture and they could find no evidence of his having been there.

Lloyd's great story was immediately taken down and rushed into print by W. F. Thompson, editor of the *Fairbanks Daily Times,* who also arranged by wire to transmit the account based on Lloyd's diary and personal narrative to the *New York Times* and other newspapers in America and England.

The *New York Sun* ran the Lloyd story on its front page, and on April 14 Tom Lloyd received a telegram of congratulations from President William Howard Taft. This telegram the *Fairbanks Daily Times* published the next day describing it as "from one big man . . . to another".

But Lloyd's story also ran into immediate doubt and challenge. The *New York Times,* which had given Lloyd's story no more than page seven treatment, two days later on April 16, 1910, announced: "McKinley Ascent Is Now Questioned".

Fourteen column inches detailed an interview in New York with Charles Sheldon, who was very skeptical of Lloyd's claims. He knew Lloyd, McGonagall, Anderson, and Billy Taylor from his numerous expeditions in the region, including a winter spent near them in the Kantishna goldfields. Sheldon concluded, "It

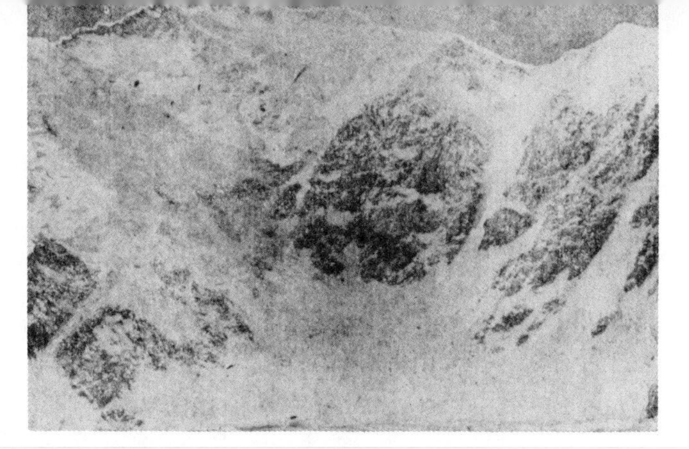

Top: This "ridge of wall on side of glacier photographed from above" seems to be the highest altitude picture the Sourdough Expedition brought back. Middle: Lloyd is the man on the left, seen reaching Chena on return to Fairbanks. Bottom: From *The New York Times,* June 5, 1910. This is unquestionably the middle Muldrow Glacier with North and South Peaks in the background. The caption states that both peaks were climbed and that the "American flag was planted" on the one marked with a circled X (the South Peak) "which was of rocky formation."

is clearly the duty of the press . . . not to encourage full credibility in the reports of the alleged ascent until the facts and details are authoritatively published . . . Only Tom Lloyd apparently brought out the report, the other members of the party having remained in the Kantishna district 150 miles away; so we haven't their corroborative evidence." A remarkably perceptive observation Sheldon's turned out to be!

Tom Lloyd in Fairbanks now found himself under pressure to produce evidence for his claim. But the films he brought back with him evidently were quite unsatisfactory. For within three weeks the *Fairbanks Times* itself ran a page one story (May 7, 1910), "This Climber Claims To Be From Missouri", quoting a telegraphed interview with Professor Parker in Seattle as follows: "Professor Herschel Parker Coming to Climb Mount McKinley, Says He Has to Be Shown Lloyd Party Got There".

Responding to all of this, Lloyd apparently sent a message by some means from Fairbanks to the boys in Kantishna to make a second climb of the mountain. The most direct evidence we have bearing on this "second climb" is the account released by Tom Lloyd in June, to newspapers in Fairbanks, New York, and London. The *Fairbanks Daily Times* ran Lloyd's account in their June 9, 1910 issue under the heading:

> "MAKE SECOND CLIMB OF MOUNT MCKINLEY. Bill Taylor, Charles McGonigle[1], and Pete Anderson Go to Top-O-The-Continent Again to Get Some More Pictures of the Flag and Summit. Because the pictures taken of the flag placed on the summit of Mt. McKinley last March by Tom Lloyd, Bill Taylor, Charles McGonigle, and Pete Anderson had not turned out quite as well as they might have done and it was thought well to have a better photographic story of the climb, Taylor, McGonigle and Anderson retraced their steps to the top of the continent and took some more pictures. They returned yesterday, having been two weeks on the trip out from the Kantishna. Lloyd had asked the boys to get as near the summit as necessary to get a good picture, and as they figured they could not get any nearer to the summit than the top, they just kept on climbing until there was no more mountain left to climb. It took a month to make the ascent and the pinnacle was reached on May 17th. They found the flag intact, although partly folded across the staff, and it is their opinion that it will bravely defy the winds and storms of many months to come. They were able to secure the necessary films, and, their work accomplished, they came home.

They believe that the Belmore Browne party will have no trouble in finding their stakes, although some of them may fall when the snow melts."

But no illustrations accompanied this story about the second 1910 Sourdough Expedition; and we know that the fourteen photographs[2] which were published with W. F. Thompson's June 5, 1910 Sunday *New York Times Magazine* article, and the three published with the *London Daily Telegraph* article of June 6, 1910 over Thomas Lloyd's signature (claiming he reached the top April 3) could not physically have got to New York or London from the *second* Sourdough Expedition, but only from the first.

A correspondent for the *Pacific Monthly* in Portland, Oregon, wrote from Alaska later in 1910:

"Alaskans are divided in opinion as to whether Tom Lloyd climbed the mountain. I know Tom Lloyd well, said a friend of mine who has been at Valdez for a number of years. If he said he climbed Mount McKinley, I am satisfied he did it. I think there is no doubt he got to the top. But—I know Tom Lloyd, said another man to me. I wouldn't believe him under oath. He can't travel ten miles a day on level ground, why, he can't even kill his own moose meat. When we were over in that country at the same time he was, we had to kill moose and give to him to keep him from going hungry!"

The fact is that Lloyd proved unable to produce summit photographs from either the first or the second 1910 Sourdough effort. Then the whole story gradually fell into a state of which Billy Taylor later said:

"We three didn't get out (from the Kantishna) until June, and by then they didn't believe any of us had climbed McKinley."

VII

Sleuthing on Mt. McKinley: The Explorers Club and the Mazamas

PROFESSOR Parker and Belmore Browne departed for Alaska in early May, 1910, determined to locate the peak which Dr. Cook had presented as McKinley's summit. They had much more to go by than the bit of another peak in the background of the "summit" photograph. There was the general description Barrill had given Browne on the Seldovia beach about the McKinley foothills which Browne himself had already seen from close by; there was the very explicit map published by Dr. Cook with his route in dotted lines. There were also the other photographs which Dr. Cook had published in his original *Harpers Magazine* article and in his book.

Parker and Browne did not attempt to bring Dr. Cook's climbing companion, Ed Barrill, back to Alaska with them. Barrill had by now become such a pawn of battle in the national press between the Cook and Peary partisans, that anything Barrill might add in 1910 would only be used further to exacerbate rather than clarify the controversy.

Originally, in the fall of 1906, Barrill had gone along with Dr. Cook's claim. And Russell Porter of the expedition had made a very fine pencil sketch portrait of Barrill[1] which was published with Dr. Cook's article in the May, 1907, *Harpers Magazine,* presenting Barrill as one of the two climbers making Mt. McKinley's historic "first ascent". In early accounts, Barrill is described by neighbors as treasuring in his home in the Bitterroot Mountains of western Montana, his copy of *To the Top of the Continent.* But after the controversy with Peary became a subject of national interest, Barrill is said to have admitted privately to his friends that he and Cook had not got above five thousand feet, and joked about the way the public had been fooled.

Finally, on October 4, 1909, Barrill stated in a notarized and published affidavit that at no time did he and Dr. Cook get nearer than about fourteen miles to the top of Mount McKinley; that the famous "summit" photograph published by Dr. Cook was actually made on a peak only 8,000 feet high and twenty miles distant from the mountain; and that the diary that he, Barrill, had kept was, in the part covering the ascent, filled in with false entries dictated by Dr. Cook.

By 1910, S. P. Beecher, Barrill's fellow horse-packer on Cook's 1906 expedition, was in print as saying: "Barrill never directly and definitely asserted to his fellow-members of the expedition that the Doctor or himself had reached the summit of McKinley . . . but he (until his 1909 affidavit) was not openly opposing Dr. Cook's story as it might interfere with his getting his wages due him from Cook."

The response to this by Cook's supporters was to allege that Barrill had been bribed to produce the affidavit. Thus both sides in the controversy were challenging Barrill's integrity. What would count now would be objective evidence from the field. Could Dr. Cook's "summit" photograph be duplicated at some place not the summit of Mt. McKinley and reasonably fitting Barrill's affidavit? And, even more important, would the true summit of Mt. McKinley when reached, be essentially like Dr. Cook's picture, or convincingly different?

So Professor Parker and Belmore Browne chose six other expert individuals, hitherto uncommitted in the controversy, to share the responsibility of trying to locate for the Explorers Club and the American Geographical Society, just where it was that Dr. Cook had actually taken his McKinley "summit" picture, photographed "September 16, 1906, ten o'clock in the morning, temperature minus 16 degrees, altitude 20,391 feet."

Professor J. H. Cuntz of Stevens Institute was the official topographer of this investigating expedition. Other members were Valdemar Grassi of Columbia University, Herman L. Tucker of the U. S. Forest Service, and Merl La Voy, the photographer, of Seattle. In addition they had general assistant Arthur

Aten of Valdez and J. W. Thompson to handle their boat engine. They left Seattle for Alaska on the 5th of May, 1910.

> "At Susitna Station we met a lot of old friends," Browne says: "The camp had changed to quite a little village (since 1906). The A. C. Co. (Alaska Commercial Co.) had erected a large store and warehouses, but the Indian cabins were still in evidence. We found the sternwheel steamer *Alice* moored at the river-front, and I imagine that the scene resembled some of the river-scenes on the Mississippi in the old days of the fur traders."

By chance they now encountered the exploring party sent out by the Mazama Mountaineering Club of Oregon, on a mission similar to their own. "This expedition," Browne writes, "consisted of four men: C. E. Rusk, the leader, Cool, a guide, Rojec, a photographer, and Ridley, an ex-forest ranger. They were a pleasant party of men." Though the two expeditions kept in touch with each other from time to time, they operated independently. Rusk, the leader of the Mazama party, was at this time sympathetic to Dr. Cook's claim. For the Mazama Club, before whom Dr. Cook had lectured in Seattle in November, 1906, had immediately afterward run in their magazine *Mazama* an article fully accepting Dr. Cook's account of the first ascent of Mount McKinley.

The two expeditions proceeded separately up the Susitna River to Talkeetna, then up the Chulitna River, just as Dr. Cook had done in 1906, to the mouth of the inrushing Tokositna, then up to its head of navigation within a few miles of the snout of the vast Ruth Glacier, so named by Dr. Cook for his daughter.

Here they found a "well constructed but tiny cabin" believed to have been built at this spot by John Dokkin, one of Dr. Cook's 1906 party. And beside it on May 31, 1910, the Parker-Browne party beached their boat and took to the glacier, whose terminal moraine they found covered by a jungle of alders and small trees.

Unlike Dr. Cook and Barrill, who with light packs had travelled northward from this point for eight days and returned in four, both investigating expeditions came heavily equipped and supplied for a full summer's campaign. The area where Parker and Browne hoped to find the fake peak—twenty miles in an air line southeast of Mt. McKinley's true summit, near the route marked in dotted lines on Dr. Cook's map—lay many a weary mile ahead, zigzagging around crevasses up the Ruth Glacier. Up this they backpacked their way, relaying their camps and supplies forward, until on June 16 they had made Camp Nine, where, as Browne writes, "the second tributary glacier (from the east) joined the big glacier from the north; and here we saw at once a striking resemblance to the type of mountain in Dr. Cook's photographs, reproductions of which I carried with me."

It was now necessary for Parker and Browne to locate the exact spot where, if their suspicions were correct, Dr. Cook's "summit" photograph had been taken. They were plagued by stormy weather. Finally, "as we pitched our tent on June 22nd the view that we saw was the same as that shown in Dr. Cook's photograph opposite page 197 *(To the Top of the Continent)*, and we could tell by referring to this picture that he had taken the photograph from a knoll about three hundred feet above us.

"Our mountain detective work was based on the fact that no man can lie topographically. In all the mountain ranges of the world there are not two hillocks that are exactly alike. We knew that if we could find one of the peaks shown in his photographs we could trace him peak by peak and snowfield by snowfield, to within a foot of the spot where he had exposed his negatives. And now we had found the peaks he had photographed, but we had found as well from the photograph opposite page 239 that at the time that he took that picture he was not going towards Mount McKinley but that he was high up among the peaks at the head of our glacier No. 2—*at least a day's travel out of his course!*

"There was only one explanation for this fact and that was that close to where this photo was taken we would find the fake peak! . . . We could see several high mountains that looked as if they might prove to be the one we were looking for, and a cliff which stood above a saddle had a familiar look to us. But the distance was too great for a definite [identification] and we decided therefore to make a reconnaissance.

"As we climbed we made important discoveries . . . the cliff we had seen . . . was the same cliff shown on the left side of the photograph opposite page 239. The scent was growing warm. But there was one fact that puzzled us. We had been under the impression that the peak Dr. Cook climbed and photographed was a moderately high peak, and yet as we advanced we could see no peaks worthy of the name in the vicinity of the cliff.

"It required but a short advance, however, to relieve our minds on this point; for turning to Dr. Cook's picture of the cliff . . . we read: 'Scene of Glaciers, Peaks, and Cliffs---shoulder of Mount McKinley, a cliff of 8,000 feet...'.

Just what Dr. Cook intended by a 'cliff of 8,000 feet' we can only surmise, for we found the top of the cliff actually rose only about 300 feet above the glacier, and its altitude was only 5,300 feet above sea-level! After this discovery we no longer expected to find that the Doctor had actually climbed a high peak.

"We had now reached the base of the saddle that led on to the cliff. We called a halt for luncheon, and as we ate our hardtack and pemican we studied the country about us. A few minutes later we began the ascent of the snow saddle on the way to the top of the cliff. Professor Parker had started a few minutes before, and, as we turned to follow the saddle we heard Professor Parker shout, 'We've got it!' An instant later we saw that it was true---the little outcrop of rock below the saddle was the rock peak of Dr. Cook's book, under which he wrote, 'The Top of our Continent-The Summit of Mount McKinley; the highest mountain of North America-Altitude 20,390 feet'.

"While we stood there lost in thought of the dramatic side of our discovery, Professor Parker walked to the top of the rock at the point where Barrill had posed when Dr. Cook exposed his negative. Parker's figure completed the picture. Then we gathered around the photograph Dr. Cook had taken and traced the contours of the rock by its cracks and shoulders. As our eyes reached the right hand skyline there stood . . . the (distant) ribbed peak on which we had based our denial of Dr. Cook's claim, and by which we had traced his footsteps through a wilderness of rock and ice . . . After taking a few photographs, we sat down on the rocks in the warm sun. Avalanches were booming and thundering among the mountains, and the view of Mount McKinley twenty miles away . . . was a picture of sublime beauty."

Half of the investigating job was now done. But the much more difficult remaining half still lay ahead. It was to follow Dr. Cook's route on his own map (or at least try to) on to the true summit of Mount McKinley, and there to photograph the real thing, and to compare it with Dr. Cook's "summit" photograph.

Top: The "Explorer" leaving Susitna Station on the way to Talkeetna Station. *(Photo by H.C. Parker.)* Below: "The author [Browne] photographing the fake peak. Tucker standing where Barrill stood. This view, including the author, is used for a special reason. As short a time ago as March, 1913, a geographer accused the author of painting (by hand) the views of this peak with which we convicted Dr. Cook!" *(Photo by H.C. Parker.)* [*Original Browne caption*]

It was upon this particular project that the Mazama expedition was already engaged. They indeed had started with this part of the project first, regarding it as the most important. With an open mind, and accepting that Dr. Cook could be believed, and regarding him as "innocent" until proved "guilty", the Mazamas were simply going to re-enact what Dr. Cook said he had done, and thereby confirm the Doctor's original account.

C. E. Rusk of Portland, Oregon, the leader of the Mazama party, was a man "of high standing in his own community as an attorney . . . of unimpeachable integrity and a sense of justice, and . . . one of the most expert and daring mountaineers in the west, yet so level-headed and cautious that he has never had a mishap." Financed by the *Pacific Monthly*, the *Portland Oregonian*, and the *New York Herald* and a number of Mazama Club members, Rusk's party was carried north from Seattle to Alaska on the U. S. Revenue cutter *Tahoma*. There was considerable interest in official government circles in an objective investigation of Dr. Cook's Mount McKinley claim, and it was felt that under Rusk the Mazama party might provide a competent, impartial, judicial approach.[2]

Free of the antagonisms which divided Cook and Peary partisans in the States, the two potentially rival Club expeditions enjoyed very cordial relations on those few occasions when they encountered each other in the field. Both recognized that while the Polar controversy might never be settled by absolutely objective proof one way or another, in the case of Dr. Cook's Mount McKinley claims a reasonable conclusion could indeed be reached by the weight of the evidence. Either the Mazamas would convince the Explorers Club that Cook had climbed Mount McKinley in 1906, or conversely, both parties would come to agree —from the evidence in the field—that he had not.

After weeks of difficult backpacking up the awe-inspiring trench of the great Ruth Glacier, Rusk's party at last came to the place, about ten miles southeast of McKinley's summit, where it is evident today Dr. Cook's 1907 map abruptly departs from reasonable accuracy into complete fantasy. Here the Ruth Glacier actually makes a sharp turn flowing in from the west, close under McKinley's sheer south wall. But Cook's map incorrectly shows the Ruth Glacier as flowing in from the east and northeast through an area in which there is in actuality, no valley glacier but a hopelessly tangled knot of high mountains.

Now impossible climbing alternatives also faced the Rusk party whichever way they turned. Camped at the bottom of their fantastic glacial trench rimmed with savage granite walls, with the summit of Mt. McKinley some nine miles away to the northwest, and still 14,000 feet above them, the Mazama party yielded to the inevitable. With only a few days' food left, they set off on their return journey back down the Ruth Glacier, leaving six gallons of alcohol fuel and the following note where the other party might find it:

> "Parker-Browne Expedition:-If you need this alcohol, use it and welcome. Our provisions are exhausted and we must turn back. Goodbye and good luck to you.
> "July 15, 1910 C.E. Rusk"

Rusk now marshalled all the evidence he had collected; it runs to many pages of detail in the January, 1911, issue of *The Pacific Monthly*. There was now not the slightest doubt in his mind or that of any member of his party that, unhappily, they had found Dr. Cook's claim to be false. They had located and identified most of the places where Dr. Cook had taken his photographs (other than the actual "summit" photograph itself, with which the Browne party was occupying itself). And these photographs of Dr. Cook's had clearly been taken between ten and twenty miles from the true top of Mount McKinley, and not high on the mountain itself as Dr. Cook had labelled them.

With the account of the Mazama expedition there is published a rather striking photograph of Dr. Cook, taken by a member of Cook's 1906 expedition who knew him well, with this comment: "He was an excellent camp man; always good-humored, ready to do his full share and more; courageous and simple; but not a man of good judgement in practical affairs. He seemed to have trouble wherever he had financial dealings. I think he claimed the ascent of McKinley, not so much through vanity and love of what glory might be in it, but because he hoped to establish a reputation that would give him backing for a polar expedition, which he always had in mind, and which he succeeded in getting."

A farewell salute to the mountain, as the Mazama party started on the return trip.

To this Rusk added:

"Dr. Cook had many admirers who would have rejoiced to see his claims vindicated, and I too would have been glad to add add my mite in clearing his name. But it could not be. Of his courage and resolution there can be no doubt. He is described as absolutely fearless. He was also considered as always willing to do his share and as an-all-around good fellow to be out with. His explorations around Mount McKinley were extensive. They were of interest and value to the world. Had he persevered, he doubtless would have reached the summit on some future expedition. He was the first to demonstrate the possibility of launch navigation up the Susitna and the Chulitna Rivers. And that one trip alone—when with a single companion he braved the awful solitude of the Ruth Glacier and penetrated the wild, crag-guarded region near the foot of McKinley—should have made him famous. But as we gazed upon the forbidding crags of the great mountain from far up the Ruth Glacier at the point of (Cook's and Barrill's) farthest advance and realized that it would require perhaps weeks or months more in which to explore a route to the summit, we realized how utterly impossible and absurd was the story of this man who, carrying a single pack, claims to have started from the Tokositna on the eighth of September, and to have stood on the highest point of McKinley on the sixteenth of the same month. The man does not live who can perform such a feat. Let us draw the mantle of charity around him and believe, if we can, that there is a thread of insanity running through the woof of his brilliant mind . . . If he is mentally unbalanced, he is entitled to the pity of mankind. If he is not, there is no corner of the earth where he can hide from his past."

"A pause for lunch on Ruth Glacier, about a mile and a half from the foot of Peak 'Six', which appears scarcely more than a couple of hundred yards away." [*Original caption, Mazama Expedition photo*]

VIII

1912: The Cairns Attempt. Parker and Browne Reach Twenty Thousand Feet

THE *Fairbanks Daily Times,* two years earlier, had blithely sold to New York and London newspapers the story that Tom Lloyd made the first ascent of Mt. McKinley. Still smarting under the embarrassment of never having been able to produce the photographic proof which had been promised, the *Times* decided to send its own expedition to make a thoroughly documented climb. On February 6, 1912, Fairbanksans read the newspaper's front page headline: "*Times* Expedition Enroute M'Kinley—Alaska Mushers, Who Are Going to Scale Mt. McKinley for the *Times*, Started from the *Times* Office Yesterday with a Flourish—Equipment is Complete. Party Will Carry the *Times* to the Summit."

Led by Ralph H. Cairns, the newspaper's telegraph editor, the party included Martin Nash, about forty, experienced Alaskan since '98, when he had packed over Chilkoot Pass, and had been "among the rescuers who dug sixty-odd people from their graves when they had met an untimely death on the great snowslide at Sheep Camp on the Dyea Trail". The third man for the mountain party was George S. Lewis, in his thirties, practical surveyor and reclamation engineer, originally from the San Joaquin Valley in California, but a Fairbanksan for three years.

And, like the Sourdoughs of 1910, none of the three had any prior climbing experience. Old Jack Phillips, who joined them at Chena, was captain of the caravan of 23 dogs transporting the expedition outward bound. "The outfit, distributed among four sleds, and including about 400 pounds of dog-salmon, weighed in at approximately an even ton, of which about 1200 pounds were in provisions and utensils, and the remainder in personal dunnage, climbing paraphernalia and so forth."

On February 27, 1912, Fairbanksans read, "Climbers Are Safe at M'Kinley's Base." Two letters dated February 20, at timberline, from Ralph Cairns and George Lewis, and brought back by Jack Phillips, told the story to that day.

Then no more word came until April 10, when the *Times* sadly reported on its front page: "Unable to Scale Heights of Mighty Mt. M'Kinley, Climbing Party Returns." The detailed story ran this way: "Failing to locate McPhee's [McGonagall] Pass, through which the Lloyd party hauled their supplies to Muldrow Glacier . . . we tried to pick a course . . . It took us a month to push our supplies and fuel through . . . the lower end of the moraine of Peters Glacier . . . to a camp on the North face of the mountain, on Peters Glacier."

Beset by many storms—Cairns nearly lost his life in a blizzard—they finally, at the end of March, were "abruptly blocked at just under 10,000 feet[1] by a series of icy pinnacles, or sawteeth, capping the ridge, with no possible alternative course presenting itself."

From their photographs this seems to have been near today's Gunsight Pass on Pioneer Ridge—a route even Wickersham so far back as 1903, had concluded would not "go". Now, of course, they saw the Muldrow Glacier some thousands of feet beneath them on their left to the south. "With another month we could have gotten our outfit onto Muldrow Glacier, but our food stores were becoming rapidly depleted. Old McKinley had defeated us . . . We gazed over the wonderful panorama of mountains and glaciers . . . then with regretful voices we muttered 'home!'."

And so ended the eighth expedition to try to reach Mount McKinley's summit—and fail.

* * *

Meanwhile, back in New York, Professor Parker and Belmore

Browne, for their 1912 attempt, had decided on a completely new approach to the north slopes of the mountain—by dog-team, in the winter, from the south. Convinced by their explorations of 1906 and 1910 that the south slopes of the mountain were impossible, they were now ready to try the northeast side of the mountain via the Muldrow Glacier. They had studied the photographs made by their friend Charles Sheldon in 1906, 1907 and 1908 during his explorations with Harry Karstens in the Kantishna, when Sheldon had pointed out the possibilities of the northeast ridge to Lloyd and his friends. And from Lloyd's published photographs made in 1910, Parker and Browne were satisfied that the Sourdough party of that year had found a successful route up this northeast ridge at least to the edge of the High Basin between the north and south peaks.

> "The next question," Browne writes, "was how we were to reach the northeast ridge. Fairbanks on the Tanana River is the nearest town to Mt. McKinley, and with the aid of dogs in winter time, the journey offers no difficulties, consisting as it does of only 160 miles of excellent snow travel. This was our logical route. But . . . it was our desire to explore the unknown canyons of the Alaskan Range east of Mt. McKinley. If we could find a pass through the high range from the Susitna River on the south we would explore a magnificent mountain wilderness that otherwise might remain unknown for years [and would further elucidate Dr. Cook's claimed approach route]. While it would be possible . . . during the summer . . . this would require too much time . . . We decided therefore to make a winter trip of it, and to depend for our transportation on the Alaskan dog.
>
> "Merl La Voy with his Graflex camera and Arthur Aten of the old party joined us. As we were to enter the Alaska Range our route would lead us up the frozen waterways of the Susitna and Chulitna Rivers. But since Cook Inlet was choked with ice during the winter time, we were forced to leave the steamer at Seward during the last days of January . . . A winter trail leads from the end of the incompleted railroad line, through the heart of the Kenai Peninsula, through magnificent mountain scenery to tidewater on Turnagain Arm, and on via Knik Arm to Susitna Station on the Susitna River. Beyond Susitna Station a winter trail now leads over the Alaskan Range at the head of the Kichatna to the Kuskoquim and the gold fields of the Iditarod. At intervals of about ten miles, 'road houses' stand offering food and rest to man and dog. They are one of the most important of Alaskan institutions, and on all the winter trails that cross

> the great land, one will find these resting places which make rapid travel possible."

In Seward they found:

> "The town was stirred by the arrival of the Iditarod gold shipment. The gold was packed in small wooden chests, one hundred pounds to the chest,[2] which were handled with grunts and groans by the bank clerks who took them from the dog sleds. The populace stood packed about, but fully one-half their interest was centered on the two magnificent, perfectly matched dog teams that had pulled the treasure from the banks of the Kuskoquim, four hundred miles to the northwest . . . The teams were hitched in the regulation Alaskan trail manner—two by two with a single leader. Their harness was perfect from the silver bells that jangled so sweetly, to the red pom-poms that bobbed gaily on each furry back . . . We said goodbye to Seward and its hospitable citizens on the first of February, 1912."
>
> Seventeen days later they reached Susitna Station. Here, "everyone showed the greatest interest in our venture. We were invited to a 'civilized dinner' by McNalley, the Alaska Commercial Co. representative—the last we were to enjoy until five months later we reached the Yukon."

Leaving Susitna Station, they turned off the winter trail of comfortable roadhouses leading west to the Iditarod country, and swung their dogs up the frozen Susitna river north into the unexplored country east of Mount McKinley, tenting out each night. By March 20 they had made it up the length of the tributary Chulitna, and were crossing the Alaska Range via an unnamed valley and pass. They then proceeded up the West Fork Glacier, over Anderson Pass and down the lower end of the Muldrow Glacier to the timber on the McKinley River, which they reached on April 17, 1912.

Now in excellent game country, they took time off to rest and hunt caribou and mountain sheep for food; and soon came upon one of the Cairns party's recently abandoned camps with tent still standing—in which they found *Fairbanks Daily Times* newspaper clippings carrying speculative stories about themselves and their plans!

Leaving Aten to hold down their tundra base camp and take care of the extra dogs, Browne, Parker and La Voy now proceeded without difficulty to dogsledge their mountain supplies

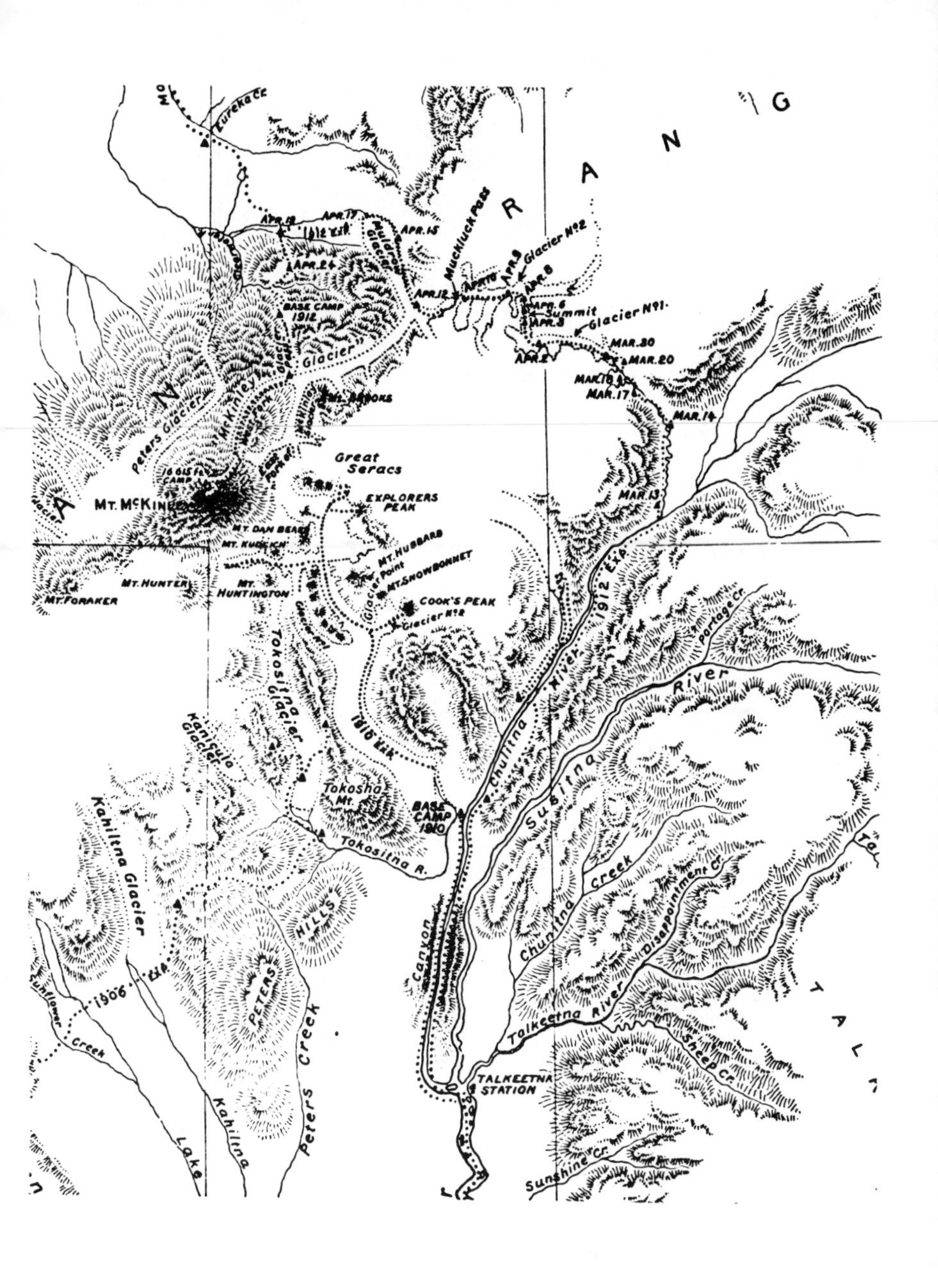

Portion of map showing route of Parker-Browne 1910 and 1912 expeditions. Though Muldrow Glacier is correctly named at its lower end, the upper end is named "McKinley Glacier." Today's McGonagall Pass is named "Glacier Pass." The Mt. Hunter name has migrated from the one that Dunn originally christened with that name to a much higher mountain southwest of McKinley.

Two dog teams hitched to one sled on "Crow Creek Pass."

through McGonagall Pass (which in their accounts they refer to as "Glacier Pass") where it emerges onto the mid-Muldrow Glacier. Then they steered directly toward McKinley's twin summits and proceeded up the gently sloping Muldrow, following its miles of turns to near the glacier's steep-walled head at 11-000 feet. Here, immediately on their left, they found the key access ridge leading to the High Basin far above. Near the bottom of this ridge they cached their dog-sled load of food, supplies and mountaineering gear, and returned to leave the dog team with Aten at the base camp.

Spring had arrived during the ten days they had been on the glacier. Back at base camp they found:

> "Our first sight of grass and flowers and running water in many months, as the lowlands had still been in the grip of late winter when we started up the mountain. We took the most extravagant delight in our new life, for living on ice is an unnatural and trying ordeal . . . We now lived largely 'off the country' and my days were filled with hunting caribou and mountain sheep, or photographing them and the nesting ptarmigan, or studying the topographical features of the magnificent mountain."

Finally, after weeks of resting in this idyll, they returned in early June for their final attack. On the upper Muldrow Glacier after a three-day snow storm, on June 8, Browne made an unusual and interesting observation:

> "The glacier has been very noisy all day; it has groaned and cracked, and at short intervals there have been deep powerful reports, sounding for all the world like the boom of big guns at a distance. We have been talking about the queer noise but are undecided as to its cause. It must be due to the settling of the great ice caverns under the tremendous weight of new snow. It was not until we reached civilization long afterwards that we found the unusual booming sound had not come from the glacial caverns, but that it was made by Katmai in eruption hundreds of miles away---Katmai, the volcano whose eruption buried Kodiak in ashes! Later we found these Katmai ashes in our teapot after we had melted snow, but again we accepted the easiest explanation and decided that the grit in our teacups was merely dust blown from the cliffs."

They reached the base of the northeast (today's Karstens)

ridge, without further incident. Then, like the 1910 Sourdough party before them, they found the climb up this access ridge no great technical problem, though very exhausting under the depth of much new snow.

Finally, after back-packing and relaying their supplies to successively higher camps and caches, Parker, Browne, and La Voy on the 27th of June . . . camped between the great North and South peaks, just below the last serac that forms the highest point of the Big Basin.

> "We arrived with our last loads after the sun had gone down, and I have never felt such savage cold as the ice-fields sent down to us," says Browne. "We were in a frigid hollow at an altitude of 16,615 ft. On the north the great blue ice slopes led up an almost unclimbable pitch between the granite buttresses of the North Peak . . . On the south, frozen snowfields swept gently . . . in an easy grade to the final South summit of the great mountain . . . Our feet and hands were beginning to stiffen as we pitched the tent . . . and we were seriously worried for fear Professor Parker would freeze . . .
>
> "The morning of our final climb dawned clear as crystal. As I came out into the stabbing cold to report on the weather, the whole expanse of country to the north-eastward stretched like a deep blue sea to where the rising sun was warming the distant horizon.
>
> "We left camp at 6 a.m. At first the snow was hard and required little step chopping . . . We moved quietly and steadily, conserving our strength . . . At regular half hour intervals La Voy and I exchanged places. Between changes both Professor Parker and I checked off our rise in altitude (from the altimeter) and found that although we thought we were making fairly good time, we were in reality climbing only 400 feet an hour.
>
> "One thousand feet above our camp we ran into soft snow, and fought against this handicap at frequent intervals during the day. When we reached 18,500 feet we stopped for an instant and congratulated each other joyfully, for we had returned the altitude record of North America to America, by beating the Duke of the Abruzzi's record of 18,000 feet made on St. Elias.[4]
>
> "Shortly afterward we reached the top of the big ridge. We had long dreamed of this moment, because, for the first time, we now were able to look down [south] into our battleground of 1910, and see all the glaciers and peaks we had

"The great avalanche that fell above our camp. It is about a mile away and the snow cloud shown in the photo is about 1000 feet high." (First view.) *(Photo by Merl La Voy.)* [*Browne's original caption*]

hobnobbed with in the 'old days'. But the views northeastward along the great wilderness of peaks and glaciers spread out below us like a map. On the northern side of the range there was not one cloud; the icy mountains blended into the rolling foothills which in turn melted into the dim blue of the timbered lowlands, that rolled away to the north, growing bluer and bluer until they were lost at the edge of the world. On the humid south side, a sea of clouds was rolling against the main range like surf on a rocky shore. The clouds rose as we watched.

"Now as we advanced up the ridge toward the South summit we felt a shortness of breath and Professor Parker's face was noticeably white, but we made fast time and did not suffer in any other way. At a little less than 19,000 feet, we passed the last rock on the ridge and secured our first clear view of the summit. It rose as innocently as a tilted snow-covered tennis-court and as we looked it over we grinned with relief—we *knew* the peak was ours! . . .

"During our ascent of the ridge and the first swell of the final summit the wind had increased, and the southern sky darkened until at the base of the final peak we were facing a snow-laden gale. As the storm increased we had taken careful bearings, and because the snow slope was only moderately steep all we had to do now was to 'keep going uphill' . . .

"As I again stepped ahead to take La Voy's place in the lead I realized for the first time that we were fighting a blizzard, for my companions loomed dimly through the clouds of ice-dust, and the bitter wind stabbed through my parka. Five minutes after I began chopping, my hands began to freeze; and until we returned to 18,000 feet I was engaged in a constant struggle to keep the frost from disabling my extremities. La Voy's gloves and mine became coated with ice in the chopping of steps. The storm now became so severe that I was actually afraid to get new dry mittens out of my rucksack, for I knew my hands would be frozen in the process.

"Professor Parker's barometer (altimeter) at last registered 20,000 feet[4] . . . As I stepped aside (alternating the lead) to let La Voy pass me, I saw from his face he realized the danger of our position, but I knew too that the summit was near and determined to hold on to the last moment.

"As Professor Parker passed me his lips were dark and his face showed white from cold through his parka hood, but he made no sign of distress and I will always remember his dauntless spirit. The last period of our climb is like the memory of an evil dream. La Voy was completely lost in the ice

Top: Avalanche falling 3000 feet on the northeast ridge of Mt. McKinley. (Second view of avalanche on page 95.) *(Photo by Belmore Browne.)* Below: Avalanche falling 3000 feet from the central northeast ridge of Mt. McKinley. (Third view.) *(Photo by H.C. Parker.)*

mist, and Professor Parker's frosted form was an indistinct blur above me. I worked savagely to keep my hands warm . . . when a faint hail from above told me my turn had come again to lead.

"When I reached La Voy I had to chop about twenty feet of steps before coming to the end of the rope. Something indistinct showed through the scud as I felt the rope tauten, and a few steps more brought me to a little crack or bergschrund. Up to this time we had been working in a partial lee, but as I topped the small rise made by the crack I was struck by the full fury of the storm. The breath was driven from my body and I held to my axe with stooped shoulders to stand against the gale; I couldn't go ahead. As I brushed the frost from my glasses and squinted upward through the stinging snow I saw a sight that will haunt me to my dying day. The slope above me was no longer steep! That was all I could see. What it meant I will never know for certain—all I can say is that we were close to the top!

"As the blood congealed in my fingers I went back to La Voy. He was getting the end of the gale's whiplash, and when I yelled that we couldn't stand the wind he agreed that it was suicide to try. With one accord we fell to chopping a seat in the ice in an attempt to shelter ourselves from the storm, but after sitting in a huddled group for an instant we all arose—we were beginning to freeze!

"I turned to Professor Parker and yelled, 'the game's up; we've got to get down!'

"And he answered, 'Can't we go on? I'll chop if I can.' The memory of those words will always send a wave of admiration through my mind, but I had to answer that it was not a question of chopping, and La Voy pointed out our back steps —or the place where our steps ought to be, for immediately below us everything was wiped out by hissing snow.

"Coming down from the final dome was as heartless a piece of work as any of us had ever done. Every foothold I found with my axe alone, for there was no sign of a step left. It took me nearly two hours to lead down that easy slope of one thousand feet! If my reader is a mountaineer he can complete the picture! We reached camp at 7:35 p.m. after as cruel a day as I trust we will ever experience. On the following day we could not climb [and rested in camp at 16,500 feet].

"Throughout the long day we talked food. We had now given up all thought of eating pemmican. In both our 16,000 and 16,615 foot camps we had tried to eat cooked pemmican without success. We were able to choke down a few mouthfuls

Top: Lowering sleds by hand to the top of the "1000 foot drop-off" below the pass. Below: Looking down the back-trail from 12,000 feet. Upper Muldrow Glacier at left. First camp ever made (figure with outstretched arms) on what is known today as Karstens Ridge.

of this food, but we were at last forced to realize that our stomachs could not handle the amount of fat it contained. The reader will no doubt wonder why we placed such dependence on one food, and my excuse is that we had put it to every proof except altitude.[5] We were now living, as in fact we had been living since leaving our 15,000 foot camp, on tea, sugar, hardtack and raisins. Our chocolate was finished. *We had lost ten days' rations in useless pemmican!*

"We were harassed not only by the thought of the food we had lost, but also by the memory of the *useless weight we had carried.* Moreover we were forced to eat more of our hardtack and raisins in an attempt to gain the nourishment we had been deprived of by the uselessness of our pemmican. This complication reduced us to four meagre days' rations, which meant that we could only make one more attempt on the summit of Mount McKinley, and that attempt must be made on the following day. The reader will understand with what breathless interest we now studied the weather conditions . . . We decided to leave at 3 a.m.

"The following day, strengthened as far as our insipid food would allow . . . we started on our final attack.

"The steps made two days before helped us, and in four hours and a half, or by 7:30 a.m., we had reached an altitude of 19,300 feet at the base of the final dome. From this point we could see our steps made on the first attempt leading up to the edge of the final dome, and from this point we also secured our closest photograph of the summit.

"But our progress up the main ridge had been a race with a black cloud bank that was rolling up from the Susitna Valley, and as we started toward our final climb, the clouds wrapped us in dense wind-driven sheets of snow. We stood the exposure for an hour; now chopping a few steps aimlessly upward, now stamping backward and forward on a little ledge we found, and when we had fought the blizzard to the limit of our endurance we turned and without a word stumbled downward. I remember only a feeling of weakness and dumb despair; we had burned up and lived off our own tissue until we didn't care much what happened!

"We reached camp at 3 p.m. and after some hot tea we felt a wild longing to leave the desolate spot . . . shouldered our light loads and struck off down the glacier. I turned for a last look . . . above, the roar of the wind came down from the dark clouds that hid the summit."

[Two nights and a day later] "bare mountain-sides greeted our snow-tired eyes, and at 3 a.m. we . . . laid our tired bodies on soft warm earth. We finally summoned enough energy

Photographic proof of the Browne party's high climb. This view somewhere about 18,000 to 19,000 feet back down the climbing route could have been taken only from McKinley's summit cone.

> to eat a little, and pitch our tent, and then we slept like dead men until the afternoon. When we awoke there was a warm breeze blowing up through the pass, and with it came the smell of grass and wild flowers. Never can I forget the flood of emotions that swept over me; Professor Parker and La Voy were equally affected by this first 'smell of the lowland', and we were wet-eyed and chattered like children as we prepared our packs for the last stage of the journey.
>
> "All our thoughts now centered on Arthur Aten. We had told him we would return in fourteen days and now our absence had stretched to twice that number . . . Our concern for Aten now drove us onward.
>
> "When we came out of the pass into the valley of the Clearwater, we encountered a band of fifty caribou, and while we rested they trotted excitably about until by a concerted flank movement they caught our scent, and floated like a great brown carpet across the mountainside. So it went, in turns of long packs and short rests while the sinking sun flooded the western sky with gold. At last the old rock above our camp came into view, and Professor Parker went ahead.
>
> "Then we saw a figure clear cut against the sky. Was it a man or a wild beast? was the thought that flashed through my mind, until a second smaller shape appeared—a dog! And our joyful yells echoed down the valley.
>
> "Aten came to us, tears of happiness running down his cheeks, and we forgot our stiff-necked ancestry and threw our arms around each other in a wild embrace, while over us, under us, and all around us surged an avalanche of woolly dogs."

One wholly unexpected and startling experience yet awaited them while they rested in their base camp at Cache Creek. On the evening of July 6,

> "the sky was a sickly green color. A deep rumbling came from the Alaska Range, with a deep hollow quality that was terrifying. The earth began to heave and roll, and I forgot everything but the desire to stay upright. In front of me a two-hundred-pound boulder turned, broke loose from the earth, and moved several feet. Then came the crash of falling caches, followed by another muffled crash as the front of our hill slid into the creek, and a lake nearby boiled with stirrings from below. Then suddenly everything was still. We stood up dazed and looked about. Our dogs had fled at the beginning of the quake, and we could hear them whimpering and running about in the willows.

"While we were restoring order out of chaos, Aten exclaimed: 'Good God! Look at Mount Brooks!'

"The whole extent of the mountain wall that formed its western flank was avalanching. The avalanche seemed to stretch along the range for a distance of several miles, like a huge wave, and like a huge wave it seemed to poise for an instant before it plunged downward onto the icefields thousands of feet below. The mountain was about ten miles away, and we waited breathlessly until the terrific thunder of the falling mass began to boom and rumble among the mountains . . . a great white cloud began to rise and obscure the range as it billowed upward, two—three—four thousand feet, until it hung like a huge opaque wall against the main range.

"We knew that the cloud was advancing at a rate close to sixty miles an hour and that we did not have much time to spare. But with boulders to hold the bottom and tautened guy-ropes, we made the tent as solid as possible and got inside before the cloud struck us. The tent held fast, but after the 'wullies' passed, the ground was spangled with ice-dust that only a few minutes before had formed the icy covering of a peak ten miles away!

"My strongest impression immediately after the quake was surprise at the elasticity of the earth. One felt as if the earth's crust was a quivering mass of jelly."

Months later they learned that this devastating earthquake was related to the eruption of Mount Katmai on the Alaska Peninsula, 380 miles away.

"We now turned our faces northward toward the Yukon. We still had two hundred and fifty miles of wilderness before us, and our days were still full of the joyous incidents of the wild life. Shouldering as much as we could carry, we put what was left on our faithful dogs, and wandered downward across the foothills looking for a likely stream to carry us to 'the outside.'" [They found and repaired a poling-boat on Moose Creek, and] "drifted down silent streams where the leaping grayling flashed in the air; we camped on birch-covered flats where moose, wet from the river, stampeded among our excited dogs, we floated past sun-drenched banks where Canada geese splashed, honking, from our path.

"Finally we camped with miners on the banks of rushing streams in the Kantishna where the gold lay yellow in the sluice-boxes . . . The sun-bronzed 'sourdoughs' took us in and lavished on us the riches of the land . . . "

The climbers were asked, of course, if they had found any evidence of Lloyd's 1910 expedition high on the mountain. The miners along the Kantishna, only thirty miles away, had not been able to spot that flagpole reported in the newspaper to have been left on the North Peak. Had the Parker-Browne party seen it?

The reply was "No." Later, in writing about the climb, Browne explained:

> "On our journey up the glacier from below we had begun to study the North Peak. As we advanced closer and closer, each pinnacle . . . stood out in turn against the sky, until the last days, close to the southern summit, every rock and snow slope of that approach had come into the field of our powerful binoculars. We not only saw no sign of a flagpole, but it is our concerted opinion that the Northern peak is more inaccessible than its higher southern sister."

Professor Parker was more outspoken. Though readily accepting that the Sourdough party had climbed to the top of the access ridge (today's Karstens)—which their 1910 photographs proved—he was skeptical of any more, and was quoted in a New York newspaper as saying that from his own observations "Dr. Cook didn't have anything on the Lloyd party when it comes to fabrications."

Since the entire Parker-Browne climb itself was so thoroughly documented to 19,300 feet with excellent published photographs which everyone accepted without question, the 1910 Sourdough North Peak expedition came now for a while to be dismissed by everyone as just another Alaskan tall tale. This situation was, however, destined to be completely reversed within a year.

IX

1913: Alaskans Make the First Complete Ascent

THE next event, in this active decade of the great mountain's history, was another brush with Dr. Cook. Surfacing in London from his strange year-long disappearance, Dr. Cook was interviewed by a correspondent for the *New York World.*

"The great international mystery of the century—the whereabouts of Dr. Frederick A. Cook—has been cleared, the *World* has found Dr. Cook", that paper's readers learned on October 2, 1910. He had been in seclusion, it was reported, working on the completion of his book, about to be published, describing his attainment of the North Pole. And Dr. Cook still had supporters. According to the London *St. James Gazette,* while Dr. Cook was in that city in seclusion, incognito and entirely unrecognized, he had joined the audience before which Robert E. Peary was being officially honored in Albert Hall by the Royal Geographical Society, with its Special Great Gold Medal. And, according to the *Gazette,* clearly sympathetic to Cook, "where the true greatness comes is that Cook, though so near, never lifted a hand against Peary and, still finer, never opened his mouth to controvert one of his statements."

"The End of the Polar Controversy", Belmore Browne had optimistically entitled his account of the 1910 exposure and documentation of Dr. Cook's "fake" peak in Alaska. But in this Browne was mistaken. Not only was the finding and documentation about Dr. Cook's "fake" peak not the end of the Polar Controversy, it proved to be merely the beginning of the great Mount McKinley Controversy, still alive indeed as we go to press in 1967. Where Tom Lloyd—as Billy Taylor once put it—"had kind of a nervous breakdown and just keeled over" after his McKinley story became discredited, Dr. Cook on the other hand, quite unabashed, came back to America in the winter of 1910-11 after his "year in exile" and actively reasserted his claim to have made the first ascent of the great mountain.

In February, 1913 the editor of the *Overland Monthly* (San Francisco) invited Dr. Cook to write an introduction to the account of the Cairns attempt on Mount McKinley. Dr. Cook used the opportunity to address himself to an entirely different aspect of the mountain's history. "We (Cook and Barrill) made the first ascent by the most eastern of the three north ridges in 1906. Herschel Parker, coming later, claimed that the northeast ridge was unclimbable, and that, therefore, our first ascent was impossible. In 1912 he started in from the north, reached the upper part of the same ridge upon which our climb was made from the east, and claimed to have reached the top. He has, therefore, disproven his own charge that we did not climb the mountain."

Nonsense, of course. Though on a first reading it seems there might be a point. The correct fact that Parker and Browne did demonstrate that the final upper mile of Cook's 1906 claimed "route" is indeed climbable, says nothing one way or the other about the hopelessly difficult, middle twenty miles of Dr. Cook's 1906 published "route".

In this same introductory essay Dr. Cook also made the following remarkable observation: "Mount McKinley has risen to a peculiar prominence. It has been discussed and rediscussed, climbed and unclimbed so often by distorted press reports that it is regarded as a joker among the trump cards of mountaineers. But why blot the white mantle of this virgin peak with controversy? There is room enough and honor enough on its great walls of alabaster for vast armies of future explorers. . .".

Then Dr. Cook concludes with this pleasing and well-done paragraph, "Mount McKinley, by sheer altitude, not by latitude, pushes its crown into the realm of the midnight sun. For centuries the Indians watched with awe and admiration this midnight, midsummer fire in all its crowning glory above the clouds, while the lower slopes were bathed in the chilly blue of the sub-

Arctic night. For this reason, if for no other, Mt. McKinley is the world's most remarkable mountain."

Dr. Cook had yet another contribution to make: this one, another expedition—apparently mythical—for the year 1911, which year otherwise completely lacks any record of climbing activity on Mount McKinley. Information about this seems first to have appeared in Dr. Cook's third, 1913, edition of his book *My Attainment of the Pole,* in whose pages, despite its title, much attention is actually devoted to his claims with regard to Mount McKinley in 1906.

Seeking to refute the argument that his 1906 climbing "route" is unclimbable and untraversable for miles in its middle portion, Dr. Cook on page 534 of his new book now stated that "the well known-engineer, R. C. Bates" in 1911 climbed to an altitude of "11,000 feet" along his (Cook's) 1906 route onto the "northeast ridge" (today's Karstens). This of course, if true, would prove that Karstens ridge can be easily reached and climbed from the Chulitna River-Ruth Glacier route, as Dr. Cook claims he originally did it. But careful search over the years fails to confirm either the supposed primary reference which Cook gives for this (the *Los Angeles Tribune* for February 13, 1913) or to reveal any other mention of Bates' supposed expedition. Nevertheless some later writers accept as fact Dr. Cook's original assertion about Bates' supposed expedition.

During these years McKinley was coming to be referred to as "The Great Mountain of Mystery" because of the confusion and uncertainty as to who had done what. A prominent lawyer in Philadelphia, who later testified before a Congressional Committee investigating the Mount McKinley Controversy, wrote in 1913, "Lloyd denies Cook. Browne denies Cook and Lloyd. Stuck denies Cook and Lloyd, and while not denying Browne, repeats over and over that Browne did not reach the top. There is a perfect epidemic of denials. So much so that it would be more accurate to nickname the peak Mount Denial instead of Mount Denali!"

It was in this atmosphere and against this background that Dr. Hudson Stuck, Episcopal Archdeacon of the Yukon, and his pioneer partner, Harry Karstens, later to become the first Superintendent of McKinley National Park, set off by dog team from

Fairbanks in mid-March, 1913, for the Kantishna country, their destination the distant summit of Mount McKinley.

Both were thoroughly experienced in Alaskan travel. Karstens had left his Illinois home, at nineteen, to join the Klondike gold rush to Dawson (See Literature References for Karstens' Autobiography). Later, after some mining on Seventy Mile Creek in Alaska, he had been one of those who laid out the town site of Eagle. After the discovery of gold near Fairbanks he became a mail carrier, driving dogs between that community and Valdez; and then between Fairbanks and the Kantishna mining district.

Here in 1906 he had his fateful meeting with Charles Sheldon the naturalist, who engaged Karstens' services during the 1906-7-8 years which Sheldon devoted to the study of the natural history of the northern foothills of the McKinley range. The results of this work later published by Sheldon, led to the establishment of the region as a National Park. Sheldon had written: "When I look back upon my experiences in Alaska and the Yukon I recall no better fortune than that which befell me when Harry Karstens was engaged as an assistant packer. He is a tall, stalwart man, well poised, frank, and strictly honorable, and peculiarly fitted by youth and experience for explorations in little-known regions; he proved a most efficient and congenial companion."

Karstens for years had tried unsuccessfully to interest Sheldon in a climbing attempt on McKinley, ever since the time that between them, in 1906, with field glasses from below, they had worked out the key to the climbing route up and along the northeast ridge (destined many years later to bear Karstens' name), into the high basin between the North and South Peaks. But Sheldon, though an active out-of-doors man was not really a mountain climber, and had always declined Karstens' repeated suggestions for an actual climbing expedition.

Hudson Stuck, in his fiftieth year by the time of the McKinley expedition with Karstens, as a young man had climbed in England and Wales, then in the Colorado and Canadian Rockies, and had also been to the top of Mount Rainier. A decade of mission work in Alaska had involved a vast amount of winter travel, out of which came his book *Ten Thousand Miles with a Dog Sled.*

In 1906 he had written of the thrill he experienced in his first climb to the top of Pedro Dome, sixteen miles northeast of Fairbanks. "Far to the southwest rose Mt. McKinley, or Tenali, as the Tanana natives call it, 160 or 170 miles away . . . yet dominating the whole scene . . . as it shimmered in its pearly beauty and grew clearer and brighter as I gazed. What a glorious, broad, massive uplift that mountain is! The Mississippi is not so truly the father of waters as McKinley is the father of mountains. It is not a peak, it is a region. I would rather climb that mountain than discover the richest goldmine in Alaska."

Stuck writes that he long ago had picked out Mr. Harry P. Karstens as the one colleague with whom he would be willing to make the attempt. This despite the fact that Karstens had had no previous mountaineering experience, and had not participated in any of the many preceding McKinley climbing expeditions.

But Hudson Stuck, unlike the wealthy Charles Sheldon, could not afford to engage Karstens' services on an employment basis. Indeed, Karstens might not have been willing to go as Stuck's employee. The result was that when Karstens in late 1912 finally accepted Stuck's proposal that they make an expedition to climb McKinley, they agreed that it was to be a partnership enterprise. Stuck was to recruit the other membership of the expedition, "providing equipment, provisions and transportation to the base, while Karstens was to provide the experience and leadership on the mountain", Stuck later wrote.

The project was approved by Stuck's immediate superior, Bishop Rowe, who released Stuck's time for the purpose, and authorized use of the mission's launch *Pelican*. It was to transport the supplies toward McKinley up the Kantishna and Bearpaw rivers to the head of navigation of the latter. At the last minute, though, it broke down and Karstens had to do this part of the work in the fall of 1912 by hand-poling the supplies and equipment upstream.

The financing of such an enterprise was no small problem: Dr. Cook by his own account had required some $28,000 to finance his two expeditions, most of which he had raised from Harpers, the publishers. Stuck explains: "A volunteer expedition was the only one within the resources of the writer, and even that strained them. The cost of the food supplies, the equipment, and the incidental expenses was not far short of a thousand dollars, a mere fraction of the cost of previous expeditions, it is true, but a matter of long scraping for a missionary."

The other four members of the expedition were all recruited by Stuck, from among his Episcopal mission people. "Mr. Robert G. Tatum, of Tennessee, just twenty-one years old, a postulant for holy orders, stationed at the mission at Nenana, had just been employed the past winter in a determined attempt to get supplies to two women missionaries, a nurse and a teacher, at Tanana Crossing, his efforts made desperate by the knowledge that the women were reduced to a diet of straight rabbits without salt."

Walter Harper, half Indian son of Arthur Harper, explorer of the Tanana in the eighteen seventies, was destined to play an important role on the final climb. He had been Stuck's attendant and interpreter, dog driver in the winter and boat engineer in the summer for three years, was twenty-one years old and six feet tall. "He took gleefully to mountaineering, while his kindliness and invincible amiability endeared him to every member of the party."

They also took along two Indian boys of fourteen and fifteen, picked from the elder boys of the mission school at Nenana, all of whom were eager to go. Johnny was with the expedition from start to finish, keeping the base camp. Esias went as far as the base camp, and then returned one of the dog teams back to Nenana.

Their dog-sled journey to the Kantishna passed through a region which had changed greatly during the decade since Judge Wickersham in 1903 had travelled out through a virtually undisturbed wilderness. In 1906 there had been a wild stampede to this region. Two or three thousand people went in, chiefly from the Fairbanks district. Town after town was built—Diamond City, Glacier City, Bearpaw City, Roosevelt, McKinley City—all with elaborate saloons and gambling-places, one at least equipped with electric lights. But next summer the boom had burst and all the thousands streamed out.

Stuck noted further, "Gold there was, and is yet, but in small quantities only. The 'cities' now are mere collections of tumble-down huts amongst which the moose roam. The few men now in the district have placer claims that yield a 'grub stake' as a sure thing every summer, and spend their winters chiefly in prospecting for quartz (gold lodes)."

Unlike the Cairns expedition of the preceding year, the 1913 party found the pass onto Muldrow Glacier without difficulty. In his later magazine account, Stuck explains: "There was no need to make reconnaissance for routes, since the (1910 Sourdough) pioneers found the way; there is no practical route other than the one they discovered."

Stuck was one of the first to appraise the 1910 Sourdough expedition correctly. From those members of it who told the truth about what they did and did not do, he had learned that the key to reaching the high basin between North and South Peaks was the great northeast ridge [Karstens]. Parker and Browne, moreover, had already climbed by the same route in 1912, and confirmed this.

But a real surprise awaited them. "Just before leaving Fairbanks," Stuck writes, "we had received a copy of a magazine containing the account of the Browne-Parker climb, and in that narrative Mr. Browne speaks of the Northeast [Karstens] Ridge as a 'steep but practicable snow slope', and prints a photograph which shows it as such.

> "To our surprise, when we reached the head of the (Muldrow) glacier, the ridge offered no resemblance whatever to the description or the photograph. The upper one-third of it was indeed as described, but at that point there was a sudden sharp cleavage, and all below was a jumbled mass of blocks of ice and rock in all manner of positions, with here a pinnacle and there a great gap. Moreover, the floor of the glacier was strewn with enormous ice blocks that we could not understand at all. Then the explanation came to us. The 1912 earthquake!
>
> "The Browne-Parker party of the preceding year had reported the tremendous earthquake on the 6th of July, two days after they had left the mountain; and, as was learned later, the seismographic instruments at Washington recorded it as the most severe shock since the San Francisco disturbance of 1906. The huge ice-blocks all around us were not the normal

discharge of the hanging glacier as we had at first wonderingly supposed. They were ripped off the rocks and hurled down from the ridge by this earthquake convulsion. It was as though, as soon as the Browne-Parker party reached the foot of the mountain, the ladder by which they had ascended and descended was broken up. The great blocks of ice hurled down from above lay apparently just where they had fallen almost a year before.

"What a wonderful providential escape those three men Browne, Parker, and LaVoy had. They would have waited in their high camp for fair weather had they been provided with adequate food; but their stomachs would not retain the canned pemmican they had laboriously carried aloft, and they were compelled to give up the attempt and descend. So down to the foot of the mountain they went, and immediately they reached their base camp this awful earthquake shattered the ridge and showered down huge bergs on both upper and lower glaciers. Had their food served, they would certainly have remained above; and had they remained above their bodies would be there now. Even could they have escaped the avalanching icebergs they could never have descended that ridge after the earthquake. They would either have been overwhelmed and crushed to death instantly or have perished by starvation.

"The difficulty of our task was very greatly increased; that was plain at a glance. This ridge, that the pioneer climbers of 1910 went up at one march with climbing irons strapped beneath their moccasins, carrying nothing but their flag-pole, and that the Browne-Parker party surmounted in a few days, relaying their camping stuff and supplies, was to occupy us for three weeks while we hewed a staircase three miles long in the shattered ice.

"Now (mid-May) began a period of suspense, of hope blasted anew nearly every morning: a period of waiting for decent weather. With the whole mountain and glacier enveloped in thick mist it was not possible to do anything up above, and day after day this was the condition, varied by high wind and heavy snow. But the tedium of lying in that camp while snowstorm or fierce high wind forbade adventure on the splintered ridge was not so great to the writer as to some of the other members of the expedition, for there was always Walter's education to be prosecuted, as it had been for three winters on the trail and three summers on the launch. An hour or two spent writing from dictation, another hour or two in reading aloud, a little geography and a little history and a little physics made the day pass busily. A pupil is a great resource.

"We were greatly interested and surprised at the intrusion of animal life into these regions totally devoid of any vegetation. A rabbit followed us up the glacier to an elevation of ten thousand feet, gnawing the bark from the willow shoots with which the trail was staked, creeping round the crevasses, and, in one place at least, leaping such a gap. At ten thousand feet he turned back and descended, leaving his tracks in the snow. We speculated as to what possible object he could have had.

"At this camp way up the glacier we saw ptarmigan on several occasions, and heard their unmistakable cry on several more, and once we felt sure that a covey passed over the ridge above us and descended to the other glacier. It was always in thick weather that these birds were noticed up here at the head of the glacier, and we surmised that perhaps they had lost their way in the cloud. But even this was not the greatest height at which bird life was encountered. Later, up above the Grand Basin, at sixteen thousand five hundred feet, Walter was certain that he heard the twittering of small birds familiar throughout the winter in Alaska, and this was also in mist. I have never known the boy to make a mistake in such matters.

"Day by day Karstens and Walter would go up and resume the finding and making of a way, and Tatum and the writer would relay the stuff from the camp to a cache, some five hundred feet above, and thence to another. Each day Karstens and Walter (worked above) . . . and more than once a passage painfully hewn in the solid ice had to be abandoned, because it gave no safe exit, and some other passage found . . . Just below was a loose snow slope at a dangerous angle, where it seemed only the initial impulse was needed for an avalanche to bear all below. And just before crossing that snow slope was a wall of overhanging ice beneath which steps must be cut for one hundred yards, every yard of which endangered the climber by disputing the passage of the pack upon his shoulders.

"Late in the evening of the 27th of May, looking up the ridge upon our return from relaying a load to the cache, we saw Karstens and Walter standing, clear-cut, against the sky, upon the surface of the unbroken snow *above* the earthquake cleavage. Tatum and I gave a great shout of joy, and far above though they were, they heard us and waved their response. The way was clear to the top of the ridge now. That night our spirits were high, and congratulations were showered upon the victorious pioneers.[1]"

Some days later, in the High Basin above, at lunch, they had an exciting moment, Stuck tells us:

Tatum, Esaias, Karstens, Johnny and Walter at the Clearwater Camp. *(Photo by Hudson Stuck.)*

"While we sat resting, we fell to talking about the pioneer climbers of this mountain who claimed to have set a flagstaff near the summit of the North Peak, as to which feat a great deal of incredulity existed in Alaska for several reasons, and we renewed our determination if weather permitted when we had ascended the South Peak, we would also climb the North Peak to seek for traces of this earliest exploit on Denali. All at once Walter cried out: 'I see the flagstaff!' Eagerly pointing to the rocky prominence nearest the summit—the summit itself is covered with snow—he added: 'I see it plainly!'. Karstens, looking where he pointed, saw it also, and, whipping out the field-glasses, one by one we all looked, and saw it distinctly standing against the sky. With the naked eye I was never able to see it unmistakably, but through the glasses it stood out, sturdy and strong, one side covered with crusted snow. We were greatly rejoiced that we could carry down positive information of this matter. It was no longer necessary for us to ascend the North Peak."

Where the Parker-Browne party had made three camps in the High Basin, the highest at 16,615 feet (and the Sourdough party of 1910 none at all above Muldrow Glacier), the 1913 party inched its way up into the High Basin making no less than five high camps above Karstens Ridge: at 15,000 feet in the Parker Pass the entry to the High Basin, at 16,000 feet, at 16,500 feet, at 17,000 feet, and the highest at 18,000 feet. And determined not to be caught by bad weather with low supplies, they laboriously back-packed to its high camp no less than "a full two weeks supply of food and fuel, which, at a pinch could be stretched to three weeks."

Stuck noted they had already been "above the perpetual snowline for forty-eight days". This expedition toward McKinley's summit was really determined, as well as prepared. Stuck writes:

"We were now (at 18,000 foot camp) within one day's climb of the summit with supplies to besiege. If the weather should prove persistently bad we could wait; we could put another camp on the ridge itself at nineteen thousand feet, and yet another half way up the dome. If we had to fight our way step by step and could advance but a couple of hundred feet a day, we were still confident that, barring unforeseen misfortunes, we could reach the top.

"But we wanted a clear day on top, that the observations we designed to make could be made; it would be a poor success

> that did but set our feet on the highest point. We felt sure that, prepared as we were to wait, the clear day would come."

Where Professor Parker in the high camps in the Upper Basin in 1912 had continually felt dangerously cold, the 1913 party:

> "always slept warm; with sheep skins and caribou skins under us, and down quilts and camel's hair blankets and a wolf-robe for bedding, the four of us lay in that seven by six tent, in one bed, snug and comfortable. It was overcrowding, but it was warm. The fierce little primus stove, pumped to its limit and perfectly consuming its kerosene fuel, shot out its corona of beautiful blue flame and warmed the tight, tiny tent. The primus stove, burning seven hours on a quart of coal-oil, is a little giant for heat generation.
>
> "We lay down for a few hours on the night of the 6th of June, resolved to rise at three in the morning for our attempt upon the summit of Denali. While Karstens and Tatum were tossing uneasily in the bed-clothes, the writer sat up with a blanket round his shoulders, crouching over the primus stove, with the thermometer at -21°F outdoors. Walter alone was at ease, with digestive and somnolent capabilities proof against any invasion.
>
> "It was of course, broad daylight all night. At three the company was aroused, and, after partaking of a very light breakfast indeed, we sallied forth into the brilliant, clear morning with not a cloud in the sky. The only packs we carried that day were the instruments and the lunch. The sun was shining, but a keen north wind was blowing. Karstens still had internal pains; Tatum and I had severe headaches. Walter was the only one feeling entirely himself, so Walter was put in the lead and in the lead he remained all day.
>
> "We took a straight course up the great snow ridge. Above us nothing was visible but snow; the rocks were all beneath, the last rocks standing at about 19,000 feet. Our progress was exceedingly slow. It was bitterly cold. We were all clad in full winter hand and foot gear—more gear than had sufficed at 50 below zero on the Yukon trail, yet until nigh noon feet were like lumps of iron and fingers were constantly numb. There is no question that cold is felt much more keenly in the thin air of nineteen thousand feet than it is below. But the north wind was really our friend, for nothing but a north wind will drive all vapor from this mountain. But (presently) we were in a measure sheltered from the north wind, and the sun full upon us gave more warmth.

"Ascension Day, 1913." (*Photo from Hudson Stuck's* Ascent of Denali.)

The Northeast Ridge shattered by the earthquake in July, 1912. The earthquake cleavage is plainly shown halfway down the ridge. The Browne Tower is the highest point in the picture. Parker Pass is along its base. *(Photo by Hudson Stuck.)*

"At last the crest of the ridge was reached . . . we were well above the great North Peak across the Grand Basin. Its crest had been like an index as we climbed. There still stretched ahead of us, and perhaps one hundred feet above us, another small ridge with a north and south pair of little haycock summits. This is the real top of Denali. From below, this ultimate ridge merges indistinguishably with the crest of the horseshoe ridge but it is not a part of it but a culminating ridge beyond it. With keen excitement we pushed on. Walter, who had been in the lead all day, was the first to scramble up; a native Alaskan, he is the first human being to set foot upon the top of Alaska's great mountain, and he had well earned the lifelong distinction.

" . . . our wind . . . recovered . . . we fell at once to our scientific tasks. The instrument-tent was set up, the mercurial barometer taken out of its leather case and then out of its wooden case, was swung upon its tripod and a rough zero established. It was a great gratification to get it to the top uninjured. The boiling-point apparatus was put together and its candle lighted under the ice which filled its little cistern. The three-inch, three-circle aneroid was read at once . . . its mendacious altitude scale confidently pointing at twenty-three thousand three hundred feet. Soon the water was boiling in the little tubes of the boiling point thermometer and the steam pouring out of the vent.

"The thread of mercury rose to 174.9° F and stayed there. There is something definite and uncompromising about the boiling point hypsometer; it reaches its mark unmistakably and does not budge, no tapping will make it rise or fall. The reading of the mercurial barometer is a slower and more delicate business. It takes a good light and a good sight to tell when the ivory zero-point is exactly touching the surface of the mercury in the cistern. It was read some half hour after it was set up, at 13.617 inches. The alcohol minimum thermometer stood at 7° F in the full sunshine all the while we were on top.

"Meanwhile, Tatum had been reading a round of angles with the prismatic compass. He could not handle it with sufficient exactness with his mitts on, and froze his fingers doing it barehanded.

"The scientific work accomplished, we indulged ourselves in the wonderful prospect that stretched around us. It was a perfectly clear day, the sun shining brightly in the sky, and naught bounded our view save the natural limitations of vision. The chief impression was not of our connection with the earth so far below, its rivers and its seas, but rather of detachment from it. Above us the sky took a blue so deep that none of us had ever gazed upon a midday sky like it—a deep rich, lustrous, transparent blue, a hue strange (and) increasingly impressive. Immediately before us, in the direction from which we had climbed, lay nothing: a void, a sheer gulf many thousands of feet deep, and one shrank back instinctively from the little parapet of the snow basin when one had glanced at the awful profundity. Fifteen or twenty miles away, sprang most splendidly into view the great mass of Denali's Wife, or Mount Foraker as some men misname her, filling majestically all the middle distance.

"Beyond stretched, blue and vague to the southwest, the wide valley of the Kuskokwim, with an end of all mountains. To the north we looked right over the North Peak to the foot-hills below, patched with lakes and lingering snow, glittering with streams. We had hoped to see the junction of the Yukon and Tanana Rivers, one hundred and fifty miles away to the northwest, as we had often seen the summit of Denali from that point in the winter, but the haze that almost always qualifies a fine summer day inhibited that stretch of vision. Perhaps the forest fires we found raging on the Tanana River were already beginning to foul the northern sky.

"We could not linger, unique though the occasion, dearly bought our privilege; the miserable limitations of the flesh gave us continual warning to depart; we grew colder and still more wretchedly cold. My fingers were so cold that I

Cutting a staircase three miles long in the ice of the shattered ridge. *(Photo by Hudson Stuck.)*

would not venture to withdraw them from the mittens to change the film in the camera, and the others were in like case; indeed our hands were by this time so numb as to make it almost impossible to operate a camera at all. Our top-of-the-mountain photography was a great disappointment.

"When the mercurial barometer had been read the tent was thrown down and abandoned. The tent-pole was used for a moment as a flagstaff while Tatum hoisted a little United States flag he had patiently and skilfully constructed in our camps below out of two silk handkerchiefs and the cover of a sewing-bag. Then the pole was put to its permanent use— a transverse piece, already prepared and fitted, was lashed securely to it and it was planted on one of the little snow turrets of the summit. Then we gathered about it and said the Te Deum.

"There was no pride of conquest, no trace of that exultation of victory some enjoy upon the first ascent of a lofty peak, no gloating over good fortune that had hoisted us a few hundred feet higher than others who had struggled and been discomfited. Rather . . . that a privileged communion with the high places of the earth had been granted . . . secret and solitary since the world began. All the way down, unconscious of weariness in the descent, my thoughts were occupied with the glorious scene my eyes gazed upon, and should gaze upon never again."

X

Tragedy on the Muldrow. The Pioneer Airplane Landings—1932

THROUGHOUT the nineteen years following the first complete ascent of Denali in 1913, its glaciers and slopes remained untouched by climbers. A long procession of events —first World War, the creation of Mount McKinley National Park, the building of the Alaska Railroad, the Roaring Twenties in the States, and the Great Depression—all occurred before the next expedition, in 1932, arrived to climb the great mountain. And then, actually, there were two expeditions at the same time, one a scientific research project, the other a sporting attempt at a ski ascent.

Allen Carpé, thirty-eight-year-old research engineer with the Bell Telephone Laboratories in New York, was a brilliant scientist who had also come to be regarded as the ablest of American mountaineers. After extensive climbing in the Alps in his younger days, and in the Canadian Rockies, he had been a member of the international expedition which made the first ascent of Mount Logan in 1925. He took part in the first ascent of Alaska's Mount Bona in 1930, and of spectacular Mount Fairweather in 1931. Carpé's pleasure in Alaskan mountaineering and exploration was now to coincide with his scientific interest in electrical engineering, particularly in cosmic radiation, a phenomenon then but little understood.

Early January, 1932, found Carpé in New York sending the following to his friend, Francis Farquhar, President of the Sierra Club in San Francisco:

> "I am writing you in regard to a development in which it occurs to me some of your members may be interested. You

may have read of the project of Dr. Arthur H. Compton of Chicago University, for a wide program of investigations of cosmic rays at high elevations in different parts of the earth. I have a grant and am collaborating with Dr. Compton in planning some of this work, particularly in Alaska and will be carrying out measurements at high elevations on Mount McKinley. One of Dr. Compton's assistants is also going to another part of Alaska to get a measurement as far north as possible, but not on a mountain (at the Kennecott Mine, in the same latitude).

"For the initial cosmic ray measurements it will not be necessary to occupy a place higher than the head of Muldrow Glacier (11,000 feet), or to transport heavy equipment up the steep northeast Karstens Ridge, the only point of real mountaineering difficulty on McKinley. You might have one or more persons in mind who would like to be considered for participation in such an expedition.

"There is a possibility of flying by airplane to the Muldrow Glacier, or at least of dropping supplies from the air to the party on the glacier. If you think any of your people would fit into such a trip, I wish you would let me know about them. Great skill in climbing is much less of a requirement than ability and willingness to live a rough camp life and pull their share of the work of packing and hauling. Ability to use skis would be an asset."

Edward P. Beckwith, a former instructor at Massachusetts Institute of Technology and consulting engineer for General Electric, joined Carpé's group; and Theodore Koven, a twenty-eight-year-old Sierra Club member living in New Jersey, was enlisted as an assistant for the scientific work.

On March 2, 1932, Carpé wrote:

"I am to get the cosmic ray apparatus from Professor Compton by April 1st. I had the opportunity of a good talk with Joe Crosson, head pilot of Alaska Airways, and the dropping of loads on the mountain seems quite feasible. Also, a short time ago I got in touch with a Mr. Alfred D. Lindley, a young lawyer of Minneapolis, who with a friend (Erling Strom, the Norwegian skier) is going up there and has the plan of climbing Mount McKinley on skis. We considered joining, but their arrangements seem a bit casual and I am not sure what advantage there would be in a close tie-up. I find however that these skiers have interested the superintendent of the Park, Harry J. Liek, and apparently expect to get dog-team transportation and other cooperation free of cost. If the Park authorities will assist a purely sporting venture to this extent, perhaps they would help us with our scientific equipment."

They would indeed, and the Director of the National Park Service in Washington wrote:

> "I am going to do all I can to help Carpé. The two expeditions are going to try to get together. It will probably fall to us to furnish most of the sleds and dogs necessary to get supplies out on the Muldrow Glacier."

The scientific party decided to try flying from Fairbanks directly onto McKinley's mountain glaciers—the first time in history so far as we know, that airplanes were used in this way. Beckwith tells the story:

> Looking back to the spring of 1932 it is hard to imagine a more interesting proposal than that of Allen Carpé to join his expedition for measuring cosmic rays at high altitude on Mount McKinley. In many ways Carpé was the ideal leader for such an expedition. His splendid mountaineering achievements in Alaska gave him a knowledge of climbing conditions which was invaluable, while his experience in electrical research especially fitted him for the scientific work. The party consisted of five members, of which Allen Carpé, Theodore Koven and I constituted the first unit . . . a second unit, Percy T. Olton and Nicholas Spadavecchia, were coming by the next steamer.
>
> We were assisted in transporting our 800 pounds of scientific equipment by the Lindley-Liek party, who were already well advanced in their attempt to climb the mountain. Earlier it had been agreed that they would transport this considerable load with their own supplies by dog-team to the head of the Muldrow Glacier, the prospective site of our observations. They had done this in March, while there was plenty of snow on the flatlands approach to McKinley. And the instruments were now cached up on the glacier awaiting our arrival.
>
> We were aware that a plane equipped with wheels only could not land on any of the glacial slopes of McKinley and that skiis must replace them. It was necessary therefore to select a starting base on a frozen river, lake, or stretch of snow.
>
> Nenana, within one hundred miles of the mountain, seemed the most promising base, since ice on the Tanana River still held, though it was fast melting, and might go out at any time. It was arranged that Joe Crosson, an Alaskan airman of long experience should pilot the plane.

Carpé was naturally anxious to land at as high an altitude as possible on McKinley; but the Alaskan pilots informed us that a landing at 11,000 feet was out of the question on account of the excessive ground speed required at that altitude (to compensate for the thinner air), which would make taking off especially hazardous even under the best conditions. We would have to be satisifed with an altitude of 6,000 feet or less; and they were not very encouraging about landing on any part of the mountain.

FIRST MOUNTAIN GLACIER FLIGHT

My diary describes this as follows:

April 24, 1932—Nenana. We put up at the "Southern Hotel" and began selecting necessities. Johnson, manager of Alaskan Airways in Fairbanks, promised over one of the two telephones in Nenana, that he would have the plane on the river by nine the next morning. He still gave little encouragement to our plan of landing on the Muldrow Glacier, but agreed to leave it entirely to the discretion of the pilot after a careful examination from the air.

April 25th. We were up at six, and transferred everything over to the grocery store to be weighed so as not to exceed the plane's capacity. Total weight was sixty pounds too great. Carpé wanted to know why my sleeping-bag weighed twenty pounds instead of twelve, and I had to admit there was an extra quilt in it. Discarding this and other things brought the weight down to the required 1,200 pounds which included our own weights.

Nine o'clock and no plane. Carpé finally getting disturbed telephoned Fairbanks, where Johnson asked that we be patient, as the plane had injured a ski in trying to take off on soft snow.

Finally the plane landed on our river. Crosson was a strong-looking Alaskan, weighing over 200 pounds, and seemed unconcerned at the prospect of attempting to land on the untried slopes of McKinley.

The plane was an enclosed, single-motored Fairchild monoplane of four hundred and fifty horsepower. With all baggage on board we were at such close quarters that there was hardly room to use my camera. We took off at about eleven, and flew toward the distant mountains. The country below was completely snow-covered and flat for a long distance. There was no sign of game or life of any kind on the white stretches of snow which were broken by irregular lines of evergreens. After three quarters of an hour we began to approach the mountains, and then there was a great deal to photograph.

The summit of McKinley was in clouds, and flying at 7,000 feet we seemed far below it. On one side were seas of peaks, unnamed and even the valleys unexplored, while on the other, the white plains reached to the horizon.

Crosson turned the plane sharply toward the mountain and flew over a ridge, bringing the Muldrow Glacier below us, the upper part of it that is, for the glacier is some forty miles long. We flew back and forth eight hundred feet above it, examining the surface carefully. It looked smooth for several miles. After considerable conversation with Carpé, which I could not hear above the noise of the motor, Crosson made his decision, apparently quickly, and dropped the plane toward the surface, landing with no difficulty whatever on about the middle of the glacier. The altitude measured slightly over six thousand feet, which was about the best we had hoped for. Carpé was delighted, and shook hands with Crosson, who took it much as a matter of course, and lit a cigar before leaving the plane.

The glacier was perhaps a mile wide with a high ridge on one side and low one on the other. Crosson had landed on the Muldrow near the opening from McGonagall Pass. The mountain above was covered with clouds, but the air was clear at the time we landed. By the time we had unloaded the plane, however, though it did not take long, there was a complete change in the weather. Clouds descended from the mountain and a wind came up across the glacier which sent some of our lighter equipment on a journey. With it came blinding, drifting snow, just at the point of freezing. It clung to every part of our baggage and melted on it as our things were warm from the plane.

Crosson seated himself in the empty plane, and at his direction we wound up the inertia starter. With no goodbyes he disappeared in the swirling snow up the glacier. It seemed a long time before he left the ice, which was not remarkable since the required speed at this altitude was seventy miles an hour, but we saw that he did get into the air. We waited to hear him overhead, as he would naturally circle and fly back. But there was no sound above the blowing wind; and we concluded he had probably crashed.

By this time we were all on skiis[1]. Carpé and Koven started up the glacier while I collected our equipment and piled it up so that everything would be protected as much as possible. I then started in the same direction, but after some time saw them returning.

Since Crosson was not with them, I thought he might be dead, since if he were injured, only one would have returned. As they approached, Carpé shouted that everything was all right. They could see no sign of the plane, and concluded that Crosson had flown over a low part of the ridge and was well on his way. So we put the plane out of our minds, and turned to making camp under the protection of an icewall across the glacier, relaying our things to that place.

Returning from one of these trips, I unexpectedly saw three figures, and supposed the extra man must be one of the Lindley-Liek party, then on the mountain. It turned out to be Crosson, on snowshoes. He had come several miles after leaving the plane which he said was undamaged. He had been unable to rise above the ridge, and had made an emergency landing, later folding the wings of the plane alone, a difficult job for one man even under calm conditions.

Crosson was the same as usual—calm and matter-of-course. He had brought no sleeping-bag so as to leave all the room in the plane for our equipment.

We all sat in the big tent and discussed the situation while we cooked supper over Koven's small gasoline stove. I suggested that I fly back with Crosson, if we succeeded in getting the plane free, and return in a week with Spadavecchia and Olton. This would make it possible for me to get a new tent-pole replacing our broken one, and look after the second load of supplies and equipment. Carpé approved, and thought of many things I could do at Nenana.

In the morning at 4:30 a.m. the weather cleared and the wind subsided, so I skied over toward the other tent. Clouds surrounded McKinley but there was sunlight on the high ridges. Crosson was on snowshoes in a few moments, and ready to start for the plane, just visible as a small red spot far up the glacier. Without thought of breakfast we all followed on skiis.

It required more than an hour to reach the plane. The latter was not in a good position and its skiis were icecovered and frozen in the snow . . . Finally with three of us rocking the wings and Crosson driving the propeller at full speed, the plane slowly pulled out and stopped to let me in.

We had a tough, long ride before leaving the ice, the skiis jumping from one frozen ridge to the next, and I thought surely one would break. Finally we were safely in the air and all was clear for the flight back, which was accomplished without incident. At breakfast in Nenana, Crosson remarked, "I have not often had a job like that to handle." [It was apparently the first time a passenger had been airborne off a glacier anywhere.]

The approaching ice break-up on the river at Nenana meant that another base had to be adopted for the second flight to the mountain a week later (for air-dropping at 11,000 feet.) So, loaded with 450 pounds of additional supplies and equipment, the plane was flown from Nenana to Birch Lake, about sixty miles from Fairbanks, where the ice was still firm. For the return flight to the mountain two planes were arranged, partly to avoid further concern about the weight to be carried, but more on account of increased safety in flying. We had discussed including a short-wave radio, but were prevented from taking the only one available through the necessity of guaranteeing its return. With two planes, in case of a forced landing, one could always mark the position of the other.

May 3, 1932. The two small planes, this time equipped with wheels, waited on the snow-free field at Fairbanks ready to take off. It was Olton's first air trip, but Spadavecchia had flown before. Our destination was the still ice-covered Birch Lake where wheel and ski landing-gear could be used interchangeably. The big cabin Fairchild was already there, ski-equipped and loaded with everything I had placed aboard at Nenana. It required about half an hour at Birch Lake to unfold the wings of the Fairchild and replace the wheels of the small plane with skiis. I then kept to the small plane, and instructed Jerry Jones, the pilot, to give me a chance to photograph the other plane against the mountain.

The country was now almost without snow. But the air was extremely cold flying in the small open plane, especially as we approached the mountains.

There was no sign of the tents or of Carpé and Koven as we dropped toward the glacier campsite at McGonagall Pass, both planes landing without difficulty on the new snow. Here I found a letter from Carpé at my small tent stating that they (Carpé and Koven) had gone to the head of the glacier.

I now asked Crosson if he would fly over Carpé's 11,000-foot camp and let me drop some provisions and my big dufflebag. He agreed, so we loaded the plane with five boxes of supplies and I went with Crosson in the Fairchild to drop them out. We climbed to 12,000 feet and then made for the head of the glacier. I soon saw Carpé's tent with skiis standing in the snow, and by them a figure which waved to us. The view of the upper part of the mountain at such close range was most inspiring. All the well known features were clearly visible. Crosson said he could see the Lindley-Liek party above Karstens Ridge, but I was unsuccessful in making them out. We then dove for the camp and Crosson told me to wait for his word before throwing out the boxes. The door was very hard to open against the wind, but I pushed out a box as Crosson said "Now!", and followed this with four others until he said "Stop!" We circled again and I threw out the duffle bag containing my sleeping equipment for use when I would reach the camp. The landing points of the boxes were necessarily some distance apart, and I could only hope that they would be found with contents undamaged.[2]

We then flew back and landed on the glacier near the other plane at McGonagall Pass, having been gone about half an hour and covered about twenty-five miles of glacier. The same work if done on foot would occupy about ten days.

The two planes took off with ease from the surface of the new snow and left the three of us to begin our life on the mountain.

A new way of travel in the mountains begins in 1932.

Top: Pilot Joe Crosson makes the first landing, April 25, 1932. "He took it as a matter of course, and lit a cigar." Bottom: Beckwith leaves in open cockpit plane.

Airdrop to the cosmic ray station. *(Photo developed from one of the scientists' cameras after they died.)*

Meanwhile, high up above in the Grand Basin on Harper Glacier, things had been going well with the ski-mountaineering party. They had originally left McKinley Park headquarters on the railroad on April 4th, and travelled the one hundred miles to the mountain with three dogteams which transported not only their own supplies but also the Carpé expedition's scientific equipment. Aided by perfect weather they had by April 20th established themselves at the 11,000 foot level at the head of the Muldrow Glacier with their own outfit of about 1,200 pounds plus 800 pounds of equipment for the cosmic ray party. At this point the other three McKinley Park rangers had returned to headquarters with the three dogteams.

Lindley, ever the ski enthusiast, wrote:

> As anticipated, and as has been the experience of all who have used skiis travelling on glaciers, the skiis proved of very great assistance because they lessened considerably the dangers of crossing snow bridges over crevasses, and because they greatly increased the range of reconnoissance trips by enabling us to run home quite rapidly once we had sounded out a safe trail.

> Karstens Ridge did not at first sight seem very formidable. But the upper half of its four thousand feet of ridge was in places either so sharp, or its slopes so steep, that skiis were out of the question there. [And everywhere above Karstens Ridge on Harper Glacier of the upper Grand Basin, the tightly packed, wind blown snow proved "too hard and rugged"; so the four pairs of skiis so laboriously dragged up above were not used at all there, even by the expert skiers.]
>
> At the entrance to the Grand Basin which Dr. Stuck named "Parker Pass", in a hollow between the largest rocks, we found an old piece of cloth which had miraculously survived the storms of nineteen years, and in a crack in the west side of the largest rock we immediately located Dr. Stuck's thermometer, placed there in 1913. We were interested to note that the recording needle of the government alcohol thermometer was way down in the bulb and that thus a temperature of lower than the minimum range of the thermometer, 95 degrees below zero, Fahrenheit, might have been recorded. We were inclined to be skeptical of the accuracy of the thermometer. but were glad to find the record of at least one of our predecessors on the mountain.
>
> While cutting steps on the ridge one day we thought that we heard an airplane motor at some distance. Two of us went to the top of the ridge to look down, and there we saw the two tents pitched at our old camp site, showing that Carpé and Koven had arrived and found their cache. That same day we were startled to see a red airplane come up the glacier, circle around over the camp site, and drop bundle after bundle to them. We had amused ourselves by leaving a tentative signal arrangement with Alaska Airways, in case they should be flying over the mountain, to let them know the precise day on which we thought we would be on the South Peak. Accordingly we rushed around to pull out sleeping bags to make the signal, but the plane stuck strictly to its business of dropping supplies, and, once through, it went back down the glacier without coming up to our altitude.

Erling Strom's narrative, from which the following is taken, gives the first description by a European climber of the ascent to the summit of McKinley; it is a literal translation from an article written for the yearbook of the Norsk Tinde Klub (Norwegian Climbing Club).

> High Camp, 17,000 feet. The 7th of May, 1932, dawned with brilliant, clear, cold weather. Even though we had provisions for more than a fortnight, and felt like resting one day before we made the last hard turn, we did not dare let the good

weather chance escape us. Each one rigged with his iceaxe, crampons, all the clothes we possessed, cameras, and a few raisins, we set out at 9 o'clock in the morning. We started with our usual 30 steps between rests, but only a few meters away from the camp we had to go down to 25 steps. We generally remained standing while resting, as it was too exhausting to get up again after sitting down. After each rest we felt as fresh as fishes, and were fully able to enjoy both being alive and the view. The first ten steps were easy going. But at the 15th step we started to doubt whether we might manage all 25. The last 5 steps were a pain. In the many books that I have read about this kind of climbing, I have always believed that all this concerning thin air and hard breathing was rather exaggerated. To make it clear what a sad reality it actually was I will repeat a little illustration. Towards the top one of my crampons fell off because a hook broke. I had a little difficulty in putting it on again, and asked the others to go on when it suited them. When I was through the others were 60 meters ahead of me. To be able to overtake them I added from 25 to 30 steps, but had right away to cut down to 29. After only three stops I had to cut off to 28 steps, but even this I did not manage to keep up. With 27 steps to their 25 I did regain the lost 60 meters in two hours. This was at the altitude of 20,000 feet, though, and that is 5,000 feet higher than Mont Blanc.

For eight hours the climb lasted. At 5 p.m. on May 7th we were standing at the top. I don't know anything in the world which satisfies me more than to stand on the top of a mountain. The more difficult or toilsome the climbing has been, the greater is the satisfaction.

For four years I had been wishing to get off on this trip, and for more than four weeks we had toiled on practically inch by inch. In that one moment did we get the reward of it all. Wherein the reward really lies I scarcely know myself. But I believe it is the knowledge of actually having reached a goal.

About the view from the highest point on North America, there is little to tell. One is simply too high up. Everything round about now appears almost flat. Only Mount Foraker was lying there, dark and mystic with sharp contours against a glorious sunset. We tried to take some snaps, but had to give it up. For four minutes only did I leave my mittens off, and in that time I froze five tips of my fingers to such a degree that after they had first been white, some weeks later they turned black, and at last fell off, with the nails and all. Not till now, six months later, do they start to look normal again.

The descent was done in a hurry; the difficulty in breathing then disappeared. One may run down where one had to crawl up. By a small group of stones which are peeping up through the snow only 300 feet below the top, we left a small specially made metal tube, containing a pad of paper and an attached pencil. Why beforehand we did not write our names on the pad I cannot understand. Perhaps we did not want to forego the move of events. As it now happened, we were standing there, struggling with frozen fingers. The names got quite undecipherable, but as the next ones who arrive will have more than enough to write their own names, it is all the same about the penmanship. Lindley and I were just about to place the tube in a cleft of the big stone, when Pearson all of a sudden disappeared. He always used to be in a hurry when he started to get cold, and we did not understand that anything wrong had happened, till we the next moment saw him standing on a plateau, waving to us. It was about 800 feet below. On a piece of ice just below the stone, he had lost his footing and rushed down. Iceaxe, crampons, sack, cap and mittens he had lost on the way, and as we later got down to him, it appeared that his nose and one ear were almost gone as well. That the edge of the iceaxe had gone right through his underarm, we did not discover till the next morning. Pearson has the name in Alaska of being a very hardy person, and I must say I have never met anybody like him. Gory and scratched as he was, with a face so swollen that he could see only with one eye, and very little with that one, he now came along with us as if nothing had happened. We reached the camp at 9 p.m., and the nursing that he received was anything but first class. We melted enough snow to clean the blood off his face. Otherwise we were too worn out to eat, so we drank a warm celebration grog and crept into the sleeping bags, immensely thankful that we had had a clear day at the top of Mount McKinley.

The next morning none of us felt particularly sprightly, and all needed a day's rest. Toward evening we had recovered to such a degree that we dared to think of a climb of the North Peak the following day. We had planned to try both if the weather permitted.

For that climb we turn to Lindley's description.

It would have been possible to reach the plateau of the North Peak by one of several steep snow chimneys leading up from the glacier at about our level, but we decided to play it safe and go way up the glacier to its head and back up a short rocky ridge to gain the plateau. On the top of the North Peak we had a grand view of the South Peak looming above us across the Grand Basin, and we scouted around trying to find the old flagpole. We observed that the easterly ridge of the north peak, up which the sourdoughs must have come in 1910, was, in its upper five hundred feet, sheer ice of considerable steepness, and that the last rock ledge on that east ridge was at the base of this upper five hundred foot stretch. It was here we assumed the flagpole had been placed, but we were not inclined to cut steps down this ridge to find it, as it was already six o'clock. So we returned by our same route and reached high camp without mishap.

[High Camp, 17,000 feet—resuming Strom's narrative]

When we woke up early in the morning of the 10th of May, the wind was tugging at the tents. Outside it was snowing, but what did that matter to us? With a light heart we might now pack up and leave. Everything we thought we could do without on the way down, we left behind. At 12 noon we had four heavy sacks ready packed. For the last time we used our little spiral scales. We had made it a rule to share evenly, as best we could. With 32 kg. (70 lbs.) each on his back, we said goodbye to our highest camp.

Down Harper Glacier we went in a hurry. We had the wind at our backs, and ran more than we walked. The worst crevasses we had marked off with the skiis that we could not use up here in any better way.

Within three hours we were back to our old camp under the blocks of ice. Here we had deposited some films and other objects which had to be found in a hurry. The plan now was to reach Muldrow Glacier the same day. We thought of resting there for one day together with Carpé and his men. At about 4 p.m. we started down the ridge. It was still blowing and snowed quite a lot. We soon discovered that the ridge would take a longer time than we had anticipated. This did not matter much, as, toward the middle of May in Alaska as with us at home (in Norway) it is light enough to move about all night long.

If our steps had not for the most part exactly followed the ridge, we would have had difficulty finding them. They were, as we had expected, altogether blown over, so that each step had to be dug out again. What we had not counted on was that this work was exceedingly more difficult down hill than up. With a heavy sack on the back it was impossible. We started a system in which we relieved each other at certain intervals. As one man passed the spade after he had dug his number of holes, he dug a hole at the side for the sack of the next man, while he himself went back to fetch his own. The number of holes to be dug we arranged in proportion to the strength and endurance of each, which we by now knew quite well. Overjoyed at being on our way down, we too easily took big risks. Lindley once slid quite badly, but remained lying on his stomach right across the ridge. The night came and went and we were still on Karstens Ridge. Not till 6 a.m. did we reach Muldrow Glacier. We could not arrive quickly enough to Carpé's tents, to have a chat which we had been looking forward to for such a long time.

It is impossible for me to describe the impression it made on us to find the tents empty. Worn out as we now were after eighteen hours of constant toil and nervous tension, I must admit that everything whirled around in our heads for a few minutes. All kinds of possible thoughts flew through our heads. That something wrong had happened we at once understood. A thick layer of fresh snow covered all tracks around the tents. Everything showed that no one had been there for several days. Our first thought was of the Ridge, where we ourselves had just spent fourteen hours in intense excitement. Had these men also wanted to try to get up, perhaps used a rope, and then slipped and pulled each other down? Could we then have passed by where that had happened without detecting it? It astonished us to find only two sleeping bags. We had expected to find four or five men. Then we soon found the two men's diaries. One belonged to Allen Carpé, the leader, the other belonged to Theodore Koven. From these it appeared that the two men were brought to Muldrow Glacier by airplane from Fairbanks more than a week earlier, that they had followed our trail up along the Glacier, found the depot, and started to take their observations. On the 7th they had written in their diaries for the last time, but their cosmic ray observations continued until the 9th. They were then worried about the three other members of the expedition, who had not been able to start at the same time, and had not yet appeared. From the diaries we might conclude that the two men had gone down the glacier to meet their three friends.

By this we became a bit relieved. We could hope that they had found the others further down the glacier, and that they were still alive, although we did think it peculiar that they had not taken with them their sleeping bags. Other things in the tents also indicated that they had expected to return the same day, but had not returned.

Having no peace of mind we did not consider the good rest we had hoped for. Neither did we take time for a meal, other than some rye crisp with butter and jam, before we started down the glacier. Our trail was not easy to follow. It was practically obliterated by 8 to 10 inches of new snow. Fortunately we had spent ten days on this glacier on the way up, and covered each section many times so we knew the route well. From time to time we saw some ski tracks in the new snow, made a few days earlier. Also these were more or less covered by the very last snowfalls. We noticed that they did not follow our trail very accurately. This frightened us again. If the men had not been able to follow the original trail they were bound to get into trouble. We should soon realize that this had been the case. Three miles or so below the camp we discovered a black spot to the left of us, well off the trail. We stopped dead. None of us said a word. None of us were in doubt.

Being in the lead on the rope I turned slowly out to the left. As we arrived close by, we stopped again. There in front of us with his face turned down was the body of a man lying in the snow. It was Theodore Koven. He was partly covered with snow, and appeared to have been lying there for several days. A wound in the head and a bad wound in the leg, showed that he had fallen into a crevasse. He was not wearing skiis. We concluded that these were broken when he fell, that he then had been able to climb out, but on account of loss of blood and exhaustion had not survived very long. We could only partly follow his tracks, but saw that they led from a very dangerous part of the glacier.

In case we might possibly discover the fate of Carpé, we followed the tracks between a maze of big crevasses. Here and there we also detected some ski tracks. All of them were almost obliterated after the snowfall of the last days, so what actually had happened, it was impossible for us to understand. Wherever Carpé might be, we knew that he was not alive. Probably he was lying in one of the twenty or thirty crevasses in our immediate neighborhood. They were all extremely deep, some of such dimensions that a whole railway train might disappear into them. After an hour's careful search of the glacier at this spot, we gave up all hopes of finding him.

Our next thought was to bring back Koven's body with us to that part of the Glacier where an airplane might land. While Liek and Pearson sat down waiting for us, Lindley and I went back for the sled. It was a long hour to wait. As we came down again, we wrapped Koven in the tent we still had with us, and tied him onto the sled with our own rope, as there was no other. One end of the rope I pulled the sled with, Lindley holding back the sled with the other. We were both on skiis, while Pearson and Liek now followed on snowshoes. They did not dare use skiis, as we now could not wear a rope. The whole maneuver was risky, but something had to be done. We scarcely advanced 200 meters before Pearson, the third in the row, suddenly disappeared. A round hole in the snow between us and Liek was all we could see. We at once started to call, but at first got no answer. With a firm grip on the rope, Lindley went to the edge of the crevasse and called again. From the bowels of the glacier we heard a voice which answered "All right! But I need a rope!" Still another hour was spent, first to get the sack and then the man up again. He had fallen 40 feet right down, but into a small crevasse, where the knapsack was so wide that it touched the sides and slacked the speed. He broke his snowshoes to bits, but was otherwise not hurt.

It became now quite clear that under these circumstances we had to leave Koven where he was. We needed the rope for ourselves and did not dare take any more risks. The sled we put up on end as a mark where we left him. We still had ten kilometers left of the glacier, with more than a hundred crevasses which we got to know about on our trip up, and at least as many which we had not yet discovered. Then also a sinister certainty that it was worth our lives to follow a trail which we could absolutely not see.

At 3 a.m. (the third day) we reached McGonagall Pass, at the spot where we might leave the Glacier. Here we found the second part of Carpé's expedition. One man (Beckwith) was ill. This was the reason for the delay. Another man (Olton) was there to nurse the sick one. The third (Spadavecchia) was wandering through the wilderness to find a hut with a telephone, so that he might call for an airplane from Fairbanks for the sick man. He had been gone for four days, and probably lost his way, but not yet in much danger, as he was in the lowlands, where ptarmigan abounded, and plenty of wood. Even without a gun we counted on his being able to kill enough for his own use.

If we now had had a tent with us, and not used it in another way (to wrap Koven's body), we would certainly have camped here. As it was, we continued to our original base camp, one Norwegian mile (10 kilometers) further down, where we already had a tent, plenty of provisions, chopped wood, and everything prepared.

This camp we reached at 5 a.m. on the third day. We had then kept going for 41 hours, each with 60 pounds on our back, and only eaten one small meal. In spite of it all I believe the psychic strain had been worse than the physical. Liek and Lindley just dropped on the floor of the tent and fell asleep, Liek with his knapsack only half off. Pearson, however, who felt better after getting off the glacier, had other things in mind. In starting to build a fire in our small tin stove he turned and said: "Well, there ain't no heroes without food, let's eat." I used my last bit of energy to open some tin cans. Having kept up with Pearson on this entire trip I could not let him get ahead of me this 42nd hour.

> When oyster stew and sausages were prepared we tried to wake up the others. As far as Harry Liek was concerned this was impossible, while the rest of us enjoyed what we thought was a wonderful meal. Then we crawled into our sleeping bags. 10 hours later we woke up and were hungry again. This time we could all eat.
>
> If I could only describe the two hours we stayed awake. The sun was just setting. The evening was clear and still. There was spring in the air. A few bare spots here and there and ptarmigan cackling all around us. It was as if we were starting a new life with only summer and sun and as if the last days and nights were the end of everything hard, cold and sad in this world. Never had we felt so happy to be alive.

But Allen Carpé's cosmic ray expedition was not yet over, for several more airplane flights were made. The Fairbanks Fire Department hosed down the snowless Weeks Field flight strip, creating enough slippery mud so that pilot Jerry Jones was enabled to take off on skis from this surface with the ski-equipped open-cockpit Stearman, fly out and land on the Muldrow Glacier, and bring the ill Beckwith back to Fairbanks. This special variant by Jones and his ingenious fellow Alaskans—for taking off a ski-equipped airplane from dry ground after the winter snow had gone—can be seen in retrospect as another historic aviation "first" in the annals of the flying north country.[3] Thus ended the pioneer airplane flights, the first anywhere in the world so far as we know, successfully to operate directly onto and off mountain glaciers.

The cosmic ray observations and measurements, which had been made at so tragic a cost, still remained in Carpé's scientific notebooks in the lonely little tent at 11,000 feet at the head of the Muldrow Glacier—being rapidly snowed up and in danger of disappearing forever beyond recovery. Since these were the only data of this particular kind which had ever been recorded, on a subject of great interest to the scientific world, an expedition was promptly organized for their recovery. Koven's mother also wished to have his body returned to the family burial plot in New Jersey. It was therefore arranged at the Explorers' Club in New York for Merl La Voy, member of the 1910 and 1912 McKinley expeditions, to leave New York in early July, and to join Alaskan sourdough Andy Taylor (companion of Carpé on the

Mount Logan, Mount Bona and Mount Fairweather first ascents), and Grant Pearson at McKinley Park. The three started up to the Muldrow Glacier in early August, the same year, 1932.

"There was only about five inches of the sled sticking out of the snow when we got there," La Voy later wrote. "Probably about fifteen feet of snow had fallen since Koven was left there in May, which fortunately had settled to about seven."

A curious event occurred at this time, illustrating the philosophers' observation that man is never quite sure just what to do with the body of his fellow man when death has claimed the spirit. While La Voy and Taylor were engaged in digging Koven's body out of the Muldrow Glacier in order to take it, with great effort, away from Mount McKinley, they noticed an airplane flying high over the mountain—a sufficiently unusual sight in those days to attract attention. Later they learned that the ashes of a pioneer Alaskan, W. H. Holmes, were from that airplane, in fulfillment of his last wish, being cast to the winds of heaven *onto* Mount McKinley!

The tent containing the scientific data, a mile farther up the glacier, was fortunately still visible, its peak sticking out of the snow; and its contents were brought back. The results of this cosmic ray research would have pleased Allen Carpé. For Professor Compton subsequently wrote to Beckwith: "You will be interested to know that the cosmic ray datum obtained by Carpé and Koven in their measurements on Mount McKinley seems to be of unusual interest. It represents the only high altitude value of cosmic rays that is available at latitudes so far north. Contrary to the results obtained at lower levels, the intensity at that altitude seems to increase as we go north of the United States. This would indicate, if correct, that there are in the cosmic rays particles which are prevented by action of the earth's magnetic field from striking the earth at lower latitudes, an important point in connection with our theory of the nature and origin of these rays."

In Carpé's tent were found several packs of exposed film, later developed by Beckwith. Some of these photographs, published here for the first time, were made with a self-timer, and show both Carpé and Koven. In one picture they seem to be on the ridge near the two peaks later to be named for them, the nearer one of which they may even possibly have climbed.

Merl La Voy, leader of the recovery expedition, in his report to the Director of the National Park Service, on September 28, 1932, suggested that some geographical feature around Mount McKinley be named in honor of Carpé and Koven. He described the ridge eastward beyond Karstens Ridge and overlooking the upper Muldrow Glacier valley, where they labored to make their cosmic ray observations. These two beautiful peaks duly appear on today's maps: Mount Koven, 12,210 feet, and Mount Carpé, 12,550 feet.

One of the scientists, recovering the airdrop. *(Photo developed from one of their cameras after they died.)*

Top: The August 1932 Recovery Expedition arrives just in time at the Cosmic Ray Test Laboratory. One or two more storms and it would have been completely covered. Below: Koven's body is dug out by the Recovery Expedition.

Scientist on Karstens Ridge views two mountains, later named for the scientists after they died. *(Film developed from Carpè's camera.)*

XI

Billy Taylor, Sourdough: The True Story of the N. Peak Climb at Last.

FADING from public memory with the passing decades, Tom Lloyd's 1910 Sourdough Expedition nevertheless continued an intriguing mystery twenty and more years after the event. In Alaska, Fairbanksans had soon learned from the other three members when they had got back from the Kantishna later in 1910, that Lloyd's original newspaper version that all four had got to the top of Mount McKinley's South Peak on April 2nd, was not true. Then, with no published photographs of consequence—nor indeed any printed account by any one of the three setting straight Lloyd's exaggerated story—critics for awhile tended to equate the whole thing with Dr. Cook's earlier and generally unaccepted claim that he had been up there in September of 1906.

But when, three years after Lloyd's expedition, in 1913, Walter Harper, Karstens, Stuck, and Tatum all agreed that they had unmistakably seen the Sourdough spruce flagstaff atop the 19,470-foot North Peak, it was realized and accepted that *some* of Lloyd's Sourdough party must have at least have climbed *that* high. But just who had done what? Anything of that sort accomplished in 1910 was clearly a mountaineering historic "first". Had some one or more of the now understandably reticent other three Alaskan old-timers perhaps actually been to the top of even the highest point, the South Peak itself? After all, a party which was capable of dragging a spruce flagpole to the top of the North Peak and erecting it there could, if they really addressed themselves to it, have climbed the higher but less steep South Peak. If so, their climb in 1910 would be the real first ascent of Mt. McKinley!

To be sure, speculative versions by such authorities as Alfred H. Brooks in 1914, and Hudson Stuck in 1915, did not actually suggest this. But then neither of their published opinions as to what had probably occurred was a first hand account by one of the actual members of the 1910 Sourdough Expedition. And though few by now thought that Lloyd's story was the correct one, it was still the only first person account published, and in the tight little world of American mountaineering a lively interest continued as to what, exactly, the other members of 1910 party had experienced, and what surprises might finally some day be revealed by one of them.

Finally, almost thirty years after the event, readers of the *American Alpine Journal*, in the summer of 1939, were delighted to come upon the following interview, written by Norman Bright, a young climber from Chehalis, Washington, while on a trip in Alaska.

> It was supper time on a hot mid-July day in 1937. The doors of the roadhouse at McKinley Park Station were open and a refreshing breeze swept through the sultry kitchen. At the counter sat several men tardily devouring the last of an excellent meal. The lady of the house was busy with the dishes. Outside a man was putting up his dogs. As he entered, removed his coat, and found a stool next to mine, the proprietress and several of the oldtimers greeted him with obvious enthusiasm and affection.
>
> Busy reading a mountaineering book, a treat which I had anticipated all day, I simply looked up, then continued reading. I supposed him to be an oldtimer himself, as everyone seemed to know him.
>
> "Is that a map of Alaska?" he asked, referring to the Alaska Steamship Company map marking my place.
>
> "Yes," I answered, handing it to him.
>
> "That's the book I was talking to you about," remarked the proprietress as she put the newly baked bread to cool and came to stand before him.
>
> "*The Ascent of Denali*", I said as I flipped the cover into view and then continued reading.
>
> "Well, this is the Mr. William Taylor mentioned in the book," she announced.
>
> I hadn't read of Mr. William Taylor being in Stuck's party. I was frankly puzzled.

"How far up the mountain did you get?" I blundered.

"To the top," he said calmly.

"What is your name again?" I asked excitedly.

"Billy Taylor," he replied, giving the nickname which everyone in the north affectionately uses.

I knew then that I was talking to one of the members of the 1910 Expedition, and one who had succeeded in conquering the North Peak. My amazement at finding one of the "old" sourdoughs still alive and not yet showing even traces of senility did not prevent me from finding out everything I could from him, between the moment of introduction a bit after 6 p.m. and the time he put his dogs on the freight and clambered aboard himself, 11:30 p.m.

The first part of the interview was carried on while Billy gave his three sled-dogs, Mickey, Spot and Ace, their suppers. Mickey, who is part wolf and part malamute, weighs 100 lbs., and is the most powerful dog Taylor has ever had. After the dogs had been attended to, we went out to the bunk house where Billy rested on the sleepingbag on top of my bunk and answered questions. A half hour later, so as not to keep the other occupants of the bunkhouse awake, we moved to the blacksmith shop across from the station. A fire still burned in the forge. Billy found a seat on a workbench while I chose an anvil near the flame where I could see to write.

Affable describes Billy Taylor. He answered my questions for almost five hours! The fact that everyone calls him Billy is only one indication which leads one to believe that Lloyd was sincere when he declared: "Taylor and I have been partners for years and (I don't claim that is because of any good qualities of mine) I have never had words with him. He is beyond question one of the finest men you ever met." Tom Lloyd was simply making a statement which many since have corroborated.

As to physical attributes, Lloyd described him as "a big man and strong as a horse." He has a massive frame with tremendous shoulders, the widest I have ever seen. At twenty-two he must have been exceedingly strong. His weight is now around 250 lbs. He wears false teeth which are especially noticeable when he talks. At twenty-two (1910) his hairline was high. Now, at forty-nine it is a trifle thin. His right thumb is cut off at the first joint; he must have lost it since the expedition, as his right hand, which rests on Lloyd's shoulder (1910 photograph) seems to be whole. He wore loose bib-overalls, a soiled shirt much wrinkled at the elbows, a blue blazer, shoepacks and a battered hat. His outfit consisted of a homemade packboard.

This huge man with his jovial laugh, for all the world like the fat plumber I knew in Fairbanks, was the conqueror of McKinley. He was the embodiment of those hearty wights of massive build to whom Shakespeare attributed the most abundant good nature.

Twenty-seven years before, this man who now wheezed when he ran had dropped his mining for a few months to make a matter-of-fact mush to the top of McKinley's North Peak. In so doing he and his companion, Pete Anderson, had unsuspectingly performed the greatest *tour de force* in the annals of mountaineering on this continent—the amazing feat of climbing from 11,000 feet to the top and back in one day!

Interview

Who were the members of the expedition? Thomas Lloyd, he was the leader, Charley McGonagall, Pete Anderson, and myself.

How did the idea get started? It got started through Cook's claims which everyone thought was a fake. Lloyd was backed by Fairbanks men, three, I think it was. He said he could pick men who could climb it and they put up the money.

Who were the backers? Gus Peterson, E. W. Griffin, and W. H. (Bill) McPhee.

Any of them living? Well, darned if I know. McPhee is dead, I know. Griffin, I don't know, I "kinda" think he is. But Peterson's alive. Leastwise, he was a year ago.

Where is he living? He's outside someplace. He *was* located in Yakima. He had a ranch there. Haven't heard of him for two or three years. But his brother was in Fairbanks a year ago.

How old were you when you went on the expedition? I think I was eighteen but I'm not rightly sure.

When were you born? March 15th, 1888. (He was twenty-one when he joined the expedition, spent his twenty-second birthday on the glacier.)

Where? Ontario, Canada.

When did you come to Alaska? 1901 or 1902, I don't rightly remember. (Mildly irritated at himself, not me) Goddamit! I never kept a diary. (He must have been only thirteen or fourteen when he came north to make his own living!)

How did you make a living? Driving teams. Owned my own teams. Sold out and went to Kantishna. (He pronounced it with one more syllable than its spelling indicates—"Kan-

Standing (left to right): Charles McGonagall, P. Anderson, W.R. Taylor. Seated: T. Lloyd.

tishina", the way nearly everyone says it.) Had pack-horses first. Sold them and got dogs.

How did you happen to be selected? Well, Lloyd just selected me. He knew me and he knew *of* me.

Do you know how he picked his men? He just knew fellers who were pretty skookum. He had been around the camps a good deal, and picked out one here and one there.

What can you tell me about Lloyd? He was probably close to sixty—well, in the fifties anyhow. I imagine he was damn close to sixty. He's been dead close to fifteen years, I guess. Died soon after the ascent—in '14 or '15. I know I went "outside" and when I came back he was dead. He was awful fat. Had kind of a nervous breakdown and just keeled over.

What sort was he? He was fine in his way, but he was lookin' for too much fame. He conflicted his stories by telling his intimate friends he didn't climb it, and told others he was at the top. We didn't get out till June, and then, they didn't believe any of us had climbed it. But Stuck verified the climb. He found the pole. The halfbreed was the first one to see it.

Did Lloyd make anything from the story? Not that I know of. Because he couldn't sell the story after he balled it up. He was the head of the party. We had to take care of our mining assessments. We never dreamed he wouldn't give a straight story. I wish to God we "hadda" been there. Of course our intimate friends believed us. But there was no proof until Stuck verified the pole three years later. Lloyd was no writer. He took the data. A fellow by the name of W. F. Thompson, newswriter, editor of the Fairbanks *News-Miner* wrote the story.

Was it published? Just in the local paper.[1] He didn't write the whole story. He kept that to sell to a syndicate. After Lloyd balled the thing up, he (Thompson) quit in disgust.

What sort of a fellow was Pete Anderson? Big husky Swede. Hell of a good fellow on the trail. Him and I'd go along and never have no trouble at all. He was a husky "sonofagun". We done all the work but we never got credit for nothin'. None of those points was named after us. I had implicit confidence in Lloyd so I never kept no data on it at all.

How old a man was Pete? He was in his prime then. I think Pete must be ten years older than me, anyway.

Where does he live? Nenana. He has a tinsmith shop. He's only home nights. Between jobs he's always building a stove or some goddam thing.

And McGonagall? Well, he—I don't know how old Johnny (he must have said "Charley") was at that time, but he used to mush dogs on the trail to Valdez (now the Richardson Highway) and he's been prospecting and doing all sorts of work before and since. I haven't seen him for several years.

(McGonagall, whom I met in Fairbanks this summer, admits sixty-eight years, although his friend Harry Karstens, who lives a few doors from him, says Charley is fudging two years, that he is seventy, ten years older than Karstens. So McGonagall must have been over forty in 1910.)

I heard that he pioneered mail service on "The Trail"? A man by the name of Ben Downing (?) did, I think, and him and Karstens were his drivers. Karstens was with Stuck. He (Karstens) used to be superintendent of the park here—just before Liek. I imagine him and Pete was close to the same age. (If so, Pete was about thirty-two at the time of the climb.)

What were you doing the winter of 1909? Prospecting.

Where? Kantishna.

When did you start on the expedition? We left Fairbanks with four head of horses the 22nd December, 1909.

What kind of supplies did you take? Oh, bacon, beans, flour, sugar, dried fruits, butter, and a general outfit.

Did you have any special high altitude rations? No. Just bacon and beans. Had doughnuts on the highest. That's all we took up with us—and hot chocolate—a thermos bottle apiece. Just took a half dozen doughnuts in a sack and started out. I had three left when I got back. That is, from the 11,000-ft. level. Of course, up to that time we used caribou meat from the country.

Did you, like Stuck, make pemmican? No, we just had steaks and stews. They took two weeks on the trip that we made in eighteen hours. No, a month, I think. Well, we made it all in one day, by God! Just breaking day, a little after three when we started, and I know it was dark—getting dusk—when we got back. I know it was an even eighteen hours. I don't know the exact time. We never paid no attention to that.

(At this point, Taylor went into the roadhouse for a few minutes to bid his friends goodbye.)

What kind of mountaineering and personal equipment did you take along? Gumshoes. (Taylor refers to the shoepacks which are worn universally in the North. They are waterproof, made of rubber with a leather top, lacing like a boot, generally around 12 inches high.) We put on moccasins when we put on our creepers. We had pole-axes and double-bitted axes for chopping wood. We started out cutting wood [steps? T. M.] with the pole-axe but finally quit it, and took our climbing poles and creepers and walked right over everything and forgot about steps. Carried knapsacks, but we had nothing to pack but a little grub, thermos bottle, rope, candles, camera. (Taylor is speaking of the final ascent.)

What did you wear? Any special mountaineering clothes? No, just bib-overalls, shirt, winter underwear, parkee and mitts.

What did you use for bedding? Down sleeping-bags. I had a wolfskin robe. (Lloyd says: "We had two caribou hides for beds and mattresses for four of us. They are the clear quill to put on the ice and snow. Pete had a sheepskin sleeping-bag as well, and besides that we had had three robes in all for the four of us—one of them was not much good—and a piece of canvas to throw over them all. You want to be sure to keep the snow and ice from thawing underneath you. We had no discomfort in sleeping at all. McGonagall and I each had a pillow, but Bill Taylor was never known to carry a pillow; neither was the Swede".)

Where did you outfit? In Fairbanks.

What kind of parkas did you have? Light duck parkees—not furlined.

Do you still have any of the equipment left from the expedition? I have a pair of creepers. I have an alpine pole somewhere in Fairbanks; I don't know where it is. Left it with Abe Stines. I don't know where Abe is now. I think he's "outside" somewhere.

What do you consider the toughest part of the climb? From the bottom of the Grand Basin to the top of the North Peak. You come to places like a knife blade and you can see down for thousands of feet below you. It's a steep climb from 11,000 ft. too, but you haven't that steep ridge to contend with.

Why didn't you use climbing ropes? Didn't need 'em.

What did you leave at the top? A 14-ft. pole 4 inches at the top end—dry spruce. We packed it and pulled it up. Where we couldn't pack it we pulled it up on a line. And a little piece of box-board, about 8 inches square, and we put all the names of the party on it. (Lloyd says the pole was 4 inches at the bottom, tapering symmetrically to 2½ inches at the top.)

Do you think it is still there? (The Lindley-Liek expedition reported no trace of it when they ascended the North Peak in 1932.) Well, it's wherever the pole is unless it got knocked off. (That's logic for you! Billy told me they chose the N. summit to put the flagpole on because the coast (S.) summit could not be seen from Fairbanks.)[2]

Did you write anything else? Yes, the date of the ascent.

What was there at the top? Little pinnacles of rock from 4 to 6 inches high. But generally speaking, it was just a mass of ice.

Did you build a cairn? Oh yes, we dug down in the ice with a little axe we had and built a pyramid of 15 inches high and we dug down in the ice so the pole had a support of about 30 inches and it was held by four guy-lines—just cotton ropes. We fastened the guy-lines to little spurs of rocks.

How did it feel to stand on the top of the highest mountain of North America and know the whole continent was beneath you? Well, of course, the altitude made you feel light-like. You had to watch yourself or your feet would come up quick.

How long did you stay on the top? Between two and two and a half hours, if I remember rightly.

What were the weather conditions like while you were on the top? Sunshine on top but cloudy below us. It shut off a lot of view.

Did you recognize any points? No. At first it was fine and you could see streaks of timber and the creeks and rivers. But on the first trip—April 1st—we had to stop four hours from the top. Had to turn back—saw a storm coming. Stormed all that night and all the next day.

Did you see Mt. Foraker? Oh yes, we could see Foraker sticking up through the clouds.

How were the weather conditions during the entire expedition? We had some awful cold weather when we started, and that day we was up there, it was thirty below. I know it was colder than hell. Mitts and everything was all ice.

Did you let your beards grow to protect your face? No. (Spits.) Didn't have long to grow anyway.

Did you have many storms? Just the one on the flats freightin' in. It was some winter all right down there! But not after we got up on the mountain. Oh, once or twice up on Muldrow Glacier.

Did you know the other summit was higher? Looking across the two of them, it didn't seem to have any elevation more, but they claim it is 300 ft. higher.[3]

About how far is it to the other summit? Between 2 and 3 miles somewheres.

What was the reason that you did not climb the South Peak? We set out to climb the North Peak. That's the toughest peak to climb—the North.

When did McGonagall and Lloyd learn of your success? (Taylor says that only he and Pete Anderson reached the top. McGonagall was outdistanced around 18,000 or 19,000 feet, while Lloyd did not go beyond the 11,000-ft. level.) McGonagall was at the 11,000-ft. level the night of the 3rd.[4] We saw Lloyd the next day—the 4th. That night we camped at the second camp below 11,000-ft. (The Willows.)

What did you have to eat the night after the climb? Beans. Meat with 'em. And bread. We made it at the lower camp on the flats. Lloyd was a pretty good baker. He done most of the cooking. Had it frozen and thawed it out when we used it.

How many days did you take in the descent? We made the descent down to 11,000 feet in 18 hours and on the day of the 4th came down to where Lloyd was camped—the Willow Camp.

What were the names of your camps? The last camp was at 11,000 feet. The next to the last was about 8 miles from the head of Muldrow Glacier. I don't know whether we called it Muldrow Camp or Glacier Camp. I've forgotten (This was what Lloyd called Pothole Camp.) Then Willow Camp. Then below that was out on the flats. The willows was the last vegetation about 4 miles below the McPhee Pass—we called it. Stuck called it the McGonagall Pass.

Just then we heard the distant whistle of a train. We both jumped. It was as dark outside as the night of the murder in *Macbeth.* The remainder of the interview took place on the run. He had to fetch his dogs.

Did your parents learn of your climb? No, my parents were dead when I left home.

What stands out most strongly in your mind concerning the climb? I can see the whole route all the way up. It was grand!

Did the climb have any ill effects on you? No, none at all.

Did you OK the newspaper story? (New York Times, June 6, 1910). No.

What is your present address? Diamond, Alaska.

Would you consider climbing the mountain again if you had the chance? Yes, if there was enough money in it. But not just for sport. (He put his dogs into a boxcar and climbed on board the freight.)

"Have you any more questions?" he asked, anxious to help me as much as he could. "No, that's all, thanks", I answered. "I'm certainly glad to have met you. I had taken it for granted that the members of the old Sourdough Expedition were dead long ago. Now that you're fixed up, I'll say goodbye and I hope to see you again." "Goodbye, Norman." "Take good care of the dogs," I said. "Oh, I will," he laughed.

As I took the road back to the bunkhouse Taylor's words, "I can see the whole route. It was grand!" rang in my ears. He will always carry with him the memory of that magnificent climb, and of himself and Anderson fighting the altitude and cold to place the American flag on McKinley's northern summit . . .

The moon broke through the clouds and sailed slowly across the sky.

This aerial photo by Terris Moore, taken at 13,000 feet from 15 miles northeast of McKinley's summit, shows the High Basin (Big Basin, Upper Basin, Grand Basin) between the South Peak (left) and North Peak (right). Karsten's Ridge descends to the head of Muldrow Glacier behind the little white blossoming cloud. Lower, out of sight on the right, McGonagall Pass opens onto the Muldrow. From the left, the broad Traleika Glacier joins the lower Muldrow.

XII

Epilogue; and a Summit Photograph to Compare with Dr. Cook's

A full generation had passed since Dr. Frederick A. Cook in 1906 claimed to have reached the summit of Mount McKinley. One might have supposed that after thirty years the whole episode would have been forgotten. Or at least that Dr. Cook, like Tom Lloyd, would simply have given up. But in the winter of 1935-6 the Doctor and his friends opened a fresh campaign for his vindication.

His life during the intervening years had lacked neither color nor imagination—his motivations, with the passage of time, an endless subject for wonder. Like the individual convinced he is Napoleon, Dr. Cook seems to have convinced himself over the years (whatever his original mental process), that he actually had been first to the top of Mount McKinley and was the discoverer of the North Pole. But, unlike the self-proclaimed Napoleon, the persuasive and often charming Dr. Cook seems always to have been able to enlist some believers in his esoteric and rather appealing claims.

The U. S. Congress, after conducting investigations into the North Pole controversy, had passed a bill, signed by President Taft on March 4, 1911, giving Robert E. Peary U.S.N. a life pension of $6,000 and the retired rank of Rear Admiral, for his "arctic explorations in reaching the North Pole." "Discovery" and "discovered" had been deleted in the amended bill in deference to the still unsettled controversy with Dr. Cook. The Doctor immediately afterward took to the lecture platform with marked success. Seventy bookings on the Chautauqua circuit, following in the footsteps of William Jennings Bryan, Robert M.

LaFollette and other well-known speakers, kept the Doctor's message and claims alive. After his lectures, well-wishers often surrounded him, eager to express sympathy and a desire to help. According to at least one source, Henry Ford, Thomas Edison and John Burroughs appeared together in one of these groups; after which Dr. Cook was for some days a house guest with them at Edison's home, reportedly receiving sympathy and verbal support from Ford.

On April 30, 1914, Senator Miles Poindexter of Washington state, introduced a resolution into the U. S. Senate proposing that the thanks of the Congress be extended to Dr. Cook "for his discovery of the North Pole." It failed to pass, but Dr. Cook was gaining in his drive for political support. Petitions bearing many names were next sent to congressmen, and in early 1915 a somewhat similar resolution was introduced into the House of Representatives; and its Committee on Education thereupon conducted hearings. Though this resolution also ultimately failed of passage, the hearings produced some arresting presentations.

Edwin Swift Balch, a distinguished Philadelphia lawyer, past president of the Philadelphia Geographical Society, and a Fellow of the Royal Geographical Society, had with Dr. Cook been one of the original founding members of the American Alpine Club in 1901. Unlike most of Cook's other adherents at the time of the Congressional hearings, Balch could not be dismissed as completely lacking in geographical or mountaineering experience. He had a considerable climbing record in Europe, though none in Alaska.

At his own expense and effort, Balch prepared a detailed analysis, printed in a 142-page booklet entitled *Mount McKinley and Mountain Climbers' Proofs.* In this he summed up his opinions: "The only conclusion which seems possible is that Cook's photograph of the top of Mount McKinley and Browne's illustration of Fake Peak represent different peaks . . . one can but think that Browne made a mistake." Balch "proved" this by presenting tracings he made of the outlines of Cook's and Browne's photographs for comparison; and the outlines were in fact not quite identical. But the ultimate quality of Balch's judgement is illuminated by the fact that he accepted unquestioningly Lloyd's claim to have reached the top of McKinley's South and

North Peaks on April 2 and 3, 1910. In Balch's opinion, Stuck in 1913 made merely the *third* ascent of Mount McKinley!

One Ernest C. Rost "of Chicago, an expert photographer", now presented testimonials from other Arctic explorers in Cook's behalf. And Rost asserted that Parker, Browne and Stuck had used the "most cruel, cowardly and dastardly methods" to discredit Dr. Cook's claims. This outburst amply confirms Belmore Browne's sad comment. "In looking back on that remarkable controversy I am still filled with astonishment at the incredible amount of vindictive and personal spite that was shown by the partisans of Dr. Cook. Men who had never seen an ice-axe or a dog-sled wrote us reams of warped exploring details and accused us of untold crimes because we dared to question Cook's honesty. I was visiting Professor Parker . . . and scarcely a day went by that we did not receive abusive anonymous letters."

But all this was soon eclipsed by the onrushing events of World War I during which Dr. Cook dropped from sight. Years later, it emerged that he and a friend had gone to India late in 1915 to attempt the ascent of Mount Everest—only to be arrested by the British authorities because they had chanced to travel with some German conspirators who were seeking to foment a revolution in India.

After the war, Dr. Cook engaged in the oil business as a geologist in the western United States, and for awhile prospered. But in April, 1923, he was ordered arrested by the Federal authorities on charges of using the mails to defraud in connection with the sale of oil stock, and surrendered at Fort Worth, Texas. In the resulting trial Dr. Cook admitted having been overly-optimistic about his company's prospects, but his company books showed all funds accounted for, none missing. He had drawn neither salary, profits nor commissions, and he himself was the largest investor in the company.

But Dr. Cook was sentenced to a fine of $12,000, plus fourteen years and nine months in Leavenworth Penitentiary. It seems the judge threw the book at Dr. Cook, regarding him as a repeater in fraud because of his Mount McKinley and Polar claims. A reporter at the sentencing commented that "while these weren't in themselves punishable offenses, the judge appeared to think that they ought to have been, and that a good time to mete out punishment for them was right then, with the doctor's conviction on an oil fraud charge as the excuse . . . " Ironically, not long after Cook's conviction, the supposedly worthless oil-field flowed profusely, and proved highly profitable to those who obtained it for a small price from the bankruptcy proceedings.

Dr. Cook turned out to be an exemplary prisoner; in addition to assisting in the prison hospital as a doctor, he organized and taught in a school for prisoners. The great Roald Amundsen, discoverer of the South Pole, and an old friend of Cook's from Antarctic days together, made a special trip to visit him in prison in January, 1926, causing considerable comment by so doing.

Amundsen publicly praised Cook, and in response to telegrams asking for further explanation replied: "I did not commit myself to an opinion as to the respective achievements of Peary or Cook. What I said was that the only evidence I could accept would be the publications of their complete observations. Recalling my acquaintanceship with Dr. Cook during our two hazardous years on the *Belgica* expedition to the Antarctic, remembering also the debt of gratitude I owed him for his kindness to me in my novitiate as an explorer, and recalling that I owed my life indeed to his resourcefulness in extricating us from the dangers of that expedition, I felt I could do no less than make a short journey to the prison and call upon my former benefactor in his present misfortune. I could not have done less without convicting myself of base ingratitude and contemptible cowardice."

Dr. Cook was paroled in March, 1930, his departure from prison being marked by tributes from his fellow inmates. And five years later, as soon as the term of his parole had expired, he and his friends immediately began a campaign for the specific vindication of his Mt. McKinley and North Pole claims.

Ted Leitzell, a writer from Chicago, now led off in 1935 with a series of articles in a publication called *Real America,* whose titles indicate their tone: "Peary's Conspiracy Against Dr. Cook"; "The North Pole Boomerang"; and "Who Stole the North Pole?"

The essential point in Leitzell's series was that Dr. Cook had been unfairly judged on his North Pole claim because enemies had discredited his earlier Mt. McKinley expedition: "Some unknown person had purchased the [incriminating] affidavit from

Edward Barrill, a laborer who had accompanied Dr. Cook on the ascent . . . " Leitzell's conclusion was that "there is ample evidence to prove that Dr. Cook, once called 'the most colossal liar in history', is really the most truthful of all our Polar explorers."

Two years after this series of articles, Leitzell (now referred to as "an executive of the Zenith Radio Company") reported that he made a trip to Alaska and with one companion went out to the site of the Fake Peak. From this he maintained that it did not look anything like Dr. Cook's 1906 summit photograph, and argued that therefore Cook's Mt. McKinley claim had not really been disproved by the Explorers Club Expedition of 1910.

Dr. Cook, promptly after the term of his parole had expired, also instituted libel suits in the courts against various writers and publishers, among them the *Encyclopedia Britannica* and the Houghton Mifflin Company.

Further adding to the picture of an unjustly maligned man, Dr. Cook in early 1936 formally petitioned the American Geographical Society to re-examine the results of his 1906 Mount McKinley expedition. It was evident by now that Dr. Cook would never regain the original acceptance he had for awhile enjoyed in 1909 for his far more important claim on history, the discovery of the North Pole, so long as he continued under the charge of the professional joint expedition which had returned from Alaska in 1910 reporting: "To sum up, our discoveries prove beyond a doubt that Dr. Cook (in 1906) wilfully and with full knowledge of the deception, claimed the ascent of Mount McKinley, when he had not even reached the base of the mountain."

But in none of his libel suits did Dr. Cook receive a favorable Court ruling. The American Geographical Society declined to reverse its original finding. And what Ted Leitzell, or anyone else in the late 1930's, had to say about the 1910 "Fake Peak" was no longer the issue it had been thirty years earlier at a time when no one knew what McKinley's actual summit looked like. For in the meantime eleven men in three different parties had been up and had a close look at the real thing—three men to 20,000 feet in 1912, four on the summit itself in 1913, and four again on the summit in 1932—and none of these eleven men would accept Dr. Cook's "summit" photograph, or his claim to have been there.

These parties had not however succeeded in bringing back their own photographs of McKinley's summit which could be compared with Dr. Cook's; that is, one taken from a distance of about fifty yards with a person standing on top for scale, holding the flag. Conditions had simply been too rigorous. But no one doubted these three parties had been where they said they had; their numerous other photographs high on the mountain were entirely convincing.

In 1936 a new figure, destined to be the most important single individual in the next thirty years of Mount McKinley's history, came to the great mountain. Bradford Washburn, young Harvard graduate who the year before had discovered and named Mount King George and Mount Queen Mary in an unexplored region of Yukon Territory, Canada, now led the first expedition to cover the McKinley range with aerial photography. In the summers of 1936 and 1937, the flights which he organized for the National Geographic Society began a long series which years later were to result in a map, receiving international recognition for its accuracy and detailed portrayal of the McKinley Range's fantastic and infinitely complex topography.

Though these flights were but the beginning of the long mapping project, they early revealed that the glacial valleys and ridges along Mount McKinley's south and east slopes differ strikingly from Dr. Cook's description of his purported "route" in 1906 from the Ruth Glacier to the top of the South Peak. These photographs strengthened long standing doubts that *anybody* could climb to the top of the mountain along the route Dr. Cook claimed he and Barrill had done in 1906. The Royal Geographical Society the next year in London, conferred the Cuthbert Peek award on Washburn, "for Alaska Explorations and Glacier studies".

Dr. Frederick A. Cook was now in his seventies. In May, 1940, while in Larchmont, New York, visiting Ralph Shainwald von Ahlefeldt, who had been his most junior companion during the very creditable 1903 McKinley expedition, the Doctor suffered a stroke. While Cook lay ill in a nearby hospital, Shainwald petitioned President Franklin D. Roosevelt to grant Cook a full pardon as an act of executive clemency, and this the President promptly did. Dr. Cook died on August 5, 1940, at the age of seventy-five, never having had to face a photograph of the true summit of Mount McKinley on a scale comparable to the one he took in 1906—perhaps the most controversial single photograph in the history of exploration.

The Wartime Expedition of 1942; and a Summit Photograph at last to Compare with Dr. Cook's

"Where can we find natural out-of-doors temperatures of at least 20 to 25 below zero Fahrenheit, *dependably* during the coming summer, on the North American continent—with the war on, Greenland has to be ruled out—reasonably accessible, where we can work on the prototype designs of some 150 items of military clothing and equipment, to manufacture late this summer and early fall, for issue to mountain and arctic troops in time for the winter of 1942-43?"

This technical question, posed by the U. S. Army's Quartermaster General in early 1942, to a handful of consultants (of whom the writer of this book was one), led to the military testing expedition which in July of that war year, placed seven men in the High Basin between the North and South Peaks of Mount McKinley. This unique location was really the only one on the continent—except for Mount Logan, even more inaccessible—where such low temperatures could be found in a a natural environment in midsummer.

The usefulness of cold-chambers is limited principally to testing the response of materials to sub-zero temperatures. For research into the design aspects of articles for field use, cold-chambers are inadequate. Ultimately, of course, performance in combat use by troops works out the most effective designs. But when the bombs fell at Pearl Harbor in December, 1941, the United States and Canadian military establishments were singularly lacking in designs using modern materials, for troops who might have to fight in mountain and arctic environments. Immediate choices of design had to be made, however, and quick field tests were urgent. So the U. S. Army Alaska Test Expedition, 1942, was sent out from Washington by military air transport to Alaska.

Base Camp, McGonagall Pass, 1942, showing Mt. Brooks across Muldrow Glacier. *(Photo by Bradford Washburn.)*

The High Basin between the North and South Peaks of Mount McKinley can hardly be described as "reasonably accessible"! The problem was solved by calling for experienced volunteers to climb up into the High Basin, to set up a research camp near the 18,000 foot level while the Air Force parachuted out the numerous items to be tested, and the necessary supplies to maintain the research party there for some weeks.

A seventeen man task force, commanded by a regular Army Lieutenant Colonel of the Quartermaster Corps, with officers representing the Army Ground Forces, Army Air Forces, Medical Corps, Signal Corps, the Royal Canadian Air Force, and the Royal Canadian Army, plus four civilian consultants, took to the field. One remained behind at Fairbanks' Ladd Air Force Base to ride in the Air Force planes and direct the parachuting. We sixteen others were trucked to Wonder Lake, and from there in June walked to McGonagall Pass, and set up a base camp on the edge of the Muldrow Glacier. From here on the expedition gradually sorted itself out, as the higher and

Equipment testing and backpacking up Muldrow Glacier. *(Photo by Terris Moore, July 1942.)*

higher camps were set up—climbing by the route of the pioneering parties of decades before, along Muldrow Glacier and up Karstens Ridge—until finally the tents of the research camp were set up at 17,800 feet in the High Basin.

Here the predicted sub-zero July temperatures were indeed found, accompanied moreover by very high winds almost constantly lashing the area. "The tents were hardly up when we were visited by two giant planes which showered the upper Harper Glacier with food, gasoline, and warm clothing (and some of the test items). For half an hour in sub-zero cold we watched the shining parachutes descend . . . Some of the parachute loads were damaged and one was never found, but most were intact. Then chilled by the wind, we crawled into our sleeping bags to get the best sleep in many weeks."

This description, from the account of Captain Robert H. Bates, in command of operations in the high research area, who with six others of us made it aloft there to do the research work, is also a fair account of the strange sight we saw on later occasions when the last of all the test items were again parachuted down.

During the ensuing weeks our party lived and worked in the High Basin, it was but natural that we should take a day off when the weather seemed favorable, and wearing the various experimental items being tested at the moment, climb the remaining 2,500 feet to the top of McKinley's South Peak, which now loomed so enticingly before those of us who were familiar with the great mountain's remarkable history.

An opportunity to make this climb came on July 23rd. In his official account covering the day before, Bates generously observes:

> "Moore and Jackman, be it noted, backpacked about 50 lbs apiece from 12,000 ft. to nearly 18,000 ft. that day, getting in late when the evening chill was numbing our thoughts and actions. The late arrival threw off our plans for an early breakfast, and cold and limited acclimatization slowed our morning efforts. Not until after eleven did Moore and I on one rope, and (Bradford) Washburn and Nilsson (Einar Nilsson, engineer and civilian consultant) on another, start out. As bad weather was apparently setting in now, we felt dubious of getting to the top.

"They were all extremely deep, some of such dimensions that a whole railway train might disappear into them," said Erling Strom about the crevasses. *(Photo by Terris Moore, July 1942.)*

Starting up Karstens Ridge, Browne Tower above, July 1942. *(Photo by Terris Moore.)*

> "We were carrying little as we set off, but each was wearing different items in order to test as much as possible. Footgear especially we were interested in, for repeated tests had confirmed that the temperature of the snow beneath the surface was 17° below zero no matter how much the sun smiled. The air temperature itself kept generally well below zero and nightly descended to minus 22° or 23°"

Almost casually we struck off toward our personal rendezvous with this mountain's dramatic history. Soon we were breaking trail through a foot of loose powder and climbing beyond the last tracks above camp—and on the historic route of the pioneer climbers of Denali, a trail so long untouched.

Before long we were leaning on our ice-axes trying to catch our breaths. The same thought came to our minds; we spoke of it again when, briefly, we halted for lunch. What a contrast between our position and that of our predecessors on this great mountain! Here we were, but a few minutes away from our high camp well-stocked with food and equipment all dropped from the skies without our effort. As Bates pointed out: "Here on these very slopes Browne, Parker, and La Voy had fought their way despite pemmican which sickened them and storms that frustrated their every chance; here Stuck, the indomitable archdeacon, had toiled upward, supported by sturdy companions and a brave spirit; here the Lindley-Liek expedition years later had found the peak dangerously cold . . . "

Slowly we ascended, changing the lead every fifty steps. No longer now were we in a high valley but rather looking down on valleys which showed, far below, in places through a sea of clouds, undercast beneath us at perhaps the ten thousand foot level.

At 2:30 we once more moved upward, as rhythmically as possible, straining to reach the high shoulder that gives the great view off to the westward from which Mount Foraker first springs into sight. Gradually the surface changed, and now we found ourselves on windfirmed snow near the place where, thirty years before, Browne and Parker sheltered among snowdrifts and the howling storm turned them back. Galeswept drifts in a little hollow, and beyond them snow hardened by many storms, were still here. But this day, mercifully, the air was remarkably calm.

Our crampons barely dented the hardened crystal snow surface compacted almost to ice; we now moved along an easy ridge to another snow crest. This proved not to be the top, for yet another summit perhaps ten feet higher, still rose to the south, separated by a fifty foot stretch of ridge that looked much longer. But now, at last, almost unbelievably, we were on the very top; keenly aware that we stood on the highest point of the continent.

Other climbers usually describe strong vivid emotions at such a time as this. And I have experienced my share of these too. But I must honestly confess that for me the memories of those moments have always been quite dim. Even more so, on the higher summits of Chimborazo and Minya Konka, my recollections of the brief charmed visits there are really strong only as our actual photographs survive. And there is every reason why this should be so; for after all, above 20,000 feet one lives in a state of partial oxygen starvation; all the body processes and movements are slowed, and the senses are appreciably dimmed. One good look at the summit photographs however, and the dreamlike memories come flooding back and all is fresh again.

Days before, at base camp in McGonagall Pass, Washburn and I had discussed carrying up extra film and photographic equipment, for a final bit of history on the summit to complete the record of the pioneer climbs. Specifically, we would try to come back with a photograph, comparable at last with the one Dr. Cook had handed the world in 1907 as being the summit of Mount McKinley taken by him when he claimed to have been there: September 16, 1906. Both pioneer expeditions which had unquestionably preceded us on the summit—we were now the third party (the fifth if one accepts Dr. Cook and Tom Lloyd!) to stand upon this rather exclusive spot—had tried but failed to get this particular picture. On our day however, we were more fortunate, enjoyed almost windless conditions on top; and lovely sunshine, whose effect however could scarcely be described as heat! Later, we were able to develop excellent summit photographs. One of these, taken by Washburn, was published in the *American Alpine Journal.* Together with one of my own we reproduce it here, the first to be directly comparable to Dr. Cook's (which was presented in Chapter Five). The reader may make his own comparisons and draw his own conclusions.

Research camp in High Basin, 17,800 feet, July 1942. The author feels cold, having briefly removed parka for photographic record of clothing just before summit climb. *(Photo by Bradford Washburn.)*

The true summit of Mt. McKinley, July 23, 1942. Taken from the same distance (50 yards) and in the same direction (southerly), this photograph is the first to be directly comparable with Dr. Cook's "summit" photographs. See pages 62 and 63. *(Photo by Bradford Washburn.)*

Our brief rendezvous with history concluded, we faced down the north slopes from the summit, toward our research camp in the High Basin, and commenced our return back to our work in a world at war.

Standing on the summit of Mt. McKinley facing northeast along its fifty-yard snow crest. North Peak to the left, the only rock slope in the entire circumference. In all other directions, a profound abyss. *(Photo by Terris Moore, July 23, 1942.)*

The pioneer climbing route viewed from the summit of Mt. McKinley: the first successful photograph of this terrain. Looking northeast, 5 p.m., July 23, 1942. Bates and Moore begin the descent, their figures 100 yards distant. Nothing remotely comparable relating to McKinley's summit can be found in the photography from the controversial 1906 or 1910 expeditions. *Photo by Bradford Washburn,* American Alpine Journal, *1943 and 1978.)*

Footnotes

Chapter II

1. Dall seems logically to have used a literal translation of the German "Gebirge von Alaeksa" of the geographer Constantin Grewingk, who in 1850 at St. Petersburg, published a map of northwest America, using that label for the mountainous region of central Alaska. We may suppose that Grewingk for his part, in the eighteen-forties had consulted with Zagoskin for the more appropriate name than the localized "Tenada" and "Tschigmit" of Wrangell's 1839 map.

2. Baron Wrangell and the Russian Science Academy of course had used "Tenada" and "Tschigmit". Although Brooks knew Wrangell's 1839 book, indeed lists it in his literary references, he seems to have been completely unaware of the important map buried behind page 332. Perhaps Brooks' particular reference copy of this rare book simply lacked the map. In any event, Brooks' statement set the pattern on this subject for later writers.

3. The Susitna Station trading post at the mouth of the Skwentna.

Chapter III

1. This cairn was located in 1954, by J. C. Reed, Jr. of U.S.G.S., and the cartridge case with note still legible is now in the McKinley Park Museum. (A.A.J., 1955.)

Chapter IV

1. Identified as about 8,000 feet by Washburn on his 1960 map; the aneroid barometers for obtaining altitude in the Judge's day were subject to large errors.

2. Although Mount McKinley stands 245 miles south of the Arctic Circle, sunlight reaches its summit at midnight on June 21st. As is well known to residents along the upper Yukon River, one does not have to travel all the way to the Arctic Circle to see the midnight sun. Because of the lift given to the sun's image by atmospheric refraction, the midnight sun on June 21st is easily seen, for example, from Circle City which lies far short of the Arctic Circle on the map. (Indeed, this was why the original settlers there in 1893 misnamed their community; they mistakenly supposed that because they could see the midnight sun they must be on the Arctic Circle.) The vast elevation of McKinley's summit accounts for the visibility over the remainder of the 245 mile distance—as residents on the University of Alaska campus know who easily see the upper half of the mountain 158 miles away across the curvature of the earth.

Chapter VI

1. He spelled his name this way in 1910; thirty years later he was spelling it McGonagall, the official spelling of the Pass on to the glacier now honoring him.

Chapter VI

2. These fourteen pictures from the first expedition were, years later, evaluated by Bradford Washburn as "unquestionably authentic pictures taken on Muldrow Glacier, and one looking eastward to Mount Silverthrone from Karstens Ridge". He does not identify any from the summit and he also adds that "a large part of Lloyds story has since been proven to be fiction". So far as is known no pictures of the second expedition have ever appeared; and it remains a real mystery, especially seeing that when he was interviewed by Washburn, many years later, McGonagall "modified the account saying that this second ascent was pressed only so far as Denali Pass (18,180 ft)".

Chapter VII

1. On this portrait and in the 1906 references his name is spelled Barrille; elsewhere it appears in the shortened form.

2. According to the account in *The Pacific Monthly* for September, 1910, the Mazama expedition hoped also to appraise the Sourdough party's claim to have made the first ascent of Mt. McKinley in April, 1910. "Four men under the leadership of Thomas Lloyd, a well-known pioneer . . . claim to have reached the summit on April 3, by methods wholly new to mountaineering . . . No one will do honor to these hardy men of the North with heartier good will than the Mazamas, if it is proved true that they reached the summit." But the Mazamas' expedition was not able to bring back anything more than Alaskans' opinions about Tom Lloyd.

Chapter VIII

1. But more like 8,000 feet, using Washburn's modern contour map for this part of the mountain.

2. Worth about $30,000, at the then price for alluvial gold.

3. The Parker-Browne expedition, although among the first to recognize the photographic proof that the 1910 Sourdough party had got up todays Karstens Ridge, did not believe—as will be seen in following pages—that the 1910 party had climbed to the top of either the North or South Peak.

4. Their altitudes match ours today because Professor Parker checked the aneroid altimeter at each camp against a boiling-point hypsometer which he carried and took the trouble to operate.

5. Theirs was the first American expedition to discover what is now so well known—that fatty foods become indigestible at high altitude.

Chapter IX

1. It was Stuck who in subsequent writings formally proposed naming the ridge for Karstens. In his *Scribners* magazine article and in his book, he pays generous tribute to Karstens, calling him "the real leader of the party".

Chapter X

1. Beckwith also was vice president of the Norseman Ski Club of New York.

2. Koven's diary for Tuesday, May 3rd, 1932 reads: (The airdrop) "landed a good way down the glacier. I set off on skiis to locate the bundles and soon saw three. Spent

most of the day packing the stuff back to camp. Opening them was a good deal like Christmas Eve. There was a lot of grub, a spare tent and lots of spare clothes, also the shovel. Went to bed quite early."

3. Soon afterward this technique was emulated by pilot Bob Reeve at Valdez, where he developed a standard operating procedure for taking off from the slithery tidal mudflats with ski-equipped aircraft, to land on high mountain glacier snow in service to isolated mining camps; and to the Mount Lucania climbing expedition of 1937 in Yukon Territory, Canada. Not until the late 1940's and early 1950's did the modern ski-wheel gear, retractable in flight, become available to mountain pilots.

Chapter XI

1. Taylor apparently was unaware of the *N.Y. Times* and London newspapers accounts published in 1910.

2. Both peaks actually can be seen from near Fairbanks, the South appearing to the left of and higher than the North. But because of atmospheric interference the pole itself could not possibly be seen from Fairbanks, even through the best telescope. Almost ten times as much atmospheric mass interposes between an observer at Fairbanks looking at the summit of McKinley as when he directs his telescope to a star overhead.

3. The South Peak is actually 850 feet higher and 2 miles distant.

4. This is the day Tom Lloyd said he was atop the South peak of McKinley with the other three, "at 3:25 P.M."!

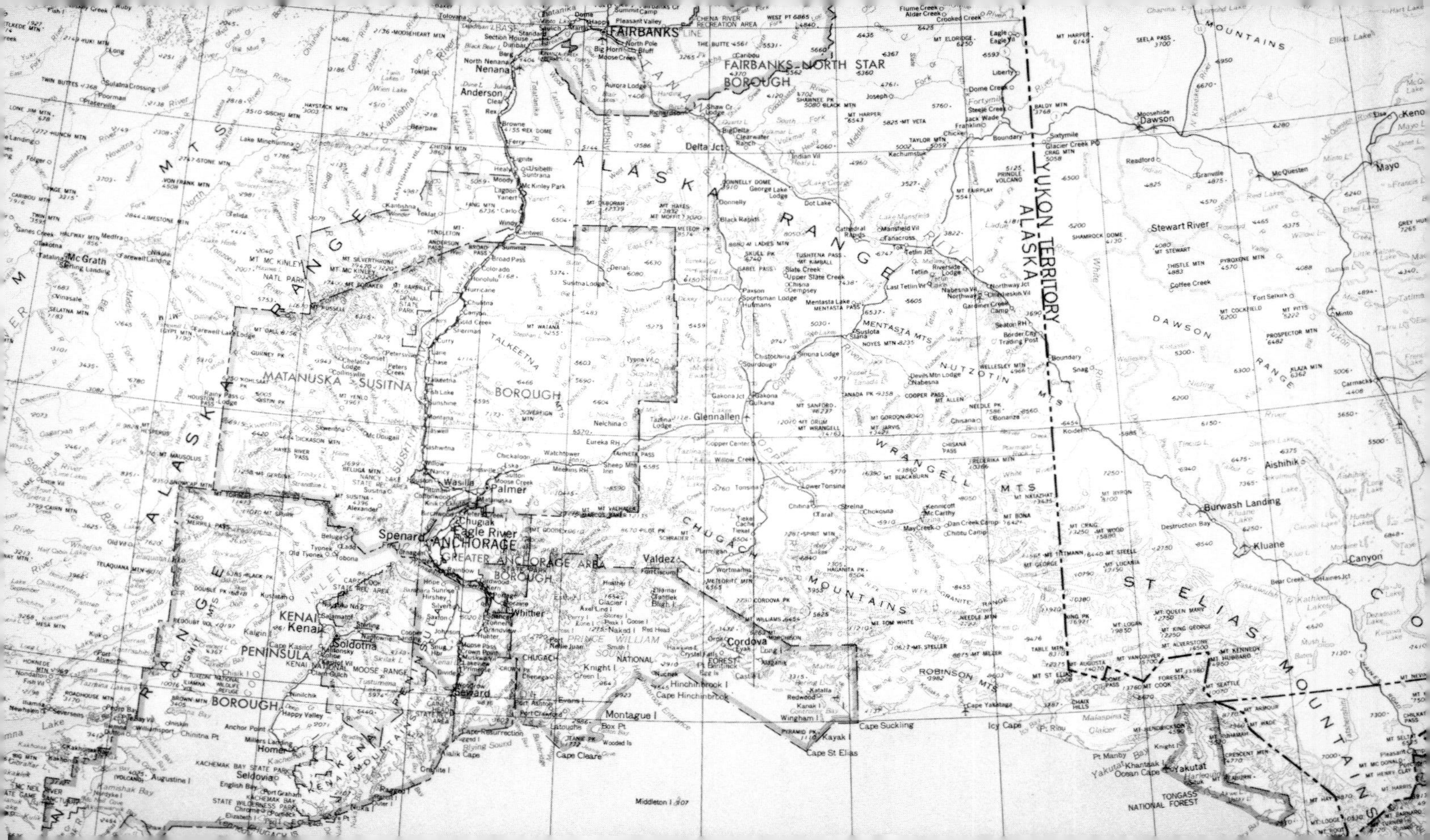

YUKON TERRITORY
ALASKA
ALASKA RANGE
FAIRBANKS
FAIRBANKS NORTH STAR BOROUGH
Nenana
Anderson
Delta Jct
Dawson
Mayo
Keno
McQuesten
Stewart River
Coffee Creek
Fort Selkirk
DAWSON RANGE
Carmacks
Minto
Aishihik
Burwash Landing
Destruction Bay
Kluane
Canyon
ST ELIAS MOUNTAINS
Yakutat
Ocean Cape
TONGASS NATIONAL FOREST
Icy Cape
Cape Yakataga
ROBINSON MTS
WRANGELL MTS
NUTZOTIN MTS
MENTASTA MTS
CHUGACH MOUNTAINS
Eagle
Chicken
Boundary
Tok
Northway
Glennallen
Copper Center
Valdez
Cordova
Cape Suckling
Kayak I
Cape St Elias
Montague I
Cape Hinchinbrook
Middleton I
Whittier
Palmer
Wasilla
Spenard
ANCHORAGE
Eagle River
GREATER ANCHORAGE AREA BOROUGH
Seward
Kenai
Soldotna
KENAI PENINSULA BOROUGH
KENAI MOUNTAINS
Homer
Seldovia
Talkeetna
MATANUSKA SUSITNA BOROUGH
MT MC KINLEY NATL PARK
McGrath
Medfra

Literature References

There is a vast literature surrounding the subject of the exploration and early climbs of Mount McKinley. The best general bibliography covering it is unquestionably Bradford Washburn's *Mount McKinley and the Alaska Range in Literature,* (Boston, 1951). "Published at the request of the University of Alaska for distribution at the Alaska Science Conference" that year, it carries 264 entries with valuable comments on each, and runs to 80 pages, a small book in itself.

Dr. Frederick A. Cook, a key Mount McKinley figure, is himself the subject of an even larger literature because of the North Pole controversy. In the bibliography sections of the two following named books will be found a very extensive list of the primary sources regarding the life of Frederick Albert Cook: *Return from the Pole, by F. A. Cook,* edited By Frederick J. Pohl, New York, 1951; *The Case For Doctor Cook,* by Andrew A. Freeman, New York, 1961.

The books, articles and letters cited in our own bibliography listed below, are not a comprehensive collection on the subject of Mount McKinley's pioneer climbs, but instead are the citations documenting the primary sources from which our book quotes. These references are given below in the order in which the subjects appear.

Chapter One - Tenada and the Tschigmit Mountains

Golder, F. A. - *Bering's Voyages* New York, 1922 and 1925.

Cook, James (and Capt. James King) - *A Voyage to the Pacific Ocean . . .* London, 1784 V. II, pp. 382-403 describes the exploration of the Alaskan coast, Prince William Sound and what was later named Cook Inlet.

Vancouver, Capt. George - *A Voyage to the Pacific Ocean . . .* London 1798 V. III p. 124 mentions sighting of the mountain.

Wrangell, F. P. von - *Statistische und Ethnographische Nachrichten uber die Russischen Besitzungen an der Nordwestkuste von Amerika* (St. Petersburg,

U.S. Geological Survey map

1839) pp. 137-160 tell the story of Glazunov's journey. Map, page 332, shows the first indication of Mt. McKinley and the Alaska Range.

Brooks, Alfred H. - *Blazing Alaska's Trails* (University of Alaska, 1953) This compilation of a great variety of geological and historical material contains an account of Glazunov's explorations (pp. 230 ff.) Brooks believed that Glazunov's "Tchalachuk on modern maps is called the Stony River . . . A conspicuous mountain was sighted to the northeast which he called Tenada and which is one of the peaks in the unsurveyed headwaters of the Stony River . . . It appears that their most easterly point was fifty miles from the Kuskokwim and not far from what are now called the Lime Hills." Brooks also says: "Glazunov lost his compass during his hard journey - a fact which detracts somewhat from the value of his notes."

Brooks' interpretation of the location of Tenada is thus not consistent with Wrangell's 1839 map of Tenada—with which map Brooks evidently was not familiar. We think that had he been familiar with it he would agree with us in placing Tenada not in the headwaters of the Stony River but where Wrangell places Tenada: identical with today's Mt. McKinley.

Zagoskin, Lavrenti A. - *Puteshestvie i isledovanie v Russkoi Amerike v 1842, 43, 44 godax* (St. Petersburg 1847). A recent edition also in Russian, which translates as *Travels and Explorations of Lieut. Zagoskin in Russian America in the Years 1842-44*, was published by the State Publishing House for Geographical Literature, Moscow, 1956; in its introduction biographical material concerning Malakov is found. The quotation about "the zealous Lukeen" is from p. 47 of the 1956 edition. There is a German version of the book, but the only English translation at present is a typescript version by Antoinette Hotovitsky, in the Library of Congress. *

Chapter Two - Prospectors Name the Great Ice Mountain

Petrov, Ivan - "The Population and Resources of Alaska, 1880", Tenth Census. 1880. VIII. Washington, D.C. 1884 - quotation is from "Geography and Topography", p. 86.

Dall, William Healey - *Alaska and its Resources* (Boston, 1870). Basic description of Alaska and personal narrative by Alaska's most eminent early scientist.

Whymper, Frederick - *Travel and Adventure in the Territory of Alaska* (New York, 1869). Entertaining account of Yukon River voyage, with drawings.

Grewingk, Constantin - *Beitrag zur Kenntniss der Orographischen Geognostischen Beschaffenheit der Nord-West Kuste Amerikas, mit den Anliegenden Inseln* (St. Petersburg, 1850). Contains first reference to "Gebirge von Alaeksa", the Alaska Range.

Brooks, Alfred H. - *Blazing Alaska's Trails* (University of Alaska, 1953). Among a vast amount of historical material, contains the story of Arthur Harper's life, pp. 312-320.

Spurr, Josiah Edward - "A Reconnaissance in Southeastern Alaska in 1898" in Twentieth Annual Report of the U.S. Geological Survey (Washington, 1900), Part VII, pp. 31-264. "Densmore's Mountain" is mentioned on p. 95.

* An English edition, *Lieut. Zagoskin's Travels in Russian America 1842-1844*, edited by Henry N. Michael, was published by the University of Toronto Press in 1967.

Brooks, Alfred H. - *The Mount McKinley Region, Alaska* U. S. Geological Survey Professional Paper No. 70 (Washington, 1911). According to Washburn in 1951, then "still the most complete and reliable single work on the McKinley region."

Princeton Alumni Weekly, May 5, 1944 (Princeton, N.J.). Obituary of William A. Dickey.

Dickey, William A. - "Discoveries in Alaska" in *The Sun* (New York, January 24, 1897) p. 6, 3 columns and sketch map.

Private communication to Bradford Washburn from George W. Dickey, citing a *Genealogical History of the Dickey Family,* compiled by Richard S. Currier (no date).

Browne, Belmore - *The Conquest of Mount McKinley* (New York, 1913). One of the great classics of mountain literature, which will be referred to more fully in Chapter 8. The story about Dickey's explanation of why he named the mountain after McKinley occurs on p. 8.

Chapter Three - McKinley's Height Measured; Mt. Foraker Discovered

Eldridge, George H. - "A Reconnaissance in the Susitna Basin and Adjacent Territory, Alaska, in 1898", *Twentieth Annual Report,* U. S. Geological Survey (Washington, 1900), Part VII, pp. 1-29.

Spurr, J. E. - "A Reconnaissance in Southwestern Alaska in 1898", *Twentieth Annual Report,* U. S. Geological Survey (Washington, 1900), Part VII, pp. 43-45, 59-61. Spurr's expedition started up the Susitna River from Cook Inlet, turned up the Yentna to the Skwentna River, and portaged from its headwaters across to the Styx River, an upper tributary of the Kuskokwim's south fork. They descended the Kuskokwim to its mouth, and returned across the Alaska Peninsula. Spurr brought to reality the unsuccessful plans of Russian explorers, Glazunov and Zagoskin among others, to find a pass through the mountains between the Kuskokwim basin and Cook Inlet, also making what is generally called the first crossing of the Alaska Range.

Herron, First Lieut. Joseph S. - *Explorations in Alaska, 1899,* War Department, Adjutant General's Office, Washington, 1901. Although Herron himself does not say so, we learn from Marcus Baker, *Geographic Dictionary of Alaska,* 1902, that Herron named the new mountain he had discovered, to honor the incumbent U. S. Senator from Ohio. Francis P. Farquhar, in his series "Naming Alaska's Mountains", in the *American Alpine Journal* 1959, pp. 211-232, adds: "Joseph Benson Foraker (1846-1917), elected Governor of Ohio, 1886, but defeated 1889; elected U. S. Senator from Ohio, 1896, re-elected 1902; exposed by the Hearst papers for accepting fees and loans from Standard Oil Company, and driven from public life; attempted a comeback for the Senate, 1914, but was defeated by Warren G. Harding. Not a very happy connotation for so great a mountain."

Brooks, Alfred H. - "An Exploration to Mt. McKinley, America's Highest Mountain"; *Journal of Geography* v. 2, no. 9, Nov. 1903, pp. 441-469.

Brooks, Alfred H., and D. L. Reaburn - "Plans for Climbing Mt. McKinley", *National Geographic Magazine,* January 1903, pp. 30-35.

Reed, John C., Jr. - "Record of the First Approach to Mt. McKinley"; *American Alpine Journal,* 1955, pp. 78-83. Describes the finding of records left by Brooks on his expedition of 1902, on the slopes of Mt. McKinley.

Houston, Charles S. - "Denali's Wife"; *American Alpine Journal,* 1935, pp. 285-297. An excellent account of the first ascent of Mt. Foraker, written by the leader of the party. For more than a generation after its discovery and naming by Lieutenant Herron, Mt. Foraker remained unvisited by climbers. In 1934 the Houston expedition made a successful ascent on the first attempt. Houston says their interest in the mountain was aroused "by Belmore Browne's great book on McKinley." They first considered approaching the mountain by air, but there was at that time no practicable landing-place near the base of the mountain; and they decided to go in from McKinley Park Station with horses—one of the last major expeditions to do this. The horses transported their expedition to the Foraker River, and the party ascended the West Foraker Glacier for thirty miles. By the west and northwest ridges they reached the site of their highest camp at about 11,000 feet, and on August 6 the three men of the high party reached the summit of Foraker's North Peak. Later they climbed Foraker's South Peak also.

Chapter Four - Judge Wickersham Makes the First Climbing Attempt; and Dr. Cook Makes the Second

Wickersham, Hon. James - *Old Yukon - Tales, Trails and Trials,* Washington, D.C., Washington Law Book Co., 1938. The account of his 1903 attempt on Mt. McKinley is found in pp. 203-320 of this very interesting collection of early Alaskan material by one of its history-makers, a Federal judge and later Territorial Delegate to Congress.

American Alpine Journal, 1946 - American Alpine Club Annals - "Biography of Frederick Albert Cook", pp. 86-88. Cook was a founding member of the American Alpine Club from May 9, 1901; he was expelled in 1910. The article concludes: "It is fair to repeat that, in his early days, Cook was regarded as a man of charm and energy, and that mental derangement may have caused his later digressions."

Cook, Frederick A. - "America's Unconquered Mountain", Parts I and II in *Harpers Monthly Magazine,* January, 1904, and February, 1904.

Dunn, Robert - A series of five articles in *The Outing Magazine:*
"Across the Forbidden Tundra" - January 1904
"Into the Mists of Mt. McKinley" - February 1904
"Storm-Wrapped on Mt. McKinley" - March 1904
"Highest on Mt. McKinley" - April 1904
"Home by Ice and by Swimming from Mt. McKinley" - May 1904

Dunn, Robert - *Shameless Diary of an Explorer* New York, The Outing Publishing Co., 1907. A candid and extremely outspoken account of the 1903 expedition, highly critical of Cook. Comments on Cook p. 93 and 97. Account of the final climb and the discovery of Mt. Hunter, pp. 213-230 passim.

Cook, Frederick A. - *To the Top of the Continent,* London, Hodder & Stoughton, 1909. The 1903 expedition is described in Part I, pp. 1-91. Cook's paragraphs on pp. 41-42 about his companions as their characters were revealed by the vicissitudes of the trail, contains this . . . "The haphazard chap who has run the life of a literary hack bewails his misfortunes, makes copy, secretes his observations of interesting things, and makes life tiresome by his egotism." No names mentioned, but this is clearly a rejoinder to Dunn!

Chapter Five - Dr. Cook's Claim: Mt. McKinley, 1906; and the North Pole, 1908

Browne, Belmore - "The Struggle up Mount McKinley", *Outing Magazine,* June 1907.

"The Conquering of Mt. McKinley" - *Hearst's Magazine,* December 1912.

"Conquering Mt. McKinley", Parts I, II and III, *Outing Magazine,* February, March and April 1913.

"An Alaskan Happy Hunting Ground", *Outing Magazine,* May 1913.

The Conquest of Mount McKinley, New York and London, 1913.

The account of Dr. Cook's and Barrill's departure and return is found on pp. 68-72.

Cook, Frederick A. - "The Conquest of Mt. McKinley", *Harpers Monthly Magazine,* May 1907.

Cook, Frederick A. - *To the Top of the Continent, - Discovery, Exploration and Adventure in Sub-Arctic Alaska. The First Ascent of Mt. McKinley 1903-1906,* New York, 1908; London, 1909.

New York *Times,* September 3, 1909, September 7, 1909 - Cook's cable and the American minister's endorsement.

Gibbons, Russell W. - *F. A. Cook, Pioneer American Polar Explorer* pamphlet, published by the Dr. Frederick A. Cook Society, Sullivan County, New York, 1965.

Euller, John E. - "The Centenary of the Birth of Frederick A. Cook", *Arctic* - Journal of the Arctic Institute of North America, December, 1964.

Parker, Herschel C. - "The Exploration of Mt. McKinley: Is It the 'Crest of the Continent'?", *Review of Reviews,* January 1907.

"Conquering Mt. McKinley", *Appalachia* XIII, 1-June 1913.

Cook, Frederick A. - *My Attainment of the Pole,* N.Y. The Polar Publishing Co., 1911; another edition, N.Y. Mitchell Kennerley 1912; a third, Chicago, Polar Publishing Co., 1913. Chapter XXXIV "The McKinley Bribery" sets forth Cook's contention that the challenge of his claim to the first ascent of Mt. McKinley was the work of a "pro-Peary cabal" of "bribers and perjurers". Earlier chapters describe his Arctic journey of 1907-1909, his announcement of success, his reception in Copenhagen and in New York.

Chapter Six - Tom Lloyd's Sourdough North Peak Expedition.

Stuck, Hudson - *The Ascent of Denali (Mt. McKinley),* New York, 1914. Quotation about the attitude of Alaskans to Dr. Cook's claim, and an account of the sourdough ascent, pp. 166-174.

Brooks, Alfred H. - "Mountain Exploration in Alaska", in *Alpina Americana,* published by the American Alpine Club, Phila., 1914. Here Brooks, instead of accepting Dr. Cook's claim to the first ascent of Mt. McKinley in September, 1906 (as Brooks' chapter in Dr. Cook's 1908 book does by implication), now rejects that, by specifically crediting Stuck and Karstens with the first ascent of McKinley's highest (South) peak in 1913. He also credits Anderson and Taylor with the first ascent of McKinley's lower North Peak in 1910, thus also rejecting Lloyd's claims. Brooks in this 1914 publication becomes the first historian to take the modern view of both Cook and Lloyd claims.

Fairbanks *Daily Times,* December 22, 1909 - "Cheers are Given as Climbers Leave".

Sheldon, Charles - *The Wilderness of Denali,* (New York, 1930).

New York *Sun* - April 13, 1910, pages 1 and 2 "Four Climb Mt. McKinley".

Fairbanks *Daily Times* - April 15, 1910 - President Taft's telegram of congratulation to Lloyd.

New York *Times* - April 16, 1910 - "M'Kinley Ascent is Now Questioned". An interview with Charles Sheldon in New York.

Fairbanks *Daily Times* - May 7, 1910 - "Professor Herschel Parker Coming to Climb M'Kinley, Says He Has to Be Shown Lloyd Party Got There".

Fairbanks *Daily Times* - June 9, 1910 - "Make Second Climb of Mt. McKinley."

New York *Times* - June 5, 1910, pages 1-3 "First Account of Conquering Mt. McKinley". W. F. Thompson of the Fairbanks *Daily Times* provided this story, and an interview with Tom Lloyd in Fairbanks, as the first complete account of the famous Sourdough Expedition to appear outside Alaska.

London *Daily Telegraph* - June 6, 1910 - Lloyd's account, claiming he had reached the top April 3; three photographs.

Rusk, C. E. - "On the Trail of Dr. Cook", *Pacific Monthly,* Portland, Oregon, January, 1911. The quotation about Alaskan opinion on the Sourdough claims, and on Tom Lloyd, is on page 62.

Chapter Seven - Sleuthing on Mt. McKinley.

Cook, Frederick A. - "The Conquest of Mt. McKinley" in *Harpers Monthly Magazine,* (New York and London, May, 1907). The first complete published account of the 1906 expedition, claiming the first ascent, with the famous "summit" photograph, and pencil drawings by Porter.

New York *Times* - October 15, 1909 - "Barrill Says Cook Never on M'Kinley's Top", Pages 1, 4 and 5. News story and summary of Barrill's affidavit that "at no time did Dr. Cook and he get nearer than a point fourteen miles in an air line from the top of Mount McKinley." The New York *Times* news columns and editorial pages on October 15 and 16 contain further development of the controversy, and express suspicion of the honesty of Dr. Cook's claims.

Browne, Belmore - *The Conquest of Mt. McKinley,* (New York and London, 1913). The 1910 expedition, undertaken partly to duplicate Dr. Cook's "summit" photographs, is described in Chapters VII through XIV. Description of Susitna Station, p. 83. Location of the "fake peak", pp. 118-123.

Browne, Belmore - "Sleuthing on Mt. McKinley", *Metropolitan Magazine* (New York, January, 1911). Contains the indictment of Dr. Cook: "To sum up, our discoveries prove beyond doubt that Dr. Cook, wilfully and with full knowledge of the deception, claimed the ascent of Mt. McKinley, when he had not even reached the base of the mountain; that he published photographs purporting to have been taken on the summit and ridges of Mt. McKinley, when the exposures were made at a point twenty miles distant from the mountain." p. 489.

Metcalfe, Gertrude - "Mount McKinley and the Mazama Expedition", *The Pacific Monthly* (Portland, Oregon) September, 1910.

Rusk, Claude E. - "On the Trail of Dr. Cook", *The Pacific Monthly,* Portland, Oregon, October, 1910. The first of a series of three articles on the Mazama expedition, which started out believing in Dr. Cook's claim, but eventually rejected it as impossible. The other two articles appear in the Pacific Monthly for November, 1910, and January, 1911. The quotation about Dr. Cook ("If he is mentally unbalanced," etc.) appears on page 62 of the final article.

Chapter Eight - The Cairns Attempt. Parker and Browne Reach Twenty Thousand Feet.

Fairbanks *Daily Times* - February 6, 1912 - "Times Expedition Enroute M'Kinley", page 1.

Cairns, Ralph H. - "Hazards of Climbing Mount McKinley", *Overland Monthly,* (San Francisco) February, 1913. Narrative, illustrated with photographs, of this little known attempt.

Fairbanks *Daily Times* - February 27, 1912 - "Climbers are Safe at M'Kinley's Base".

Fairbanks *Daily Times* - April 10, 1912 - "Unable to Scale Heights of Mighty Mt. McKinley, Climbers Return".

Browne, Belmore - *Conquest of Mount McKinley,* (N.Y. 1913). The account of the 1912 attempt by the Browne-Parker party is taken from this famous classic of mountaineering, Chapters XXVI and XXVII.

New York *Sun* - September 6, 1913, p. 16. An article relating Archdeacon Stuck's McKinley climb quotes Professor Parker's opinion on Dr. Cook and the Sourdoughs.

Chapter Nine - Alaskans Make the First Complete Ascent

New York *World,* October 2, 1910 - Reappearance of Dr. Cook in London.

St. James Gazette (London), quoted in New York *World,* October 4, 1910 - story of Dr. Cook's incognito attendance at Peary's lecture.

Cook, Frederick A. - "Introduction" to Ralph H. Cairns' "Hazards of Climbing Mt. McKinley", in *Overland Monthly,* (San Francisco), February, 1913.

Balch, Edwin Swift - *Mt. McKinley and Mountain-Climbers' Proofs,* Philadelphia, 1914. "Mount Denial" - p. 67.

Sheldon, Charles - *The Wilderness of Denali,* New York, 1930. Description of Harry Karstens, page 4.

American Alpine Journal, 1959 - Biography of Hudson Stuck, p. 276.

Stuck, Hudson - *The Ascent of Denali,* New York, 1914.

Farquhar, Francis P. - "Henry P. Karstens 1878-1955" in *American Alpine Journal,* 1956, pp. 112-113.

Fairbanks *Daily Times,* July 10, 1913 - "Climber is Home Again". The story of Karstens' return to Fairbanks after the climb.

Harry Karstens: Notes for an Autobiography

The colorful life of Harry Karstens often found expression in the published narratives of his associates, through the pages of their books: the naturalist Charles Sheldon detailing the 1906-7-8 seasons in McKinley's northern foothills, Hudson Stuck describing McKinley's first ascent in 1913, and Grant Pearson's accounts of life among the rangers running McKinley National Park under Karstens' superintendency during the ninteen twenties.

In later years Karstens, retired and in his seventies, was at last persuaded to make at least a start on his own autobiography. A beginning at this, written in the form of a letter to his old friend Francis Farquhar in California, published now for the first time, appears below.

I reached Dawson City on November 1st, 1897, having whipsawed lumber and built a boat on Lake Lindemann. On the way down many outfits were wrecked and men drowned. We came through in good shape. Our party consisted of a cocky young Irishman, (who was supposed to be my partner, but we separated a short time after we reached Dawson), and two elderly Germans whom we took in with us. They had a large outfit and, as we had very little grub or anything else, agreed to share and share alike if we would take them down. I being the youngest (just past 19), and the only one who knew how to handle a boat, was elected steersman. We had a rough passage over the lakes, and bad ice on the Yukon. We landed in Dawson on Nevember 1st, 1897, with three feet of ice under the boat, so could not pull out. Next morning the river jammed and then opened again, and the boat was gone. We were camped on the beach. Tom and I went up town to look things over. When we got back, the old men were gone with all their grub, leaving us with a small A-tent, no stove, two bearskin blankets apiece, and a small amount of grub we originally had. We never did run across those two again.

We went up the Klondike a ways to timber, and built a bear-trap cabin (small, with a flat roof), and holed up for part of the winter. We had a tough time pulling through that winter. Grub was almost impossible to get; flour sold for $125. a sack, butter $5 to $10 a one-pound can, milk $2.50 a can, and other things in proportion.

Tom was too speedy for me, and I saw little of him. In February I doubled up with another young fellow to make a trip to American territory. We heard that Mission Creek and Seventy Mile River were fairly rich, shallow diggings. We had no dogs, and pulled the sleigh ourselves. We were forty days on the trip. We took in Mission Creek (about 110 miles below Dawson), staked some claims, then elected a recorder, as there were a number of other people there at the time. This was accomplished by a Miners' Meeting; at the same time a townsite was laid out and called Eagle City. This meeting was called after we returned from staking on the Seventy Mile River, twenty miles below Eagle on the Yukon. At this meeting they voted me the Seventy Mile Kid, which stuck to me for a good many years. Even now, though I am past 70, some of the oldtimers call me Kid, or Seventy.

In the spring some of the men who were on that stampede furnished me with supplies, and were to pay me $900. each on my return, for representing their interests. I failed to collect. So I pulled out for Eagle again, which had grown considerably during that past winter and summer; also Judge Wickersham and his court came in. Preparations were being made for a mail route from Valdez to Eagle through Seventy Mile River to get the news and supplies. A mail carrier was located here to take out the first mail for Valdez; he was to meet another carrier at Tanana Crossing. He was supplied with plenty of money and a fair dog team. In one of the saloons he got drunk; they got him to gambling, and cleaned him out. For a week a number of us took turns staying with him, as he tried to hang himself several times. At the end of the week he seemed to be rational, so we let him alone. That night he hung himself. This left no one to take out the mail. Everyone else in town had an out, and it seemed I was the only one who could do the job. Not thinking of the future, I held up my right hand and signed on. No money; just a dog team, and the contractor in faraway Valdez. I knew some supplies were left at the Tanana Crossing, so I borrowed and ran in debt, but got enough to pull out with the mail on time, - me, 20 or 21—out of a big city; my only experience one dog and a sled on the Seventy Mile, and four days with a nine-dog team on the Yukon. [I travelled] over the hills with no trail to Forty Mile River, to Steel Creek, up Steel Creek, and over the divide to Jack Wade Creek; then down Jack Wade to Hackers [?] Fork and Mosquito Fork, across the Ketchumstock flat; over a low range down to Lake Mansfield and the Tanana Flats, and eight miles from Mansfield to our camp on the Tanana River, where the mission is today [Tanacross]; then double back and down to Circle City. Well, I found out that I had signed on, and was sworn in and couldn't break away during the contract. I lost all my mining ground, as I couldn't get away to represent it, and had not enough money to hire anyone. I stayed with the mail, and had many a tough and exciting time. In fact, since that time, I have been living on borrowed time.

After leaving the mail, I was in Eagle, I think in 1900 or 1901, when Lieutenant Billy Mitchell of airplane fame came in to the post in charge of the construction of the telegraph line between Eagle and Valdez. I guided him and his outfit over the route, which entailed some exciting times.

Returning to Eagle I was in pretty bad shape, with pains across the shoulders, so I took a trip out to my home in Chicago. I had been away five or six years; everything was strange, and I didn't fit in. I held out as long as I could, then hit north to Valdez to take the first mail into Fairbanks. That was the fall of 1903; [Charles] McGonagall was in Valdez; he and I were to work opposite. It was a monthly contract; our run was from Gakona on the Copper River to Fort Gibbon on the Yukon at the mouth of the Tanana via Fairbanks - a 900-mile round trip each month.

To record the things that happened to us that winter is too much to write here. Suffice it to say our first trip from Valdez to the Tanana watershed was all guesswork; we could find no maps or anyone to guide us. There was a trail from Valdez over the range and up the Copper River past Gakona, and up the Chistochina River to Chesina, which was a cache place for the Slate Creek mines. From that point we were on our own. We loaded down with willow shoots for staking the trail, for it was far above timberline. After going about fifteen miles, we crossed the headwaters of the Gakona River, loaded down with more willows, and kept on going, always following the high mountains on our right. After about fifteen more miles we dropped down into a wide gravel moraine sloping both ways; part of the waters from a big glacier ran down to the Copper and part to the Tanana (though we didn't know it them). We camped in some cottonwoods. Next day we started out, keeping the big mountains to our right, through canyons, until we came out on a big delta stream, looking down onto a broad valley. Before we got to the mouth of the Delta we were out of grub, except cornmeal, and had no dog feed. When we reached the mouth, the Tanana wasn't frozen, but the dogs smelled something, and away they went along the shore ice, then up in the woods. Before we could get to them, they were in a tent, tearing things to pieces. We had a time clubbing them off. When the men who owned the tent returned, they gave us something to eat, and told us of a big meat cache down the Tanana on the opposite bank; they gave us such directions that we couldn't miss it. But no soap. We had to make it to the Salcha River road house, then just building, where we got some supplies. The forty miles to Fairbanks we made the next day. We bought another team and sleigh, and after a couple of days getting equipment in shape, we started for Fort Gibbon at the mouth of the Tanana on the Yukon. After a few days it was time to start back with the first mail out. We tossed a coin, and I had to double back alone, and Charles had fifteen days' rest.

Well, I made it on time to Gakona on the Copper. The willows we planted on the divide were a wonderful help; the trail had mostly disappeared. The lead dog got onto those willows, and between them and feeling the trail, I made good time. To write the rest of the story would take too long. Mac [McGonagall], losing the trail over the summit, got caught in a storm in green willows. He went snowblind, cut the handlebars off the sleigh to start a fire, couldn't see, burnt his snowhoes trying to get the ice off them.

I was camped in the willows at the head of the Gulkana River, and had made a run over to the head of the Delta with one of my trail-breakers. The other was in the tent with a frozen foot (amputated at instep later). Coming back from the head of the Delta, I looked down the bleak moraine of the Gakona and saw a dark spot moving slowly up toward the tent. As it came closer I saw a man with three dogs pulling a sleigh behind him. Well, it was lucky I was camped there, or I'm afraid Mac would have been done for. He was the wildest looking man I ever saw. All he had left was three of his seven dogs; no handlebars on his sleigh. But he had the mail and his robe. I fed him up for a day, then gave him one of my dogs and rigged him up to haul the frozen-foot man and the other helper back with him. The reason I had trail-breakers with me was that there had been severe storms up in the hills, and I thought it would be safer, to get me over and get Mac back. I was supposed to have met him at the head of the Delta, but the son of a gun wouldn't wait.

On that trip down the Delta I made the fifteen miles to the head of the Delta, and continued fifteen or twenty miles more to good timber for shelter for the dogs and myself. I was very tired, and dozed off while cooking dog feed on the stove. I woke up with a start; the whole tent was ablaze. I managed to save the front and back part, and a strip two feet wide which I laced together. I managed to feed the dogs. My moccasins and mitts were burned, but I had a pair of light moccasins. I had to use two pair of socks for my hands, so had only two pairs for my feet. I tried to sleep, but it was too cold, and impossible. So I hooked up and started for the mouth of the Delta - about forty miles to go. I made it, but I hardly remember much about the last miles. At the mouth I was lucky; there was someone camped there. I don't know whether they fed me or not. I didn't wake up for many hours. The boys took good care of the dogs. When I pulled out, I had their trail to the Salcha River, which helped some.

Well, that is part of what happened on one trip. I travelled in all kinds of very cold weather, breaking through overflow, fording open streams, breaking trail in deep snow—going ahead a few hundred feet and bringing the dogs up, the trail blowing full after me in a very short time; trying to go through a canyon in extreme cold, with a gale of wind to face, freezing nose and face and unable to make the dogs face it, so go back several miles to timber, and camp.

Here the MS breaks off

After his 1921 to 1928 service as McKinley Park Superintendent, Karstens engaged in business enterprises in Fairbanks; and in later years usually spent the winters in Texas or Colorado with his son. The end finally came November 28, 1955 in Fairbanks; he was survived by his wife, and son, Eugene, a Colonel in the U.S. Air Force.

Chapter 10 - Tragedy on the Muldrow. Pioneer Airplane Landings.

Carpé, Allen-Letters of January 10, 1932 and March 2, 1932, to Francis P. Farquhar, outlining plans for the McKinley Cosmic Ray Expedition.

Carpé, Allen-Letter to the Director, National Park Service.

Director of National Park Service-Letter to Francis P. Farquhar.

Beckwith, Edward P.-"The Mt. McKinley Cosmic Ray Expedition, 1932", *American Alpine Journal,* 1933, pp. 45-68.

Strom, Erling-"How We Climbed Mt. McKinley". Translation of an article written in Norwegian for the Yearbook of the Norsk Tinde Klub (Norwegian

Climbing Club). Describes the 1932 ascent by the Lindley-Liek party, and the discovery of the deaths of Carpé and Koven.

Lindley, A. D.-"Mt. McKinley, South and North Peaks, 1932", *American Alpine Journal,* 1933, pp. 36-44.

LaVoy, Merl - Report to Director of National Park Service, September 28, 1932.

New York *Times*-August 11, 1932-"Plane Sees Searchers for Body of Koven'

Chapter 11- Billy Taylor, Sourdough.

Bright, Norman-"Billy Taylor, Sourdough", *American Alpine Journal,* 1939, pages 274-286.

Farquhar, Francis P.-"The Exploration and First Ascents of Mount McKinley", Parts I and II *Sierra Club Bulletin,* June 1949, and June 1950. Farquhar's interview with Charles McGonagall in 1948 in Fairbanks corroborates Billy Taylor's story. In a letter to the writer of this book, Farquhar gives the following account of the interview:
"He said that Tom Lloyd never got beyond the 'Willows.' Billy Taylor and Anderson carried the pole up to the col below the North Peak. Charlie did not make the final climb because, as he said, it was not his turn to carry the pole. The Swede carried the big end all the way, and Charlie and Billy took turns carrying the other end. A little below the peak Charlie dropped out because 'it was not my turn', so Billy and the Swede were the only ones to go to the top. I said some of the stories were that you, Charlie, were not feeling well. 'That was not it at all. I was feeling perfectly OK, but it was not my turn, so why should I go up to the top just to say I'd been there.' Continuing, I said, 'The newspapers say there was a second trip up to the col and that you came down after three days. How did you carry your blankets and food all the way up and down in such a short time?' 'Why the hell should we take blankets? It was broad daylight, and we were skookum'. I asked him if they climbed the other peak, and he said no. I believe that what Charlie told me was the truth."

Chapter 12 - Epilogue: And a Summit Photograph to Compare with Dr. Cook's.

Gibbons, Russell W.-*Frederick Albert Cook, Pioneer American Polar Explorer,* Hamburg, N.Y. 1965, published by the Dr. Frederick A. Cook Society, 23 pp.

Hall, Thomas F..-*Has the North Pole Been Discovered?* Boston, 1917, Ch. II; Part II, "Mt. McKinley" quotes extracts from speech made by Senator Poindexter defending Cook, pp. 394-396.

Balch, Edwin Swift-*Mt. McKinley and Mountain Climbers Proofs*, Philadelphia, 1914. "Cook's photograph of Mount McKinley and Browne's illustration of Fake Peak represent different peaks."-p.81. (But see Washburn, below-T.M.)

Rost, Ernest Christian-*Mt. McKinley and its Bearing on the Polar Controversy*; Washington, D.C., 1914. "The author is a skilled artist and traveler. He reproduces Cook's photograph of the top of Mount McKinley, also a photograph by Belmore Browne of what Browne calls Cook's Fake Mountain, bringing the two pictures to the same scale, thereby exposing the counterfeit nature of Browne's picture. He also exposes the shuffling of Browne and the Reverend Archdeacon Hudson Stuck in a most convincing way.". (But, again, see Washburn, below.-T.M.)

Browne, Belmore-*The Conquest of Mt. McKinley*, New York and London, 1913. "I am still filled with astonishment at the amount of vindictive and personal spite . . . " is from page 72.

Leitzell, Ted-"The Untold Story of the Cook-Peary Controversy", *Real America*, October 1935 and January 1936. Reprinted and distributed by the Frederick A. Cook Society.

Bates, Robert H.-"Mount McKinley, 1942", *American Alpine Journal*, 1943, pp. 1-13. Narrative of the Mt. McKinley Test Expedition by the officer in command of the high party.

Life Magazine, March 22, 1943-"Mt. McKinley - Quartermaster Corps Tests Winter Equipment There", pp. 69-73, 20 photographs.

* * *

The definitive study of the "Fake Peak" controversy between Belmore Browne and Dr. Cook was made by Dr. Bradford Washburn (and Adams and Ann Carter) in 1956-7. Unlike the Balch and Rost theorizings, Washburn's study was made in Alaska at the site of the Cook-Browne "Fake Peak". Reported in the *American Alpine Journal*, 1958, pp. 1-30, with 33 photographs, Washburn's exhaustive study completely supports Browne's earlier findings. It is the most important single reference on the subject. The editor of the *Journal*, Francis P. Farquhar offered it with this comment: "It is believed that Mr. Washburn's report and his article in this issue presents the Cook-McKinley controversy with fairness to all concerned and clearly upholds the decision of the A.A.C. Council which saw fit to drop Dr. Cook from membership in 1910."

* * *

DOCTOR COOK'S POLAR JOURNEY

Perhaps the interest of the reader in the remarkable journeys of Dr. Cook will continue on to the Doctor's North Pole claim, and the way that is viewed today.

We are far less certain about what latitude Dr. Cook reached on his 1907-9 polar journey than we are as to just where he got on Mt. McKinley. Unlike the spectacular topography surrounding the mountain, which lends itself to objective proof from photographs of just where a man has been, the sea ice looks alike for hundreds of miles around the North Pole, and there is no positive way of determining whether the picture "At the Pole" presented in Dr. Cook's book *My Attainment of the Pole* was actually taken on that spot, or hundreds of miles away. And since everything there is shifting, floating ice, his "Record Left in Brass Tube at North Pole" could not possibly be found by any later visitor to the Pole, and even if it turned up somewhere else in the Arctic ice-pack or adrift in the Atlantic, would have proved nothing.

The only thing which could have maintained Dr. Cook's polar claim at the high level of acceptance which it enjoyed for some weeks in September and October 1909, would have been supporting evidence by travelling companions capable of independently determining their latitude on the Arctic ice-pack and reporting to the world where they had been. This he lacked. Peary's claim, which was substantially supported by just such evidence, steadily gained acceptance over the years, while Dr. Cook's declined.

During the four years after Cook and Peary returned from the Arctic, some thirty learned geographical societies and public bodies, American, European, and other, conferred medals, awards and recognitions upon Peary. About half these citations use the phrase "for Arctic explorations 1886 through 1909", and thus sidestep entirely the question of who discovered the North Pole. Admiral Peary's gold medal from the Royal Geographical Society (London) is an example of these. A second group of awards, of which the Italian Geographical Society's is an example, honor Peary for having reached the North Pole but refrain from calling him the discoverer of it, clearly out of reluctance to challenge Dr. Cook's claim to priority. But most of the American societies in their awards, and also the Paris Geographical Society and the Royal Geographical Society of Antwerp in theirs, refer to Peary as the "discoverer of the North Pole", thus specifically repudiating Dr. Cook's claim. Contrary to widespread impressions, the Danish honors conferred upon Dr. Cook were not subsequently withdrawn. What happened was that the University of Copenhagen, *after* awarding the honorary degree, insistently asked Dr. Cook for proof of his claim to have reached the North Pole; and after an examination of the material then submitted, the University authorities concluded that "it does not contain . . . proof that Dr. Cook reached the North Pole." The Royal Geographical Society's Journal promptly pointed out that this was neither an endorsement nor a repudiation.

What was it that revived Dr. Cook's claim after 1913? A seemingly interminable flood of books and magazine articles on the subject. As Jeannette Mirsky the Arctic historian has pointed out: "The Cook-Peary question was one that divided the world . . . People with no idea of the real points involved took sides and argued vehemently and bitterly . . . Dozens of books, thousands of articles, were written to defend one of the men as a hero and to belittle the other."

But in all this flood of literature there was only one man who had the opportunity of locally questioning Dr. Cook's two Eskimo companions, and thus really had something to contribute on the subject of Cook's polar journey. This man was Donald B. MacMillan, who had been with Peary in 1909. In 1914 MacMillan made a sledge journey with Dr. Cook's two Eskimo companions, travelling a hundred and fifty miles out over the sea ice northwesterly from Axel Heiberg Island, searching (vainly, as it happened) for Peary's "Crocker Land." On his return MacMillan published in the Geographical Review (New York) for February, 1918, the following account of what the two Eskimos had told him about their journey with Dr. Cook:

"Dr. Cook with a single white companion, by the name of Francke, the cook of the fishing schooner *John R. Bradley*, was landed at Annoatok, some fifteen miles north of Etah, late in August, 1907. There were living here at this time about six families of the so-called Smith Sound tribe of Eskimos. This number was supplemented later by the arrival of several families from the south.

"Shortly after the sun returned in February, the expedition left Annoatok, aiming west across Smith Sound for the head of Flagler Bay. Ascending the river valley Dr. Cook crossed the heights of Ellesmere Island into Bay Fiord and on up Eureka Sound to the northern end of Axel Heiberg Island but did not reach Cape Thomas Hubbard, which is some five miles west, this accounting for his not finding Peary's cairn and record. Game was plentiful throughout the trip; the dogs and men were well fed.

"At this point a cache of food and a few small articles were left. Four Eskimos returned to Etah. Four Eskimos accompanied Dr. Cook during the first day's march on the Polar Sea, a march of about twelve miles. Upon completion of the snow home, two Eskimos returned to land, leaving E-took-a-shoo and Ah-pellah ("E-tuk-i-shook" and "Ah-we-lah" in Dr. Cook's book) alone with Dr. Cook.

"Dr. Cook and his two Eskimo boys did not proceed beyond this point, which is about 500 miles from the Pole. A flag was raised over the snow house and a picture taken. For instruments Dr. Cook had with him a common watch, a compass, and a full sextant. The sledges were loaded with food.

"After sleeping at this camp two nights, the party returned to the cache on the shores of Axel Heiberg Island, took everything from the cache, and proceeded south, following the western shores. Two low islands were discovered in about latitude 79°, very low and about five miles from land. The party crossed to the eastern shore of Amund Ringnes Island, where camp was made and one or two caribou killed. Returning, they made camp a little east of Cape Southwest of Axel Heiberg Island. They now journeyed southwest to the shores of North Lincoln (southern part of Ellesmere Island), crossing the land into Gaase Fiord. Upon reaching the entrance they turned west, then north into the narrow channel known as Hell Gate. Here the small canvas boat was launched, one of the two sledges placed on board, and all dogs abandoned. The boat proceeded south, then east, following the southern shore of Jones Sound to Baffin Bay. Encountering heavy ice which barred their progress south, they returned west and landed at Cape Sparbo on the northern shore of North Devon. Here an old Eskimo igloo was prepared and furnished for the winter to come. Game was plentiful, and the igloo, well stocked with meat, was warm and comfortable.

"Early in the spring of 1909 these three men packed their sledge and began their long walk back to Etah, the two Eskimo boys generally pulling the sledge and Dr. Cook pushing on the upstanders.

"Between Cobourg Island and North Lincoln two uncharted islands were discovered. On the retreat northward the party followed a course well away from land, because of the depth of snow prevalent here in the spring of the year. Food gave out. All became very tired and hungry. Finally a bear was secured, enabling the men to reach Cape Sabine. Here a seal was found in a cache, placed there one year before by Panik-pa, the father of E-took-a-shoo. With renewed strength, thus acquired, the party succeeded in crossing Smith Sound to the headquarters of Dr. Cook at Annoatok. Following a few days rest Dr. Cook proceeded south by dog team to Upernivik.

"Many of the photographs in Dr. Cook's *My Attainment of the Pole,* New York, 1911, are recognized by both E-took-a-shoo and Ah-pellah. The photographs facing page 244 marked 'Bradley Land Discovered', etc., were taken off the western shore of Axel Heiberg Island about 550 miles from the Pole.

"Facing page 282: Photo 'Mending Near the Pole' was taken on West side of Axel Heiberg Island.

"Facing page 286: 'At the Pole---We were the only pulsating creatures in a dead world of ice.' Photos taken in the spring of 1909 near Cape Faraday on east coast of Ellesmere Island about 780 miles from the Pole. The musk-ox boots worn by Ah-pellah were made in the igloo at Cape Sparbo in Jones Sound, following Cook's return from the north.

"Facing page 298: 'First Camp at the Pole, April 21, 1908.' Photo taken in spring of 1909 a little south of Cape Faraday on the eastern shores of Ellesmere Island.

"Facing page 310: 'With eager eyes we searched the dusky plains of crystal, but there was no land, no life, to relieve the purple run of death.' Photo taken near Cape Faraday. Ah-pellah is wearing a musk-ox coat made at Cape Sparbo in Jones Sound.

"Facing page 332: 'Back to Land and Life.' Taken near Cape Southwest, southern coast of Axel Heiberg Island.

"Facing page 332: 'Saved from starvation, the result of one of our last cartridges.' Taken near Cape Svarten on the north shore of North Devon. The boys had many cartridges at this time. They had four in fact, when they reached Etah."

This account by Admiral MacMillan, a man of unimpeachable integrity, is probably the most effective summation of the case for "Dr. Cook's Non-Attainment of the Pole", the title under which it was published. And one might have expected that interest in Dr. Cook would have faded out at this point. But it did not, because Dr. Cook's numerous friends and supporters discounted MacMillan's account and refused to accept it. Captain Roald Amundsen, discoverer of the South Pole and first man to make the Northwest Passage through the Canadian Arctic in 1903-6, commented: "My experience with Eskimos is that they will give you the kind of answer you want. MacMillan said to the Eskimos: 'Dr. Cook only away from camp one sleep?' and laid his head on his hands to denote the passing of one night, and the Eskimos nodded, 'yes'. That kind of evidence was used to discredit Dr. Cook." (*New York Times,* 24 Jan. 1926).

"E-Tuk-I-Shook" (E-Took-a-Shoo), Dr. Cook's Eskimo companion in 1908-9, and Commander MacMillan's in 1914-7.

Where now does all this leave us? In December, 1964, the Arctic Institute of North America in its magazine *Arctic* published the following: "The year 1965 will mark the 100th anniversary of the birth of Frederick A. Cook . . . best remembered for claiming to be the first man to reach the North Pole . . . Cook's cause continues to find support among a small number of sceptics who seek a true verdict in place of what some feel was a decision forced by newspaper propaganda . . . At least seven arguments emerge that support the view that it was very probable that in April, 1908, Cook was the first man to reach the North Pole . . . The case for Cook is strong, and should be reviewed by fair-minded men."

What approach should such a review take? First one must decide whether there is any real possibility that Admiral MacMillan's account from Dr. Cook's two Eskimos could be honestly mistaken. And today it does seem that there is at least a possibility. Since 1918 there has emerged the example of an honest mistake of this very sort with stories told by the primitive Greenland Polar Eskimos of that day. The example relates to the report brought back by Peary's men in 1909 that their colleague Ross Marvin of the civil engineering faculty at Cornell, had been drowned breaking through the ice while leading one of Peary's returning polar support parties. This was the account given by the two Eskimos who had been with Marvin, and was accepted by all. But years later it emerged that the true facts had been quite otherwise. For one of the two Eskimos subsequently confessed to having murdered Marvin through a tragic misunderstanding of intentions. So the entire story as interpreted by Peary's men from the two Eskimos and published in 1910 in good faith, was apparently not what had happened at all.

The identification of Dr. Cook's purported Polar photographs by the two Eskimos actually raises more questions than it settles. How did Dr. Cook get *original* 1908 Polar films when publishing his book in New York in 1911? He always complained, repeatedly and bitterly, that he had permanently lost all his original Polar journey records on his return to Annoatok because of Peary's subsequent actions there. How then would *any original* photographs from Cook's 1908 Polar journey appear in his book at all? The same question applies to the even more important navigational notes, which are printed in this book as "Exact copy from original Field Papers." If the originals were lost at Annoatok, from what did he copy?

The effect of all this is scarcely to increase confidence in Dr. Cook's Polar claim. But it does however keep alive some mystery as to what actually happened, some possibility, though probably small, that the real story never did come through from Dr. Cook's Eskimo companions after all.

Could Dr. Cook and the two Eskimos have travelled to somewhere near the North Pole? It has generally been accepted (and the MacMillan account confirms it) that in the first month of the fourteen that Dr. Cook was away from his base at Annoatok, he with eight Eskimos, sledges and about a hundred dogs easily travelled nearly five hundred miles of his chosen route to the Pole. At this point he was at the north end of Axel Heiberg Island, nearly halfway to his goal, and apparently all was going well. He had with him the pick of the best Eskimos and dog-teams, which Peary had trained over the preceding years and indeed had originally planned to use himself in the 1908 season. Cook and his Eskimos now had just passed through the relatively plentiful game country of Ellesmere Island. They had shot more game than they needed, and made caches of food for men and dogs for the return journey. Ahead, at an average travel of 15-16 miles per day, Dr. Cook's life objective now lay only a little over a month away. Even with the Arctic largely unknown, it was obvious that this was a promising route north from the point of view of drift currents, and from the point of view of navigational problems on the way home, probably the safest. Axel Heiberg is the only land on the rim of the entire Arctic basin toward which an ultra-simple "follow-the-north-seeking-end-of-the-compass" type of navigation could be expected to steer a returning explorer back from the North Pole. Crude though his navigational methods seem to have been, Dr. Cook is known to have been well aware of this particular phenomenon.

Is it really credible that, with the prize he and others had so ardently sought for so many years at last within his reach, Dr. Cook would at this point travel merely twelve miles out on the ice, build a igloo, sit down in it, and then do nothing toward his goal for months on end? This seems improbable, for Dr. Cook (as he amply demonstrated on his 1903 McKinley expedition) was not a man to lose his nerve or hesitate to take long chances. And there is yet another reason. If, when he got himself into this favorable position at the north end of Axel Heiberg Island, he had then decided to fake the whole thing, would he deliberately (and for that purpose quite unnecessarily) have spent *thirteen more* months, including the rigors of a whole winter in the open away from his Greenland base? We think not, especially since by returning in a few months, he could have got back to New York in 1908 and thus have beaten Peary by a whole year. It seems much more likely that he must actually have done something toward a real North Pole attempt, got lost far out, and thus was forced to spend an unexpected winter away from his Greenland base.

The article in *Arctic* considers it "very probable" that Dr. Cook reached the Pole during that period. We would think that unlikely. There are persuasive reasons to doubt he got that far. But it just could be that Dr. Cook and the two Eskimos did make it to somewhere near the Pole, or just conceivably all the way, and thus of course a year ahead of Peary. We find it easier to accept this possibility than to believe that he reached the top of McKinley. What an ironic through forever unverifiable twist of history, a sort of poetic justice, if the real discoverer of the North Pole was denied permanent recognition and acceptance for his feat because when he returned, there arose to haunt him the spectre of his claim to have made the first ascent of Mount McKinley!

Glossary of Mountaineering Terms

THE appearance of special mountaineering terminology in the accounts of American mountain climbing is not really an affectation. The reason is that mountain climbing as a sport originated a little over a hundred years ago in the Alps. English climbers employing Swiss, French and Italian guides inevitably came to use the native words and terms exactly as they learned their meaning. The very word Alp has special local meaning; but it happens to be one of the few whose meaning came to be changed after being brought into general English usage.

ALP—when used in the singular the word still carries its original European meaning: a high meadow pasturage or grazing land. In the spring of the year Swiss livestock is driven up into these alps, at around 7,000 to 8,000 feet and not brought down to valley shelter until the fall to be wintered below. In the plural the word in English is, of course, usually taken to mean not just the high meadow but the mass of high mountains centered in Switzerland and running out into France, Italy, Austria and Germany.

ALPENSTOCK—the predecessor of the modern ice-axe. The staff was about twice as long, and the cutting head small. It was actually superior for probing for crevasses on glaciers, but quite awkward for step-cutting. No longer used. Ideal is an even longer pole for glacier probing, plus the shorter modern ice-axe for step-cutting.

ARÊTE—the French word for a ridge. The use of this word instead of the perfectly adequate English word might, in Alaska, be regarded as an affectation, but it is in general use in the Alps.

AVALANCHE—this term, originally a technical one requiring explanation, is now in general English usage referring to a large mass of sliding or falling snow, or ice, or indeed even of rocks.

BELAY—used as a verb, the act of taking the climbing rope and in any one of a number of ways arranging a secure attachment around a boss of rock, around the body of a stationary climber, or around an ice-axe deeply driven into firm snow, more securely to protect the climbers who are tied to the rope.

used as a noun it refers to the structure and the rope arrangement itself by which this is done.

BERGSCHRUND—there will be many crevasses or schrunds in a glacier, but if the valley walls are steep there is likely to be a single specific uppermost one which is *the* mountain's (the *berg's*) schrund. This one tends to provide the separation between the fast moving part of the glacier and the essentially landfast upper edges of the glacier. There is no equivalent English word.

CIRQUE—this French word is used by geologists and mountaineers to denote the characteristic deep hollow in a mountainside which has been eroded and plucked out by glacial action.

COL—the French word for pass. But in English mountaineering usage it means only very high passes or saddles connecting high peaks with each other, and not the kind of ordinary pass through which a road for general use might be made.

CORNICE—the overhanging lip of snow built out over the crest of a ridge by a prevailing wind. On snow covered mountains these are very common; and they are treacherous for they are liable to collapse unexpectedly and either drop a climber into the abyss below; or, perhaps fall off from above and start an avalanche down upon the climber.

COULOIR—French. As a mountaineering term it means gully down a mountainside. May be a snow couloir or a rock couloir.

CRAMPONS—a special spiked footgear strapped to the soles of climbing boots for the particular purpose of being able to climb steep snow and ice slopes without the necessity of having to cut steps for security. There are varieties of crampons: eight, ten or twelve points (1" to 1 1/2" in length) on each foot. Also referred to in this book as ice creepers, or, simply, creepers.

CREVASSE—a wide and deep split in the surface of the glacier caused by its motion over an uneven rocky bed below the glacier. Though wide and deep it may be completely covered by fresh snow, not evident to the climber, and hence a trap into which he may fall. In Alaska in the early days use of this word might be regarded as an affectation, the old-time Alaskan gold-rushers being more likely to use the simple word "crack". There are however many insignificant cracks in glaciers of no consequence. Perhaps the word "crevasse" should be confined to those cracks in a glacier which are wide enough and deep enough for a climber to fall into.

DYKE—a sheet of igneous rock forced upward toward the earth's surface through a cleft while in the process of solidifying. A term more frequently used in geology than in mountaineering.

FIRN—this German word seems to have two uses. One a general term similar to névé meaning the catchment or feeding ground of a glacier. More specifically among glaciologists the firn line means the lowest line on the glacier where the winter snow does not melt in summer.

GENDARME—this French word denotes those singular rock towers or pinnacles which develop on ridges, sometimes as spectacular spires more than 200 feet high.

GLACIER—a slowly moving stream of ice; mountain glaciers are bodies of ice flowing down mountains, their position and movement determined by local topography; valley glaciers form when the accumulation (as on Mt. McKinley) is sufficient to drive ice out from the steep sides of the mountain itself, for example, the lower two-thirds of the Muldrow Glacier. Piedmont glaciers are found at the foot of mountains in Alaska where valley glaciers spread out into adjacent lowlands, an example being the Malaspina Glacier south of Mt. St. Elias which covers 1400 square miles. Rate and nature of movement of glaciers vary greatly, and conditions determining them are complex.

GLISSADE—a voluntary, controlled descent of a snow slope by sliding and skating on the feet, a sort of skiing without skis, (often controlled by use of the staff of the ice-axe) in a standing or squatting position.

HIP BELAY—a preferred way of using the body, instead of a rock or ice-axe, to give security to other climbers on the active rope.

HORN—this German name, used for whole mountains in the Alps, in Alaska has been applied to pinnacles near their summits.

ICEFALL—the fractured surface of a glacier where it passes over a particularly steep drop in its rocky bed; place where the glacier is deeply cut by crevasses.

MASSIF—a general mountain mass.

MORAINE—accumulation of earth and stones carried down by a glacier. Lateral moraines form along the sides of a glacier; medial moraines are carried down the center of a glacier below the point where two glaciers meet; terminal moraines are heaped up at the lower end of a glacier.

MOULIN—French; a spectacular round vertical hole in a glacier formed by a stream of water pouring vertically downward toward the glacier bed.

MUSKEG—a boggy region in northern countries, characterized by grassy tussocks and sphagnum moss, and trees, if any, dwarfed.

NÉVÉ—partly compacted granular snow which is in the process of being changed to ice.

PEMMICAN—concentrated food for polar and mountain expeditions, made by various formulas usually including dried meat and fat, sometimes also fruit and sugar, designed for high energy output.

PITCH—section of a climb.

PITON—an iron peg 3 to 8 inches in length with a ringed head of varying designs and shapes, to drive into the thin cracks of rock walls as an artificial aid in climbing to increase the security afforded by the rope. There are also ice pitons, necessarily of somewhat different design.

SADDLE—the lowest point on a ridge between two summits.

SCREE—loose slope of small rocks.

SÉRAC—a pinnacle of ice among the crevasses of a glacier, especially a part of an ice-fall.

TALUS—a loose slope of rocks and boulders; similar to scree.

TRAVERSE—the crossing of a mountain peak, ascending by one route and descending by another. Often, more loosely, to traverse across a face or slope, meaning simply to cross it.

VERGLAS—thin film of ice formed on rocks by rain and freezing. An extremely dangerous condition for rock-climbing.

Index

The author, seen here on Mt. Mc-Kinley in 1942 at age thirty-four, is a State of Mainer, professionally based in Cambridge, Massachusetts. Alaska has been his second home, off and on, since he first went there at the age of twenty-two. Moore made the journey with a cosmic ray scientist who, two years later — as described in this book — was lost on Mt. McKinley in the pioneer scientific expedition.

Moore did the academic work for his undergraduate, master's and doctoral degrees at Williams and Harvard. He seems, however, always to have had two quite different strings to his bow, one a conventional indoor professional life, and parallel with it, the adventurous life of an out-of-doors explorer. He has been a classroom teacher, author of diverse publications, head of a science museum (Boston), and president of the University of Alaska from 1949 to 1953. His more unconventional side led him to learn to fly a glider and then a power-plane at the age of twenty-two, make pioneering ascents of peaks in Alaska and Ecuador, and at the age of twenty-four, become rope leader of the climbing team that reached the top of 24,900-foot Mt. Minya Konka in eastern Tibet. For twenty-five years thereafter it continued to be the highest mountain climbed by Americans.

"Maine and Alaska are both part of the same great North Country which stretches from Alaska's Bering Strait to Cape Race, Newfoundland, and I love it all," he says. But he adds that his two lives join "only at the University of Alaska, where the solid values of conventional learning may be found together with the charm of the unconventional."